The Uses of Delusion

The Uses of Delusion

Why It's Not Always Rational to be Rational

STUART VYSE

OXFORD
UNIVERSITY PRESS

OXFORD
UNIVERSITY PRESS

Oxford University Press is a department of the University of Oxford. It furthers the University's objective of excellence in research, scholarship, and education by publishing worldwide. Oxford is a registered trade mark of Oxford University Press in the UK and certain other countries.

Published in the United States of America by Oxford University Press
198 Madison Avenue, New York, NY 10016, United States of America.

Library of Congress Cataloging-in-Publication Data
Names: Vyse, Stuart, author.
Title: The uses of delusion : why it's not always rational to be rational / Stuart Vyse.
Description: New York, NY : Oxford University Press, [2022] |
Includes bibliographical references and index.
Identifiers: LCCN 2021046186 (print) | LCCN 2021046187 (ebook) |
ISBN 9780190079857 (hardback) | ISBN 9780190079871 (epub) |
ISBN 9780197621547 (online)
Subjects: LCSH: Defense mechanisms (Psychology) | Delusions. | Self-deception.
Classification: LCC BF175.5.D44 V97 2022 (print) | LCC BF175.5.D44 (ebook) |
DDC 155.2—dc23
LC record available at https://lccn.loc.gov/2021046186
LC ebook record available at https://lccn.loc.gov/2021046187

DOI: 10.1093/oso/9780190079857.001.0001

1 3 5 7 9 8 6 4 2

Printed by Sheridan Books, Inc., United States of America

In honor of
Howard Rachlin and Daniel M. Wegner

Contents

1

Ridiculous Reason

To develop a thought's meaning we need only determine what conduct it is fitted to produce; that conduct is for us its sole significance.
— William James, "The Pragmatic Method"

In 1972, as I was starting graduate school, a friend died in a car accident. He was a troubled man, a Vietnam veteran who never quite settled into life after returning home from the war. Late at night while his wife Susan slept in their bed, his car crashed into a tree many miles away from where he should have been.

In the weeks that followed, a group of us spent a lot of time with Susan. We took her out and taught her how to get drunk. We hugged her. We tried to make sure she was with other people as much as possible.

Susan worked in the university library. Her desk was at a window seven floors up, and before her husband died, at the end of each day, she would see him down below, walking to the library to pick her up from work. Catching sight of him was her signal to put away her things and go home.

One evening, months after his death, Susan told me that she still looked down to the street near the end of each day, expecting to see her husband walking toward the library. It wasn't just a habit. She was unwilling to accept that this man who survived a war had somehow slipped away from her once he was safely back home.

"Sometimes I think he's just going to walk through a door," she said.

There are times when we need a little delusion in our lives, and death is often one of those times. In her memoir *The Year of Magical Thinking*, Joan Didion described her experience of mourning the sudden death of her husband:

On most surface levels I was rational. To the average observer I would have appeared to fully understand that death was irreversible. I had authorized the autopsy. I had arranged for the cremation. I had arranged for the ashes to be taken to the Cathedral of St. John the Divine.[1]

Yet Didion insisted on spending the first night after her husband's death alone, "so that he could come back."[2] Bringing her husband back became the focus of the next several months, during which she kept his shoes in the closet—because he would need them when he returned.

To me, one of the most endearing of all human characteristics is our propensity for paradoxical behavior. There is little doubt that we are the most intelligent species this planet has produced, and yet, on an hourly basis, completely normal people do things they know full well they probably shouldn't do. Others cling to ideas that they have good reason to believe are false. Often, we have complete awareness of our inconsistencies: "I know I probably shouldn't do this, but I can't help it. I'm going to do it anyway." In contrast, other species seem enviably free of these conflicts. Dogs and cats do things that seem utterly crazy to us, but their commitment to the project is complete and uncomplicated. They don't give it a second thought.

This book is about some of these human paradoxes. It is about beliefs we cling to and actions we take that don't entirely make sense—paradoxes that are, nonetheless, quite valuable because they help us survive difficult times, navigate the social world around us, and achieve our personal goals.

Like Didion, I am a rationalist most of the time. I am a behavioral scientist who has published research on the psychology of superstition and belief in astrology, and I write the "Behavior & Belief" column for *Skeptical Inquirer*, a magazine "for science and reason." I've spent much of my career promoting the idea that logic and evidence should be our guides. I believe our capacity for reason has been essential to all of our greatest achievements and, if humanity is to survive, we will need reason and evidence to get us through. But slowly, over a period of many years, I have come to a more nuanced understanding of truth and illusion. Human beings are often biased, superstitious, and irrational, and usually these characteristics are flies in the ointment. Most of the time we should throw off our delusions and strive for rationality if we hope to perform at our best. However, this book is about the other times: times when we cannot—or should not—discard our delusions.

Useful delusions come in several varieties. Some of them seem to be built in at the factory, as much a part of us as our teeth and bones. In that regard they share an affinity with perceptual illusions. Figure 1.1 shows the famous

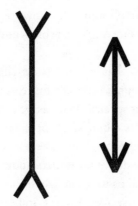

Figure 1.1 The Müller-Lyer illusion.

Müller-Lyer illusion. As anyone who has taken an introductory psychology course can tell you, the two vertical lines are the same length. I created this graphic on my computer, and I made the line on the right by duplicating the one on the left. So, I know they are exactly the same length. If you are unconvinced, I encourage you to make your own measurements.

Despite the evidence, to most people, the line on the left looks longer than the one on the right. The most common explanation for the illusion is that, for those of us who have grown up around boxes and cubes, the figure on the left looks like the inside corner of a cube that is a bit farther away from us, and the one on the right looks like the outside corner of a cube that is pointed toward us. Finally, in judging the size of objects, our brain makes an adjustment for their distance from us, boosting the apparent size of far-away objects. This calculation keeps us from mistaking a distant oncoming car for a toy car. Therefore, according to the common depth-perception explanation for the Müller-Lyer illusion, the line on the left looks longer because it appears to be farther away.

But telling you the two lines are the same length doesn't eliminate the illusion. Even measuring the lines and knowing about the depth-perception explanation doesn't help. The lines still look different, and we are powerless to see them any other way. In a similar fashion, some of the delusions in this book are just as sticky. Knowing that we are under the sway of a delusion doesn't help us shake it off. These stickier delusions appear to be part of our basic equipment. Other delusions are more amenable to modification. We can allow ourselves to fall under their sway or not. But unlike a simple perceptional illusion, all of the delusions we will encounter in the following chapters have important implications for how we live our lives. Although delusions sound like things we ought to avoid—and usually they are—some delusions help.

Part of the problem is that we are so intelligent. Philosophers and psychologists point to the human capacity for reason as an essential trait that distinguishes us from other species. As far as we can tell, humans alone have the degree of consciousness required to appreciate and comment on their own lives. Indeed, existentialist philosophers—never a cheerful bunch—considered reason and the desire for understanding to be uniquely human burdens that inevitably lead us to recognize the absurdity and meaninglessness of life. In *The Myth of Sisyphus*, Albert Camus put it this way:

> If I were a tree among trees, a cat among animals, this life would have a meaning, or rather this problem would not arise, for I should belong to this world. I should be this world to which I am now opposed by my whole consciousness and my whole insistence upon familiarity. This ridiculous reason is what sets me in opposition to all creation. I cannot cross it out with a stroke of the pen.[3]

Reason and the sheer processing power of our brains have produced great cities, art, and technologies, but even without falling into Camus' existential despair, we can recognize that our intellectual gifts are not without drawbacks. Among our many talents is the ability to anticipate death—our own and that of our loved ones—and, as a result, we experience illness and loss in a way that a tree or a cat cannot.

Furthermore, we are not just of one mind. Science's dominant theory of human cognition suggests we have two separate motherboards running in our brains at the same time—one thinks fast and the other slow. System One (clever name!) is our quick intuitive brain that helps us maneuver the world in real time without having to engage the more powerful machinery. It uses our past experiences and simple rules of thumb to process the billions of bits of data that wash over us every hour of every day. In contrast, System Two is a slower supercomputer capable of doing math and figuring out the things System One can't do. System One wants to make a quick decision and get on with it; System Two needs a minute to weigh all the pros and cons. When you are going on a road trip, the methodical System Two figures out how to fit all your family's stuff into the back of the station wagon, and System One probes your gut feelings to decide what to order for lunch.

Although there are many advantages to having two motherboards pro-cessing information, there are disadvantages, too. The last four decades of be-havioral economic research have shown that System One and System Two are often at odds with each other. Psychologist Daniel Kahneman received the 2002 Nobel Prize in economics for work he did with the late Amos Tversky, a research program the writer Michael Lewis called "The Undoing Project."[4] In a long series of simple but clever experiments, Kahneman and Tversky showed that quick-acting System One, while accurate most of the time, sometimes made important mistakes—mistakes it would be best to undo.

One of the most dramatic examples of this kind of conflict is ratio bias, a phenomenon studied by psychologist Seymour Epstein.[5] Consider the fol-lowing choice. Imagine that you can win a dollar if you draw a red jelly bean from a bowl, but you must choose which of two bowls to draw from. In one bowl, there are ten jelly beans total, one red and nine white. In the other bowl there are one hundred beans in total, ten winning red ones and ninety white (see Figure 1.2). The deliberate, mathematically inclined System Two moth-erboard tells us that the chances of winning are exactly the same in either bowl. You only get a single chance to pick a red bean, so you should be indif-ferent between the two bowls. Flip a coin and choose one. But, as you might suspect, the intuitive System One motherboard is distracted by the ten win-ning jelly beans in the larger bowl. Far from indifferent, System One often wants to draw from the larger bowl because it appears to have so many more winning red beans. When Epstein and his colleagues gave college students these choices, as many as 80 percent of them chose the larger bowl.

So what? Yes, System One is biased in favor of the large bowl, but there's no harm in that. The chances of winning are the same. But, of course, that wasn't the end of the story. The researchers went on to test the strength of System One's ratio bias by removing red beans from the larger bowl. They used the same small bowl with one red out of a total of ten jellies, but now

Equal Probabilities

Small Bowl	Large Bowl
1 red	10 red
9 white	90 white

Figure 1.2 The arrangement of jelly beans in two bowls with equal probabilities of choosing a red jelly bean.
Based on Denes-Raj and Epstein (1994).

they paired it with a large bowl that still had one hundred beans total but now contained only nine red beans. In this case, the System Two motherboard was able to determine that the chances of winning with the small bowl remained at 10 percent, but the chances of winning with the large bowl had dropped to only 9 percent (see Figure 1.3). To be certain this fact was not lost on the participants, the experimenters pointed out the probabilities of winning with each bowl before the students were asked to make a decision, and they still found that 61 percent of people chose the larger bowl despite the odds being worse. When they dropped the number of red beans in the larger bowl down to five—a 5 percent probability of winning, only half that of the small bowl—they still found that 23 percent of participants went for the long-shot larger bowl.[6]

Now you see the conflict. While the intuitive System One motherboard was going for the big bowl, the more numerate System Two motherboard must have been blowing its circuits. It knew that as soon as the probability of winning in the big bowl dropped below 10 percent, the best choice was the small bowl. *Choose the small bowl!* Furthermore, when confronted with choices like this, people are often aware of the paradox of choosing against their better interest, but the power of intuition is just too strong to get them to do the right thing. A substantial number of very intelligent adults kept choosing against their better judgment.

Ratio bias is a kind of mental illusion, akin to perceptual illusions, such as the Müller-Lyer. It is an illusion produced by our mental processing motherboards. But ratio bias is different from perceptual illusions in an important way. As we have seen, nothing helps the Müller-Lyer illusion. You can tell us the two lines are the same length as many times as you please, but the one on the left is still going to look longer. There is no cure. In contrast, ratio bias feels much more like a choice. People who knowingly choose the big bowl have a sense of giving in to intuition. You can imagine that a

Unequal Probabilities

Small Bowl	Large Bowl
1 red	9 red
9 white	91 white

Figure 1.3 The arrangement of jelly beans in two bowls with unequal probabilities of choosing a red jelly bean.
Based on Denes-Raj and Epstein (1994).

bunch of people who were safely under the control of their rational System Two motherboards might be able to get together and try to convince the System One people that it is better to choose the smaller bowl. The Müller-Lyer illusion is sticky, but ratio bias and many other mental biases are less so. You have the impression the error can be undone in a way that perceptual illusions cannot.

Over the last few decades, much of behavioral economic research has been of this nature. Psychologists have discovered biases in our thinking—many of them conflicts between System One and System Two—with the hope of undoing them. In the case of ratio bias, it is easy enough to stand to one side and see the right path. Intuition is often a very helpful tool, but in this case, it obviously leads some of us to choose the wrong bowl. By shining a light on these quirks in our nature, psychologists hope to nudge us toward a truer path.

This book is a very different kind of project. It is not about undoing anything at all. Instead, the following chapters will describe a number of equally paradoxical human characteristics that are better not being undone. It's not that all bets are off. It would be unwise to abandon logic and reason in favor of intuition and blind belief. But the following chapters will present a more balanced view of human nature, revealing a creature who is capable of great intelligence and clarity, as well as predictable lapses in rationality. Furthermore, there is a growing recognition that some of our irrationalities are features, not bugs—aspects of our hardware that at times confuse one or both of our motherboards but are, nonetheless, very useful to us.

What's a Delusion?

The word delusion often suggests something abnormal. The American Psychiatric Association defines delusions as "fixed beliefs that are not amenable to change in light of conflicting evidence"[7] and lists delusions among the features of schizophrenia, one of the most debilitating of all mental disorders. But the word delusion was around long before there were any psychiatrists, and it is commonly—and quite appropriately—applied to healthy, nonschizophrenic people. Our modern English word stems from the Latin verb *deludere*, the root of which is *ludere*, "to play." Deludere is to "play with" or "make a mockery of," particularly by instilling a false belief in your victim. This sense of the word is used by Joan of Arc in Shakespeare's play *Henry the VI, Part I:*

> O, give me leave, I have deluded you:
> 'Twas neither Charles nor yet the duke I named,
> But Reignier, king of Naples, that prevail'd.[8]

Merriam-Webster defines a delusion as "something that is falsely or delusively believed or propagated."[9] This definition does not get us very far, but the kind of delusion that most concerns us is holding a belief despite good evidence that your belief is false. Although few if any of them have schizophrenia, there exists a group of people who believe that our planet is flat, despite considerable evidence to the contrary.[10] As a result, most of us would consider flat-Earth belief to be a delusion. However, flat-Earth belief is different from the delusions we will consider in the coming chapters, because— like believing in ghosts or alien visitors—it has few practical implications. Flat-Earthers are not a well-researched group, but they appear to go about their lives neither helped nor harmed by their delusion—except, perhaps, having to endure a bit of ridicule. The delusions that concern us here are both more common and more consequential—delusions that, somewhat paradoxically, we are better off keeping than discarding.

Delusions have something to do with the ideas or beliefs we hold, but to be helpful or not helpful, these ideas need to lead to some kind of action. Belief that your house is haunted by the ghost of a previous owner is a kind of delusion, but unless your belief turns into a debilitating fear, you are unlikely to do anything with it. Alternatively, ratio bias is an intuitive delusion that can produce bad gambling decisions, so, unless you like losing your money, it is clearly a harmful delusion. As a result, our greatest concern is for delusions that are not merely private beliefs but are likely to lead to illogical actions. But before we can go much further we need to get a bit deeper into how we weigh our beliefs and behavior.

Today, the value of a given action is sometimes judged by whether it is rational or not. But what does that mean? Scholars in several fields have described rationality and reason in a variety of ways. For example, philosophers and cognitive scientists sometimes divide the topic into *epistemic rationality* and *instrumental rationality.*[11] Epistemology is the study of knowledge, how we do and should acquire it, and as a result epistemic rationality is concerned with having good beliefs that are based in evidence and logic and that describe the world accurately. Instrumental rationality is about whether your actions are appropriate to your goals in light of your beliefs.

Some of the most dominant theories of rationality have come from economics. The eighteenth-century Scottish philosopher Adam Smith proposed that humans are purely rational animals who usually make optimal choices for a given situation. Smith saw people as self-interested beings, making decisions that maximized their happiness through the satisfaction of their personal tastes and preferences. In the marketplace, individual buyers and sellers were thought to make the best possible transactions to achieve their goals, and the beauty of the theory was that this mutual contest of selfishness, when loosed on an unrestricted playing field, benefited all.

This idealistic view of human decision-making became a basic assumption of economics until the mid-twentieth century when The Undoing Project got underway and Kahneman, Tversky, and other researchers began to reveal our built-in decision-making flaws. However, even as behavioral economics was tarnishing the image of our unwavering brilliance, the traditional view of a self-interested decision-maker was regarded as a standard that we should aspire to. Indeed, the biases and reasoning errors revealed by people like Kahneman, Tversky, and Epstein were so compelling because they were obviously in conflict with what we should be doing. If you want to win the dollar prize, there is no upside to drawing from the bowl with the lower probability of success. It just doesn't make sense.

Building upon philosophical and economic theories of thinking and acting, *rational choice theory* emerged as a way of understanding good decision-making. Figure 1.4 presents a schematic diagram of a popular conception of rational choice.[12] Actions that satisfy a person's preferences and desires are rational, and sometimes there is little thinking involved. I like sharp cheddar cheese, and if there happens to be some within arm's reach, I can satisfy that desire without engaging my powers of reasoning. However, in another situation, satisfying the same desire might require some thought. For example, if I am in a strange place far away from home when the urge for cheddar strikes, it would be a mistake to stop at a car repair shop. If I see that the only establishment nearby is a car repair business, I might engage in a hopeful fantasy that it would fulfill my cheddar desires, but any serious belief that the shop might have what I need would not be based on an understanding of the available information.

As in the cheddar cheese example, rational choice theory suggests that many of our actions are based on beliefs about the state of the world. The

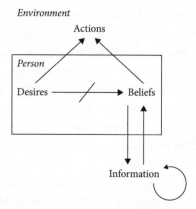

Figure 1.4 A model of rational choice theory. Solid arrows represent methods of appropriately grounding actions in beliefs, which, in turn, are based on the available information. The broken arrow between desires and beliefs is an irrational path by which beliefs are shaped by what the individual would like to be true.

Based on Elster (2009).

theory portrays us as brainy intellects who think about things and then decide what to do based on the results our motherboards spit out. To be rational, our actions must be appropriately grounded in our best available beliefs. That's all that is required, which means that we can be acting in a perfectly rational manner, even when we are dead wrong. Many of us grew up being told you should never swim immediately after eating—an idea that, as it turns out, was not based on solid data. The rule made a kind of sense at the time, and so we spent many a frustrated hour on the beach or poolside, just a few feet from where we really wanted to be. We now know our parents were wrong. Drinking alcoholic beverages before swimming is quite risky—and there is mortality data to back up that conclusion—but eating lunch before jumping in the pool is perfectly fine.[13] So, the original practice of waiting an hour before getting in the pool was rational, given the available information at the time, but, when better information became available, it turned out to be wrong. Our pool behavior today is no more rational than in the past, but it is more reality-based. As long as you don't have a martini at lunch, it's fine to get right in the water.

Another requirement of rationality, according to the theory, is the responsibility to have good beliefs—to be epistemically rational. To form good beliefs, you should value evidence and make a reasonable search for relevant information. There are times when the circumstances create obstacles to finding good information. Soldiers on the field of battle may not be able to do much research before choosing a line of attack because time is short. But a parent who chooses an herbal remedy for a sick child based on the testimonial of a friend is acting less rationally. Ideally, the parent should pursue other sources of information about the best course of action. Similarly, it is not rational to make a substantial financial investment based on a hunch. In Figure 1.4, the arrows going both directions from beliefs to information are meant to suggest that new information can alter beliefs and that beliefs, once established, should be supported by good data. The circular arrow indicates that the search for information may need to be repeated until a solid basis for belief and action can be established.

One of the most interesting aspects of rational choice theory—and one that is particularly important for us—is the broken arrow from desires to beliefs. This arrow represents one of the most common paths to irrationality. According to the theory, it is never acceptable to believe something merely because it fits your desires, because you would like it to be true. This is the fallacy of wishful thinking, which will often appear as a kind of delusion. Indeed, the broken arrow points to the cases of my friend Susan and Joan Didion. On some level, both women held on to the belief that their husbands were alive—or would return—because they desperately wanted it to be true, despite the available evidence.

In setting a standard of rationality, rational choice theory also suggests a number of ways the system can break down, leading to irrationality. As we have seen, allowing your desires to determine your beliefs is a well-traveled road to irrationality. In addition, failing to ground your beliefs in sufficient evidence is irrational, as is failing to use good logic to move from information to belief or from belief to action. In constructing their system of beliefs, flat-Earthers fail to apply the logical principle of parsimony, also known as Occam's Razor, which suggests that, when evaluating two possible explanations, the simpler one is preferred. Instead of accepting the many photographs and videos gathered by NASA and other space agencies, as well as the testimony of astronauts and cosmonauts, flat-Earthers implicate an elaborate conspiracy that has created a decades-long series of faked space missions and manipulated satellite pictures, all aimed at concealing the Earth's flatness.[14] According to believers, this conspiracy has been so successful at maintaining secrecy that none of the people (probably thousands) involved in this ruse has come forward to unburden themselves of the lies they told as part of a scheme to defraud the public. This theory is highly unlikely, and believing it requires a failure of epistemic rationality.

The idea of irrationality is much larger than delusion. For example, the college student who has an important exam in the morning yet spends an hour watching cat videos on Facebook probably knows that this is not a good use of time. Similarly, the shopper who puts a $300 pair shoes they can't really afford on a Visa card often does so with some awareness that this is a mistake. These are examples of instrumental irrationality and, in particular, a kind of irrationality that Aristotle called *akrasia* or weakness of will. Given competing interests, we often have a failure of self-control and choose a smaller immediate reward (amusing cat videos) over a much more valuable delayed reward (a good grade on the exam). Akratic behavior is central to many of our most important social problems (e.g., indebtedness, obesity, addiction), and in some cases it does involve a kind of delusion or self-deception. The shopper pondering the $300 pair of shoes may try to rationalize that the purchase really does fit into the budget. It will all work out somehow. This is another example of broken-arrow wishful thinking in the rational-choice diagram. But many failures of self-control involve less thinking than this and are driven by impulsive System One decision-making. As a result, for the most part, this book will not be about the varieties of irrationality that come from lapses in self-control.

Finally, many have interpreted Adam Smith's classic economic model as a justification for cold-blooded selfishness, but Smith knew better. We often aim our efforts outward toward other people. In his 1759 book, *The Theory of Moral Sentiments*, he wrote:

> How selfish soever man may be supposed, there are evidently some principles in his nature, which interest him in the fortune of others, and render their happiness necessary to him, though he derives nothing from it except the pleasure of seeing it.[15]

Of course, if you think about it, this moral sentiment can apply to helping people you will never know, and even to helping other species. When we give money to charities or volunteer for a service organization, we need not experience "the pleasure of seeing" the happiness of others. We can imagine it, and that is often enough. When considering rational choice in an economic framework, we tend to think of narrowly self-interested goals, but even the father of self-interested economics understood that some of our personal goals are not about us at all. They are selfish only in the sense that we are interested in the fortunes of others. A number of the useful delusions in the chapters ahead involve these other-directed goals.

What Should We Believe?

The rational-choice model is based on the assumption that people act on their beliefs, and as a result the quality of our beliefs is important. When should we allow ourselves to believe something, and when should we withhold belief? A classic debate on this subject was carried out by William Clifford, a British mathematician, and William James, an American psychologist and philosopher. In 1877, Clifford published an essay called "The Ethics of Belief," in which he carved out the hardline skeptical position: "it is wrong always, everywhere, and for anyone, to believe anything upon insufficient evidence."[16] Clifford used the example of a shipowner who was about to send his vessel out to sea filled with people emigrating to a new land. The ship was old, and he began to have doubts about whether it was seaworthy. The shipowner's doubts made him worried and unhappy, so he chose to push the troubling thoughts out of his mind. Having done so, the shipowner was comforted as the ship left port:

> he watched her departure with a light heart, and benevolent wishes for the success of the exiles in their strange new home that was to be; and he got his insurance-money when she went down in mid-ocean and told no tales.

Clifford went on to argue that, had the ship sailed safely, the owner would remain just as guilty of unethical behavior. The outcome of the trip was irrelevant to the ethics of the shipowner's behavior. In either case, he would be just as wrong for holding a belief without adequate justification.

Taking the point further still, Clifford argued that even holding a completely private belief that was not supported by evidence was unethical. Even if the person never expressed the belief or acted on it in any way, the mere act of holding it could lead to a general gullibility:

> The danger to society is not merely that it should believe wrong things, though that is great enough; but that it should become credulous, and lose

the habit of testing things and inquiring into them; for then it must sink back into savagery.

Clifford's view is what philosophers would characterize as an extreme evidentiary position. Beliefs can only be ethically held if evidence supports them, and where there is insufficient information, the individual is obligated to "test things and [inquire] into them." The implications of Clifford's stance for religious belief were clear, and he made them quite explicit, quoting this passage from the poet Samuel Taylor Coleridge:

> He who begins by loving Christianity better than Truth, will proceed by loving his own sect or Church better than Christianity, and end loving himself better than all.[17]

Nineteen years later, the American psychologist and philosopher William James responded directly to Clifford's challenge in an address given to the Philosophical Clubs of Yale and Brown Universities entitled "The Will to Believe,"[18] which was later published as an essay. James was a rationalist and a scientist who agreed with Clifford in many respects, but he also described Clifford as "that delicious enfant terrible" who expressed his viewpoint "with somewhat too much of robustious pathos in the voice." In most cases James and Clifford would agree, signing on to a style of reasoning consistent with modern rational-choice theory, but James' essay was designed to drill a tiny hole in Clifford's "Ethics of Belief" large enough to pull God through. To do this, James outlined three special conditions that made it acceptable to allow passions to determine belief—in other words, he was making a special case for mending the broken arrow from desires to belief. James' special conditions were:

- *Living hypothesis*: a living hypothesis is one where the belief and its absence (or opposite) are both still plausible and under consideration. James' example of a pair of living hypotheses was "Be a Christian or be an agnostic."
- *Forced question* (not avoidable): the question under discussion cannot simply be left hanging and put off for another day.
- *Momentous* (not trivial): there must be something at stake in the acceptance or rejection of the belief.

For some people in the nineteenth century—just as today—the existence of God was not a living hypothesis, but for James it was. Furthermore, the question could not be delayed because there was too much at stake. James' case was built on the foundation of Pascal's wager, an argument made two hundred years earlier by the French philosopher and mathematician Blaise Pascal. Simply put, Pascal suggested that living a Christian life was a good bet. The value of everlasting life in Heaven was infinite, and so if you neglected to live a Christian life and lost out on Heaven, the forgone reward would be enormous. In comparison, diligently living a Christian life, only to discover there was no Heaven after all, would be a relatively minimal loss. James and others have pointed out that Pascal's wager did not say much for God's valuing of genuine belief over self-interested calculation, but nonetheless James endorsed Pascal's basic argument. He believed that, when the three conditions he outlined were satisfied, it was acceptable to base a belief in passion. In stark contrast to the skeptical Clifford, James proposed that, in the special case of religion, belief built on passion could fill the gap left by reason. As Pascal put it, "Le cœur a ses raisons que la raison ne connaît point" (The heart has reasons that reason doesn't understand).[19]

William James was an unusual man for his time. When Mary Calkins, a Smith College graduate, wanted to get a doctorate in a psychology, Harvard University refused her admission because she was a woman. James invited Calkins to sit in his classes, and although she never received a degree from Harvard, she excelled as a student, completed all the requirements for the degree, and went on to become the first woman president of the American Psychological Association.[20]

James was also not afraid to turn his scientific investigations to topics that opened him up to criticism from his contemporaries. He rejected what he considered the two opposing dogmatisms of religious belief and scientific skepticism, and he had a long interest in psychic phenomenon, motivated in part by his belief that the soul survives beyond death. James was a founder and vice president of the American branch of Society of Psychical Research, and he attended many seances with spiritualists and mediums of the day— exposing a number of them as frauds. He was particularly impressed with a famous Boston trance medium, Leonora Piper, whom he became convinced had true psychic powers. Five years after publishing "The Will to Believe" James would give a series of lectures that were published as one of his most famous books, *The Varieties of Religious Experience: A Study in Human Nature*.

In *The Varieties* James criticized his fellow scientists for ignoring the study of religious experience, which he considered as worthy of investigation as any other aspect of human nature. His former student, the philosopher George Santayana, claimed the book had a "tendency to disintegrate the idea of truth, to recommend belief without reason and to encourage superstition."[21]

Clifford and James represent two ends of a spectrum. They were both rationalists who looked at the world through the lenses of science and evidence. Indeed, despite his enthusiasm for spiritualism, James established one of the earliest psychological laboratories in the United States at Harvard University.[22] However, as we have seen, James parted ways with Clifford, arguing that certain "live hypotheses," including religious experience, could be believed without sufficient evidence. He endorsed a kind of wishful thinking that many contemporary theorists in psychology and philosophy would say is not rational.

As we encounter various forms of delusion in the following chapters, we will find some ideas that both Clifford and James would agree are false. For example, I suspect they would agree that ratio bias is a false belief—a kind of nonpathological delusion—and that deliberately choosing a lower-probability gamble is a bad idea. In other cases, we will encounter beliefs that are more in the James camp—beliefs for which evidence is either lacking altogether or somewhat tipped against the hypothesis. Yet there are good reasons to believe. However, the particular forms of delusion we are interested in are not merely examples of people being stubborn and sticking to favored ideas; they are false beliefs that we adopt because they help us in important ways.

Looking Ahead

The subtitle of this book, "Why It's Not Always Rational to Be Rational," is something of a play on words, but in one sense, it is an accurate description of the book's viewpoint. The delusions in the following chapters may not meet the standards of the rational-choice model, but they are rational in the sense that they meet an important goal. The psychologist Jonathan Baron expresses a similar view in this passage:

> The best kind of thinking, which we shall call *rational thinking*, is whatever kind of thinking best helps people achieve their goals. If it should turn out that following the rules of formal logic leads to eternal happiness then it

is rational thinking to follow the rules of logic (assuming that we all want eternal happiness). If it should turn out, on the other hand, that carefully violating the laws of logic at every turn leads to eternal happiness, then it is these violations that we shall call rational.[23]

This view is consistent with the philosophy expressed by William James, Charles S. Peirce, and other American pragmatists of the 1870s: the proof was in the pudding. James put it this way:

> If there be any life that is really better we should lead, and if there be any idea which, if believed in, would help us to lead that life, then it would be really better for us to believe in that idea. . . .[24]

As always, James was concerned about religious belief and saw the practical value of religion as a possible response to "tough-minded" philosophers who were empirical, materialistic, and irreligious. And, similar to belief in religion, there are some delusions in this book that will not appeal to everyone. For example, many people love their spouses very deeply but, when tragedy strikes, do not—and could not—entertain the kind of magical thinking experienced by Susan and Joan Didion. Grief takes many shapes. In contrast, some helpful delusions are impossible to avoid. But, in every case, the delusions we will encounter have a pragmatic value that justifies their existence.

The examples of beneficial delusions in the following chapters are not meant to be an exhaustive list. There are undoubtedly many others. But the delusions presented here are some of the most important and valuable delusions we possess. They are ridiculous bits of unreason that are, nonetheless, central to our humanity.

2

A Bright Future in Sales

Every man who is 5'7" earnestly believes he is 5'9."

—Tweet by @evepeyser[1]

In my sophomore year of college, I satisfied a general education require-ment by taking an introductory course in the Communication Department. Although there was a standard curriculum for this class, our graduate stu-dent instructor proposed that we put it aside and form an *encounter group*. During the late 1960s and early 1970s of my college years, encounter groups were all the rage. In 1969, *Journey Into Self* won the Academy Award for Best Documentary. The film presented highlights from an encounter group made up of eight adults and their leaders, Carl Rogers and Richard Farson. Farson would go on to be president of the Esalen Institute in Big Sur, California, the center of the *human potential movement* and a gathering place for all manner of popular psychology.[2] Rogers was an important humanistic psychologist, the developer of *person-centered therapy*, and a proponent of encounter groups.

The eight members of the *Journey Into Self* group had never met before, but for sixteen hours they sat in chairs arranged in a circle, drank cups of coffee, smoked cigarettes, and shared some of their most intimate thoughts and feelings. At one point an Asian-American woman cried out, "I don't want to be a goddamned lotus blossom! I'm a real person!" The balding and bespec-tacled Rogers guided the participants with a calm, avuncular manner, and both men and women wept at regular intervals. Even Rogers cried briefly. The documentary was quite moving, and viewers came away thinking some-thing very important had happened to these eight people during their time together.

Despite having little idea what we were in for, our class agreed to the en-counter group idea. I suspect we were secretly calculating that this plan might involve fewer tests and assignments than the standard material, which turned out to be true. Some of us later speculated that the instructor was studying us as part of his doctoral dissertation research. I don't remember much about the actual group sessions. I'm not sure whether anyone cried. But I recall that I started a small rebellion, organizing a subset of our class to meet at an apartment off campus to discuss something that bothered me about the sessions. When we later confessed to the larger group that we'd met separately, rather than being upset, the instructor could hardly contain his delight. At the next class, he came in waving a journal article in the air that he claimed predicted that defections like ours might happen in some encounter groups. His reaction further cemented our impression that we were his research guinea pigs.

Self-Flattering Delusions

The *Journey Into Self* encounter group had been given two questions to examine:

1. What is it like to be oneself?
2. What are other people like when they are themselves?

As these questions suggest, an important goal of the encounter group process was for members to understand themselves better. Rogers believed that, in a successful group, individuals would drop their defenses and share their true thoughts and feelings. This, in turn, would lead to greater self-knowledge and improved functioning in everyday life.[3] All of this makes perfect sense, but making sense is not always the most important goal.

Encounter groups have largely gone the way of bell-bottomed pants and disco music, but Rogers' person-centered approach had a lasting impact on clinical psychology. Indeed, much of the stereotype of the supportive therapist comes from the humanistic approach he pioneered: "How did that make you feel?" But in the 1980s, as social and cognitive psychology began to have greater influence on psychotherapy, a different idea emerged to challenge the standard view that clear-eyed self-understanding was the best medicine.

In a classic article, psychologists Shelley Taylor and Jonathan Brown argued that most people engage in daily self-deceptions that they're better off keeping than shedding.[4] No encounter groups required. In particular, Taylor and Brown identified three categories of self-flattering delusions:[5]

1. We have an unrealistically positive view of ourselves.
2. We believe we have more control over events than we do.
3. We have overly optimistic views of our futures.

I'm amazing. The first of these delusions, sometimes called the Lake Wobegon effect, is the popular view that we are all—or, at least, most of us—above average. In a famous study published in 1980, 87.5 percent of Americans surveyed said they were above-average drivers with respect to safety.[6] This is, of course, a mathematical impossibility. Sixty percent of the respondents said they were in the top 20 percent of drivers—also impossible. In the same study, Swedish drivers had a slightly less inflated view of themselves, with 77 percent saying they were above average. In a study of college students' impressions of their popularity, one and a half times as many students said they had more friends than average as said they had fewer. Similarly, three times as many students said they had more friends than their friends had, compared to those who said they had fewer.[7] Both of these results are at odds with reality. Due to a mathematical phenomenon known as "the friendship paradox," the average number of friends your friends have tends to be larger than the number you have. Some people really do have more friends, but thanks to a numerical quirk I will explain in a footnote[8] but not here, on average, most people's friends have more friends than they themselves do. Nonetheless, we tend to see it the other way around.

I'm in control. If you happen to be a gambler or you are at all superstitious, you likely have experienced a psychological phenomenon known as the *illusion of control*. Human beings generally crave control. Unfortunately, many important things in life are not under our control or can't be controlled as much as we would like. For example, health. Most of us know someone who appeared to be bursting with vitality and yet was suddenly struck down by disease. Marathoner and author of *The Complete Book of Running*, Jim Fixx, dropped dead of a heart attack during his daily run at age fifty-two.[9] Often we want something very badly—a job, a romantic partner, a healthy baby—and yet we can't be completely certain it will happen. At these times, many people do something—*anything*—in an effort to increase their chances of success.

Merely taking some kind of action makes us feel like we've gained a bit of control—even when control is impossible. In a classic study, college students were invited into the lab for what they were told was an experiment on psychokinesis—mind over matter.[10] In a dice-rolling exercise, two participants were asked to concentrate on a single die and try to influence the outcome. One participant rolled the die, while the other merely looked on. Although it was impossible to influence the die under these circumstances—dice are random number generators and, of course, psychokinesis doesn't exist—the participants who actually tossed the die were more confident in their ability to influence the outcome than the passive participants. Greater involvement in the task produced an illusion of greater control. In many situations, normal people believe they have some influence over things that are uncontrollable.

My future looks great. My children will tell you that, in the course of their upbringing, I repeated a number of maxims they got tired of hearing. At the top of this list of Annoying Dad Phrases was, "Everything takes longer than you think it will." In general, people have unrealistically optimistic views of how the future will play out. Our health will be fine; we will do well in school; we will get a great job; and we will have a wonderful life.[11] We think our futures will be better, both in comparison to other people's futures and in comparison to an objective standard of what we should expect.[12] These happy delusions about the future are not mere idle daydreams. They tend to be somewhat grounded in reality and based on our current plans. Nonetheless, in general, our view of the future tends to be rosier than we have any right to expect.

Why Are We So Optimistic?

For obvious reasons, we are motivated to be optimistic. It feels good. Life is a more pleasant enterprise if we see happy times ahead. The alternative would be no fun. It is also reassuring to believe our lives are just a bit better than the next person's. So, once we are driven to be optimistic, a number of predictable reasoning errors—commonly known as *biases* and *heuristics*—kick in to help us maintain our pleasant outlook. One of the most common biases involves the way we explain successes and failures. Whenever we achieve some good outcome, we are quite happy to accept whatever praise comes our way. The college student who receives a good mark on a term paper thinks "Yes, I am an excellent writer, and I worked really hard on that assignment." But when they fail, suddenly all the surrounding obstacles come to mind: "Well, I had a bad cold, and I couldn't get any decent sleep because my roommate was partying every night." This is known as the *self-serving attribution bias*. We take full credit for successes and blame external factors for our failures.[13]

We are also quite unbalanced in the way we confront positive and negative feedback. Most people savor praise and skip over criticism. If we linger on negative feedback at all, it is in an effort to pick it apart and minimize it, whereas we accept positive feedback on its face. Similarly, the past is often better on reflection because it is easier to remember the good bits than the times we screwed up. In addition, when we compare ourselves to other people, we have a tendency to make downwards comparisons with those who aren't doing as well as we are,[14] and when we consider the future, we believe it will work out better for us than for others.[15]

We don't overestimate our status in all situations. For example, when working in groups, people are more clear about where they stand in relation to the other members, probably because in a group we get regular feedback about social ranking, making it more difficult to overestimate your position.[16] Bob Slocum, the main character of Joseph Heller's novel, *Something Happened,* demonstrated this kind of clarity in his obsessively detailed view of his place among his coworkers:

> In the office in which I work there are five people of whom I am afraid. Each of these people is afraid of four people (excluding overlaps), for a total of twenty, and each of these twenty people is afraid of six people, making a total of one hundred and twenty people who are feared by at least one person. Each of these one hundred and twenty people is afraid of the other one hundred and nineteen, and all of these one hundred and forty-five people are afraid of the twelve men at the top who helped found and build the company and now own and direct it.[17]
>
> —Something Happened by Joseph Heller

But in situations that are lacking immediate feedback, we often slide into a reassuring posture of self-flattery. Everything will be just fine.

Is All This Optimism Good for Us?

In general, people have an unrealistically inflated views of themselves—of how much control they have over events, and of their prospects for the future. Is all this rosiness a good thing? The honest answer is a definite, "Yes and no." It is not difficult to come up with examples of optimism that led to disastrous outcomes. The Great Recession of 2008 was caused by bankers who believed that they had devised a way to take the risk out of investments built on shaky mortgages and by homebuyers who were overconfident about their ability to pay for their mortgages. Both beliefs were supported by a housing market that had been strong for several years, but the result of this unwarranted optimism was double-digit unemployment, the worst economy since the Great Depression, and a very slow recovery. In more than one instance, US presidents have launched wars they thought would be quickly won, only to have them drag on for many years and, in the cases of Vietnam and Afghanistan, end in defeat.[18] But overconfidence about war was also common during the Crusades, when Christian armies were convinced that God would lead them to victory. They were frequently surprised by humiliating defeats.[19]

In addition, psychologists David Dunning and Justin Kruger have identified the now-famous overconfidence effect that bears their names. It is one thing to be routinely overconfident, but according to the Dunning-Kruger effect, those who perform the worst are the most likely to be overconfident about their abilities. For example, in one study, students who had the lowest scores on an exam thought they had ranked in the sixtieth percentile when they had actually scored at the fifteenth.[20] Students who scored the highest on the test slightly *under*estimated their performance.

Similarly, seeing is believing, but believing is not always seeing. Over several decades, there has been extensive research on the accuracy of eye witnesses to various crimes, and the evidence points to two important conclusions. First, eyewitnesses are often wrong. Although the practice seems to have gone out of fashion, for many years, professors staged a mild disturbance in their introductory psychology classes. Midway through class, someone might burst into the room, shout at the professor or a student, perhaps throw something, and run away. At some point, well after the actor has left the scene, students are asked questions about the intruder. Was he wearing anything on his head? Did he have anything in his hand? What did he say? Typically, the students were remarkably bad at this exercise. Despite their power to sway juries, eyewitnesses are notoriously unreliable.

Second, the degree of confidence expressed by the witness bears little relationship to their accuracy.[21] In a trial, if a witness points at the defendant and says, "I am one hundred percent certain he is the killer," the statement of confidence may influence on the jury, but research suggests it shouldn't. In a study of 250 convictions that were overturned with DNA evidence, 70 percent involved a mistaken eyewitness who was very confident.[22]

When psychologist Daniel Kahneman was asked what single human error he would most like to eliminate, he said overconfidence.[23] At the time he was asked that question, US involvement in the war in Afghanistan was in its fourteenth year, and the memory of the Great Recession was still fresh. Without question, when being wrong could lead to disaster, overconfidence is something to be avoided. But the evidence shows that, most of the time, a general attitude of moderate overconfidence leads to important benefits.

Research in *depressive realism* provides some of the most frequently cited examples of positive delusions helping us get through the night. According to the evidence, the difference between people who are depressed and those who are not depressed is the difference between a realistic and an unjustifiably rosy view of the world. Rather than seeing things in a darker hue than is warranted by the facts, depressed people see themselves realistically. For example, in a laboratory test, depressed and non-depressed people pressed buttons to try to turn on a light. Rather than have each press turn on the light—as we might normally expect—the experimenters varied the probability that a press would turn on the light, and on occasion the light came on when the participants hadn't pressed at all. For example, in one condition only 25 percent of presses turned on the light and 25 percent of the time the light came on when the participant hadn't pressed. When the experiment was over, each participant was asked to estimate how much control they had over the light. Moderately depressed individuals were remarkably accurate in their judgments and non-depressed participants substantially overestimated how much control they had over the light. The depressed button-pushers showed depressive realism. They were sadder but wiser.[24] Although the results showed only a correlation between mood and accuracy, this research suggests that optimism—and not the realism of the encounter group—is a component of good mental health.

One of the most often mentioned examples of dangerous optimism is starting a business. By some estimates, approximately 50 percent of small businesses make it to their fifth birthday.[25] If you live in a place long enough, you get to witness the natural selection of various local businesses, and in hindsight it often seems obvious why some didn't survive. In my little town, I can recall the restaurant that substantially misjudged the palates and pocketbooks of the neighborhood, as well as several specialty shops that were just too precious for a place with limited foot traffic. But each of these shuttered establishments was someone's American dream, and hopeful entrepreneurs put all they had into chasing it. Furthermore, even when successful, starting your own business often doesn't make economic sense. According to one analysis, on average people who entered self-employment made 35 percent less than if they had remained a paid employee.[26]

Overconfidence among entrepreneurs comes in at least two forms. People make overly optimistic predictions about their future prospects, and they make inaccurate assessments of their skills relative to others.[27] In other words, we are overconfident in both the absolute sense and relative to the competition. Because the dire statistics about entrepreneurial failure are widely known, overconfidence about your prospects versus those of the other schmucks seems particularly relevant. In a simulation study, business school students played a game in which they chose whether to start a business in an environment with a known number of competitors. When the game was designed such that income was based on the player's skill rather than random luck, the students inflated their own capabilities and failed to adequately account for the skills of their competitors.[28] They thought that their competitors' profits would be negative, whereas theirs would be positive. Similarly, in a large multi-national study of entrepreneurs and non-entrepreneurs, the strongest indicator that a person would start a new business was the strength of their belief that they had the skills to succeed. Unfortunately, across all countries in the study, the entrepreneur's self-confidence was not related to the ultimate success of the business.[29]

Starting a business involves much risk. If successful, the new business can produce reliable income, but if not, it can lead to substantial losses. Furthermore, in most cases, the outcome of the decision will not be known for some time. Buying a house is a similar gamble. Signing the mortgage is an act of faith that you will have sufficient future income to keep making payments for many years. Home ownership has generally been considered a reasonable gamble, in part because mortgages are backed by a valuable asset, but as we saw in 2008, housing prices sometimes fall, leaving the homeowner "under water"—owing more money than the house is worth.

Despite his stated wish to eliminate overconfidence, in an article written with his long-time collaborator Amos Tversky, Daniel Kahneman proposed a more nuanced view.[30] Not all uses of overconfidence are the same. For example, starting a new business, launching a war, or buying a home are decisions that have some features in common. First, they are rather discrete choices. There is a moment of decision, and once you have passed it, it is difficult—if not impossible—to go back. In addition, as mentioned earlier, the outcome of the decision is delayed. It may take a year or several years before you get clear feedback about whether it was a good idea or not. Finally, each of these decisions risks a substantial downside: financial failure or, in the case of war, massive loss of life.

Kahneman and Tversky recognized that overconfident optimism was dangerous in these situations. When setting a goal or launching a new enterprise, too much of a warm glow can have disastrous consequences. Unfortunately, overconfidence at the moment of decision is common. All of the reasoning errors and biases discussed previously encourage us to remember our successes and forget our failures. So, our prediction of the outcome is likely to be rosier than it should be. This kind of delusion is decidedly not constructive.

But Kahneman and Tversky also observed that optimism often carries us along when we are beyond the decision point and in the throes of executing the plan. In our daily effort to get ahead, optimism—even to the point of overconfidence—can be a big boost. Sports competitions are a good example because playing with confidence may both sustain an athlete and intimidate the opponent. In competitions that have a time limit, often the game will reach a point where it is physically impossible for the trailing team to catch up. If your basketball team is behind by twenty points with thirty seconds left on the clock, there just isn't enough time for even the most skilled team to score that many points. But until the moment of doom arrives, overconfidence can sustain a team's effort. You never know when a star player on the opposing side will sprain an ankle or be ejected from the game. It can happen.

Interestingly, the absence of a clock makes confidence and resilience in the face of adversity much more important. In 2016, during David Ortiz' final season, I managed to get a ticket to a Yankees-Red Sox game at Fenway Park in Boston.[31] For several innings the Yankees were ahead, 5 to 1. In the eighth inning, Boston added another run, but, with the score 5 to 2 entering the final inning, most of the fans headed for the exits. As luck—or optimism— would have it, in the bottom of the ninth the Sox added two more runs on singles by Ortiz and Mookie Betts. Finally, with two outs and two men on base, Hanley Ramirez hit a 441-foot home run to center field to win the game 7 to 5. When I looked around me after the game ended, there were very few fans remaining, but the ones who'd stuck it out were very happy. Many die-hard baseball fans have similar stories of games won long after most of the fans had given up. Obviously, the players never gave up.

Similarly, tennis is known for its unlikely comebacks. In the 1984 French Open Final, Ivan Lendl was soundly beaten in the first two sets against John

McEnroe, 2-6 and 3-6, but he rallied to win the last three sets 6-4, 7-5, and 7-5. It was Lendl's first Grand Slam win, and at the time, McEnroe had won two Wimbledon and three US Open titles and was ranked number one in the world.[32]

Because there is no time limit, winning a baseball game is never a physical impossibility until the last out. The longest game in organized baseball was played in Pawtucket, Rhode Island on the evening of April 18 (first night of Passover) and the morning of April 19 (Easter), 1981. After eight hours and twenty-five minutes of play the International League Pawtucket Red Sox beat the Rochester Red Wings 3 to 2 in the bottom of the 33rd inning.[33] Both teams played under extremely difficult circumstances. The Red Wings catcher played for twenty-five innings and batted eleven times. But neither team gave up until the end.

Similarly, until a tennis player wins the last point of their third set (for men) or their second set (for women), it is never physically impossible to come back and win. Under these circumstances, confidence is likely to help a team or a player take advantage of any opportunity to turn things around. "I saw hope as soon as I broke him," Lendl said. "I felt that once I could break him, I could do it again."[34]

Bluffing Yourself

I'm a terrible poker player. For years, I've played with a group of friends, and we all know who the good and bad players are. Fortunately, the stakes are quite low (nickel ante; quarter limit), making it possible to win as much as $20 but difficult to lose more than $5—although, on occasion, I've managed to do so.

Part of the reason I'm bad at poker is that I'm not a good bluffer. Although there is a lot of luck in poker, successful play involves the skillful use of a number of strategies, one of which is bluffing. If you have been dealt a bad hand, in some cases, it is still possible to win by giving off signals that you have a strong hand. For example, you might raise the size of the current bet, forcing others to choose between risking more money and folding. In an ideal scenario, the bluffer succeeds in convincing the remaining players to drop out and wins the pot with a very weak hand. But if the bluff is to work, your competitors must be sufficiently concerned that you might be holding a full house and not a pair of queens.

Of course, in everyday non-poker life, we often encounter people who lie and engage in various forms of deception. Sales people lie about their services, politicians lie, children lie to their parents and teachers, and parents lie to their kids. Unfortunately, evidence suggests that we are bad at detecting lies, and as a result there are still many con artists among us.[35] In what seems like a natural career path, Maria Konnikova, a psychologist, science writer, and author of *The Confidence Game: Why We Fall for It . . . Every Time*, is also a professional poker player.[36]

But lying is rational. The person who lies is not deluded. Liars know the truth but present a different picture in order to gain something of value. Of course, lying is often frowned upon, but if you are more interested in getting ahead than protecting your public image, lying can make sense and be completely rational. Indeed, non-human species lie in a number of ways. Insects, fish, and land animals have evolved camouflage that allows them to escape predators by blending into the background, and nut-burying squirrels will dig and cover empty holes to confuse those who might want to steal their reserves.[37] Humans have the ability to reason and make plans, and if you knowingly lie or dissemble, it is often a rational decision whose potential costs and benefits you've taken into account. In which case, you are far from deluded.

The problem with lying is that it is difficult to do well. Family and friends who know our tricks can often tell when we are trying to pull a fast one, and if you have been socialized to feel guilty about lying, evidence of your discomfort may leak out in your tone of voice or non-verbal behavior. You may stop making eye contact, start twirling your hair, raise the pitch of your voice, or talk more quickly. Finally, liars have to remember their lies and tell a story that is consistent with the tangled web they've woven. Although most people are bad at detecting lying, choosing to lie entails considerable risk. For all but the conscienceless sociopath, being an effective liar is no walk in the park. Self-deception makes it easier.

If we are going to reap the benefits of unwarranted optimism, it helps if we believe our own hype. The evolutionary biologist Robert Trivers has argued that humans have acquired the ability to deceive themselves, in part, because it makes us more effective at deceiving others.[38] Take, for example, the overconfident athlete. Presenting an air of confidence—no matter the odds against you—will be more effective if it isn't an act, if you truly believe you will be successful and don't have to talk yourself into it. Your confidence may not be entirely rational, but if you believe it nonetheless, you can't be accused of lying. You are operating under a kind of delusion. Alternatively, according to Trivers, if you are just acting and are not convinced that you can win, your rival may detect your inner weakness and be encouraged rather than intimidated. Just as liars who believe their own untruths are more persuasive, people who are authentically overconfident will not encourage their opponents by revealing hints of weakness.[39]

Over the years, I have watched a number of tennis players go off on explosive tirades when things went wrong, sometimes directing their anger at rackets or umpires, but often directing it at themselves. Commentators frequently explain this behavior as the athlete's attempt to get "psyched" into playing harder and better, but research does not support this view. In individual sports like tennis, in particular, negative mood prior to the match is associated with poorer performance, and self-confidence is the strongest predictor of winning.[40] But even if the sports commentators were right, they are not considering the effect of these displays on the opponent. If I were in the middle of a difficult match, nothing would boost my confidence more than seeing the person on the other side of the net explode into a tantrum. A much more effective signaling strategy would be to simply keep moving ahead with determination, even as you make errors or fall behind. The zombies of *The Walking Dead* and the cyborgs of the *Terminator* movies are terrifying because, no matter what you throw at them, they just keep coming at you. You have to admire the determination of those zombies and cyborgs.

When trying to present a strong front, there are other reasons why believing in yourself may bring benefits. If you recognize that you're putting on an act—that you don't really feel as powerful as the image you are projecting—you may experience cognitive dissonance. This famous psychological concept suggests that, when our actions and our values or beliefs appear to be in conflict, we often reduce the resulting uneasiness by changing our beliefs. The original demonstration of the concept involved participants in a very boring experiment who were paid a sum of money to tell the next participant that the study was actually enjoyable. Some were paid a small amount of money and others a larger amount, and those who were paid just a small amount later rated the boring task as more fun than those who were paid a large amount.[41] According to theory, cognitive dissonance was created by the participants saying something that they presumably did not believe in return for such a small sum of money. Being paid a larger amount to lie provided its own justification, resulting in less dissonance. But those who heard themselves say the experiment was fun in return for a small reward, could only eliminate the conflict between their actions (reporting that it was a fun experiment) and their prior beliefs (that it was dull) by changing their beliefs (actually, it was kind of fun). As a result, if you resolve any dissonance about your strong approach by changing your belief about yourself—"I really *can* do this!"—it can only help, but if the dissonance goes unresolved, it can have a detrimental effect.

In the current service economy, many people spend their work days painting a smile on their faces for the benefit of customers and employers. This is sometimes called emotional labor, and studies of service workers show that "surface acting" can lead to emotional exhaustion and job dissatis-faction.[42] The negative effects of surface acting are particularly pronounced when the employee places great personal importance on being authentic. According to cognitive dissonance theory, this inner conflict is sometimes relieved by changing your self-concept. Service workers who resolve their inner conflict by changing their attitude toward their jobs and learning to enjoy their contact with customers have greater psychological well-being. Furthermore, research suggests that customers can detect fake emotions, which can be reflected back on the employee in the form of unpleasant cus-tomer interactions.

In some cases, there may be a middle ground between conscious faking and true delusion. One college summer, I worked in the machine shop of a factory that fabricated bleachers for use in gymnasiums. The raw steel we worked with was covered in carbon, and each night I came home with soot in my nostrils and hands that never got clean. But I was a middle-class town kid, a summer hire, and the regular employees, some of them my own age, came from poor rural areas outside of town. I was just starting college, but even then I spoke differently than they did. Despite this being the upper Midwest, my coworkers had the drawl of farm people and used colloquial expressions I'd never heard before. I liked the work but was aware of being a kind of mi-nority in this world of the machine shop, and I wanted to fit in.

Over time, I found myself adopting their way of speaking. Today it might be called code switching. I learned what vowels to extend and started using some of their expressions. At home, I would revert to my usual manner of speech, but at work, I spoke their language. And it helped. No one ever men-tioned the change in my speaking style, and I think my coworkers felt more comfortable around me. I know I felt more comfortable around them. I was faking a kind of persona that was not my own, but the work environment supported my charade and rewarded me for it. As a result, I did not expe-rience putting on a work personality as labor, because my code switching reduced a conflict between my natural behavior and that of the people in my work environment. Similarly, a study of flight attendants found that those who were the healthiest in their jobs had learned to regulate their emotional displays.[43] They offered all passengers a basic level of friendliness which they did not extend further unless their customers reciprocated. This ability to adapt to a supportive or non-supportive environment prevented them from feeling emotionally beaten down by their jobs.

But in the case of overconfidence in a competitive environment, Trivers' theory suggests that we will be more effective if we truly believe our own overly optimistic story. While no one wants to be a sociopath, a zombie, or a cyborg, in competitive situations such as sports and business, being consistently and boldly optimistic without a visible chink in the armor is more likely to bring success.

There is also evidence that overconfidence is rewarded in a number of social environments. For example, confident entrepreneurs are more resilient during setbacks and more likely to take on subsequent ventures after an initial failure, but they are also able to draw more committed and motivated people to work with them.[44] Furthermore, in group settings, people who are overconfident about their abilities are granted higher social status, and—somewhat paradoxically—when their actual level of performance is revealed, they are not penalized by the group and they maintain their high status. In a series of experiments people were recruited to answer some general knowledge questions, sometimes alone and sometimes working together with others.[45] After working both alone and together, group members privately ranked each other on status, influence, and leadership ability. As had been shown in other research, confident participants were given higher status by fellow group members. Next, each person's performance during the individual testing was revealed to the group, which meant that, in some cases, people who had expressed great confidence were revealed to have been overconfident, with scores no better than other group members. The surprising result was that, in subsequent secret ratings by fellow group members, these overconfident test-takers maintained their high ranking from the other group members, despite achieving scores that were no better than participants who were given lower-status scores. So, in this case, overconfidence paid off and was equally or more important to group status than actual performance.

In a direct test of Trivers' theory, researchers in Munich, Germany placed participants in a job interview context. Prior to the main experiment, half the participants were led to believe that they had performed at a higher level on an IQ test than most of the other applicants, a procedure that was designed to boost confidence.[46] Then, participants were interviewed by people playing the role of an employer, and applicants were told that they could earn money by convincing the employers that they were better than most of the other participants. Participants who were led to believe that they actually were superior were evaluated better by employers than participants who were not. The researchers concluded that, when success requires being persuasive, overconfidence translates into better performance. In the words of Mark Twain, "When a person cannot deceive himself, the chances are against his being able to deceive other people."

The Motivational Value of Overconfidence

One of the most common justifications for overconfidence is motivation. If entrepreneurs were not dreamers, no one would start a business. Yes, many businesses fail, but without a good dose of hubris, the spirit of innovation would die and economies would stagnate. To encourage entrepreneurial enthusiasm, there are a number of protections for those who venture onto the field of battle. Many countries have laws that limit the personal financial responsibility of business owners and make it possible to escape from creditors through bankruptcy—an option that, in his work as a real estate developer, at least one US president employed several times.[47] But without a belief that you are more than your résumé, no one would take on the challenge of opening a restaurant, building a house, starting a college degree program, training for a marathon, or writing a book.

Although the motivational benefits of overconfidence make intuitive sense, we need not rely on intuition. A recent laboratory study illustrated how overconfidence sustains motivation and diminished confidence reduces it. Using a group of people primarily drawn from local colleges, a pair of researchers in Bonn, Germany asked participants to perform a tricky computerized perceptual task.[48] The computer screen showed eleven horizontal lines or "sliders" labelled 0 and 100 on each end (see Figure 2.1). The participants' job was to use the computer mouse to slide a pointer to what looked like the center of the line—where 50 would be. For each screen of eleven sliders, the participants were allowed only 55 seconds, and they were told that there would be 20 screens of sliders to complete. Importantly, they were not given any feedback on the accuracy of their performance other than

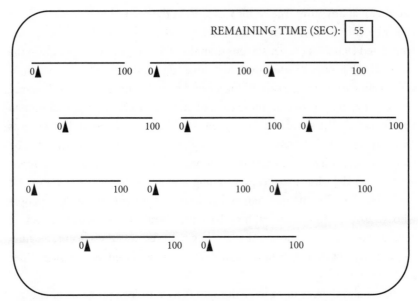

Figure 2.1 An illustration of the computer screen for the slider task. Participants were allowed 55 seconds to use the computer mouse to place each of the eleven pointers at the midpoint of scales. In the first phase of the experiment, participants completed twenty screens of this type.

Based on Chen and Schildberg-Hörisch, "Looking at the Bright Side: The Motivational Value of Confidence," *European Economic Review* 120 (2019).

their own visual judgment because the only numbers displayed on the sliders were the 0 and 100 endpoints. Participants were told they would be paid the equivalent of approximately 5 cents for each correct placement of the slider.

After completing the twenty screens of sliders, participants were asked to report their belief about how well they did at the task.[49] Then came the crucial manipulation. Half the subjects were allowed to compare their reported belief about their accuracy with their actual results, and half were not. This meant that, for half the participants who were overconfident, their balloons were burst, but the other half proceeded as usual believing they were awesome. Showing some of the participants their actual scores was meant to be a "de-biasing" procedure that would eliminate overconfidence and give people a more accurate view of their performance.

Finally, participants in both groups were allowed another shot at up to twenty more screens of the slider task, continuing at the same pay rate of a nickel for each correct placement, but this time they were also told they could quit at any time. The result was that, in the second round of the slider task, the formerly overconfident participants in the burst-balloon group completed 19 percent fewer screens than the still-overconfident people in the no-feedback group. In addition, the de-biased participants showed a significant decline in their accuracy in the second round, whereas the un-debiased participants whose overconfidence had not been challenged maintained approximately the same level of accuracy in the second round. So here was clear experimental evidence of something that had long been assumed to be true. Overconfidence has motivational value. In a work context, overconfidence is a delusion that keeps us going and sustains the accuracy of our work. Incidentally, the German researchers had no trouble finding people who were overconfident at this task. Based on the gap between people's actual accuracy on the slider task and what they believed was their accuracy, fully 94 percent of participants in the study were overconfident about their slider skills.

These helpful delusions can be thought of as Jamesean pragmatic beliefs—beliefs we hold, not because they conform to reality, but because they lead to better outcomes for us. Norwegian economist Hans Hvide has proposed a scenario that shows how a job applicant's overconfidence could lead to a higher salary.[50] The scenario goes like this: There are two companies that may make offers to a prospective employee, Suzanne. To simplify matters, both companies will make a one-time, take-it-or-leave-it offer. Suzanne can accept or reject the offer at Company 1, but if she rejects, she knows she can go on to accept or reject another offer at Company 2. However, if she rejects at Company 2, she cannot go back to Company 1. She will have to soldier on and extend her job search to other firms (see Figure 2.2).

According to the setup, the employer at Company 1 knows Suzanne's value to the company and also understands the current job market and the average salary Suzanne is likely to be offered at Company 2. However, there is some randomness in the labor market, and as a result, there is a chance Suzanne will be offered something slightly above or below her average market value at Company 2. In contrast to the employer's accurate information, Suzanne has only her beliefs about her value to Company 1 and the offer she is likely to get from Company 2.

So, what should the employer at Company 1 do? For the moment, let's assume that both Suzanne and the employer have accurate information about her value. Suzanne's beliefs match her reality. In this case, if Suzanne's value to Company 1 is greater than what she is likely to be offered at Company 2,

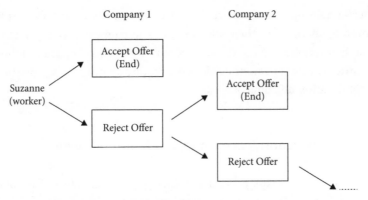

Figure 2.2 Suzanne's job-seeking dilemma.

the Company 1 employer should match what Company 2 would offer, and Suzanne should accept. If Suzanne's value to Company 1 is lower than the amount Company 2 is likely to pay, the employer at Company 1 should make a low offer, which Suzanne would presumably reject, taking her chances with Company 2.

What if Suzanne has an inflated view of her market value? She will expect more than what Company 2 will likely offer her, but if her inflated expectation is still less than her value to Company 1, according to the scenario, Company 1 should match her inflated salary expectation, or else they will lose her. There is a limit to how much overconfidence will be rewarded. If Suzanne has a wildly inflated view of her worth, she will end up being rejected by Company 1 and being forced to either accept Company 2's offer or extend her search to other employers. But according to Hvide's analysis, a moderate degree of overconfidence will benefit Suzanne because, given the randomness in the job market and the degree of knowledge the Company 1 employer has about her value to the company, it will often be in Company 1's interest to match Suzanne's inflated assessment of her worth.

In a similar approach, political scientists Dominic Johnson and James Fowler argued that evolutionary pressures encourage overconfidence in competitive situations.[51] They developed a theory that suggested that when an animal is competing for a resource and the capabilities of the competition are uncertain, individuals who are overconfident about their own capabilities will be more successful and grow to dominate the population. In addition to the benefits of gaining the resource—which strengthens the fitness of the possessor—Johnson and Fowler's model assumes that there are costs to both parties in fighting over the prize. Under these conditions, individuals who are overconfident about their own abilities will be more successful and increase their numbers. As in the case of Suzanne the job applicant, Johnson and Fowler's evolutionary model does not require bluffing the competition— it simply requires deluding oneself.

Overconfidence Good/Overconfidence Bad

Kahneman and Tversky's general approach to overconfidence still holds.[52] Overconfidence at the beginning of an enterprise, when adopting a plan or setting goals, is more likely to lead to calamity. This is undoubtedly the kind of overconfidence that, in the shadow of the Great Recession, Kahneman said he wanted to eliminate. But overconfidence later in the process—during the execution of a plan—can be a fortifying delusion.

Based on what we have discovered so far, we can summarize when overconfidence is helpful and when it's not. As we have seen, overconfident workers in the slider study who were not given deflating feedback continued longer and performed better than those who learned how badly they were doing. Day-to-day overconfidence keeps athletes and entrepreneurs moving on in the face of adversity. It also keeps all of us from being more depressed than we would otherwise be. As a practical matter, the big decisions of life come up much less often than the daily grind. If we can just calibrate our overconfidence to the circumstances and, in particular, be cautious when planning a new venture that could have a significant downside, we can be free to let our belief in ourselves loose at other times. Based on what we have learned in this chapter, we can summarize the contexts that will lead to dangerous or helpful overconfidence as follows:

Dangerous Overconfidence
Discrete choices that:

> Involve risk of substantial downside
> Are difficult or impossible to reverse
> Involve long-term obligations
> Depend on factors that are unknown or difficult to estimate

Helpful Overconfidence
Daily or repeated actions that:

Involve modest risk
Require persistence and skill
Have Short-term or cumulative impact
Depend on known factors

The risks of overconfidence are particularly obvious in cases such as signing a mortgage, taking out a business loan, getting married, or having children. Typically, cultural norms support making all these decisions, but they can lead to substantial difficulties. Furthermore, the greater power an individual has at their command, the greater the potential damage of overconfidence. Overconfident small business owners risk their financial investments and the livelihoods of a relatively small group of people. Pan American Airways was founded in 1927 and became a legendary pioneer of international flight. But, after a number of mergers and bad corporate decisions weakened the company's finances, as well as the oil crises of the 1970s and 90s and losses following the bombing of Flight 103 over Lockerbie, Scotland, the company could not survive. The once legendary and glamorous Pan American Airlines succumbed to bankruptcy in 1991, and an estimated 9,000 people in the Miami area alone lost their jobs.[53] Similarly, in the last half century, a number of very costly wars were launched because leaders failed to give adequate weight to the possibility of failure. Michael Cohen, a Senior Fellow at the American Security Project, described George W. Bush as the worst US president in history with respect to foreign policy, "in a category all his own." Bush's decision to start the Iraq war, which Cohen described as "unnecessary and pointless," is considered by many to be the worst foreign policy decision in the history of the United States.[54] It is estimated that 600,000 people died in the Iraq War.[55]

But most of us are not corporate moguls or commanders of powerful armies. Our most important life decisions are much less monumental and are widely spaced in time. When they do appear, these moments of decision can have lasting implications, so it is best to step back and be more coldly rational than we are otherwise prone to be. A slightly pessimistic attitude might be in order. I once met a woman who decided to go back to school to get a law degree. She had always been a good student, and she expected that pattern would continue. Several years later, she had flunked out of two different law schools and was holding $50,000 in student loan debt with nothing to show for it. Signing on for a student loan is a good example of a potentially dangerous context for overconfidence. For decades, the evidence suggested that, on average, young people with student loan debt arrived more quickly at the markers of the American Dream, such as getting married and buying homes and cars, presumably because their higher incomes more than compensated for the drag of their student loan payments. In recent years, that relationship has reversed. For the first time, on average, young people without student loan debt achieve these goals sooner than those with student loan debt.[56]

But those big decisions aside, when it comes to the struggles we face every day, a moderate degree of overconfidence can get you through the night. Excessive overconfidence is to be avoided, but fortunately (or not), the world often keeps us from getting too cocky. Basketball players who think they are invincible may repeatedly call for the ball, but if the three-pointers aren't falling, their teammates will pass it to somebody else. Similarly, you may think you are destined to date the most beautiful and interesting people on the planet, but a little time on an Internet dating site will recalibrate your expectations. In other cases, however, life spares us this kind of immediate feedback, and our glowing self-image is sustained. As I write these lines, I am buoyed by the conviction that I really am a very smart and skillful writer. This is going to be a great book. Tomorrow I will wake up and get to work again, comforted in the knowledge that it will be a long time before anyone has a chance to read these words and tell me otherwise.

the utility of those values is dramatically different for the two parties. For Redford, the utility of losing of a million dollars is almost trivial in relation to his total wealth, but for the young couple the addition of a million dollars takes them from zero to a million and has enormous importance. This case shows how utility and not mere face value is the most important quantity for weighing a gain or loss, and utility can vary depending upon a number of factors, including a person's current level of poverty or wealth.

When the outcomes of a decision are uncertain, economists use the idea of *expected utility* to weigh the potential results. Back in the 1960s, Nobel Prize-winning economist Paul Samuelson offered several other economists a simple bet that now bears his name. Samuelson's Bet was a single coin flip in which the colleague would win $200 for a head and lose $100 for a tail. He offered the bet to a number of economists who all turned it down, despite the average outcome being quite favorable. The first step in evaluating the bet is to calculate its expected value, which is simply the sum of the probabilities of the outcomes times their value. For example,

The Expected Value of Samuelson's Bet			
Probability			**Value**
Heads:	.5	x	+$200 = +$100
Tails:	.5	x	−$100 = −$50
			Expected Value = +$50

So, the expected value of the bet was +$50, but the more important concept in deciding whether to take the bet is *utility*, not value. Among the many contributions of psychologists Daniel Kahneman and Amos Tversky was their identification of our natural *loss aversion*: in most cases, we are much more concerned about avoiding losses than we are about making gains. In the case of Samuelson's Bet, although the expected value—the mathematical average—of the possible outcomes is +$50, for most people the actual average utility—the happiness or unhappiness experienced—is negative, because the unhappiness of having to give up $100 that you already have is greater than the happiness of winning an additional $200. One of Samuelson's colleagues put it this way: "I won't bet because I would feel the $100 loss more than the $200 gain."[6]

Gains and losses of equal value do not have equal power over us. In order to get more than half of people to accept Samuelson's gamble, you would have to raise the value of the winning flip to somewhere in the vicinity of $250, while keeping the loss at $100. This would raise the expected value of the gamble to +$75. Alternatively, you could lower the probability of losing considerably—for example, if the outcomes remain the same, $200 win vs. $100 loss, but in this case, you roll a die for which five of the six sides produce a win and only one side results in a loss. The expected value of this gamble based on a single roll of the die could be calculated as follows:

Die roll	Probability		Value
2,3,4,5, or 6	.833	x	+$200 = +$166.67
1	.167	x	−$100 = −$16.67
			Expected Value = +$150.00

In this case, the chances of experiencing a loss of $100 have been greatly reduced, and many people would gladly take the bet. The most famous response to Samuelson's Bet came from a colleague who said, "No, I won't play the game just once, but if you are willing to play a hundred times, I'm game." Samuelson turned down the multiple play option and went away confused by his colleague's response. Nonetheless, if you assume the kind of loss aversion that Kahneman and Tversky found is typical of most of us, a game that involves multiple coin flips at +$200 vs. −$100 makes sense.[7]

This kind of expected utility analysis seems quite rational, but can it be applied to more complicated everyday decisions? Could it have helped my friend decide whether to go to his pandemic seder? In some real-world cases the risks are fairly well defined, and although we don't actually put numbers on the outcomes, we are clearly making judgments based on expected utilities. Experienced drivers acquire a degree of confidence that allows them to assume the risks associated with pulling out into traffic. But coin-flipping, die-rolling, and pulling out into traffic have some features that the seder problem does not. In all three of the former cases, the probabilities are relatively transparent, and the effect of the action is immediate. Unfortunately, when it comes to maintaining our health, choices we make today often will not have an effect until much later, and the probability of loss—that you will be struck by illness or infirmity—is far more difficult to estimate.

During the SARS-CoV-2 outbreak of 2020 we engaged in a number of activities aimed at avoiding both getting infected and infecting others. Early on it became clear that some people were asymptomatic spreaders: infected and capable of infecting others but not experiencing symptoms. As a result, some of the disease was being spread by people who felt just fine and were unaware that they were carrying the virus.

Because there was a dearth of testing in the United States, most people were walking around not knowing their infection status. There were three possibilities: You might be uninfected, in which case you needed to take precautions to avoid infection until such time as a vaccine or an effective treatment was available. You could be infected, in which case your challenge was to survive the disease and not infect others. Finally, you could have recovered from the disease, possibly providing sufficient immunity that you could return to a more normal pre-COVID life with reduced fear of reinfection.

Except for the relatively few people who got tested and the unlucky people who got sick, everyone was entirely in the dark about their own infection status and that of the people around them. Life during the early months of the pandemic was a gamble for which the probabilities were impossible to know. With universal testing, it might have been possible for people to walk around wearing wristbands labeled "uninfected," "infected," or "recovered"—or an app on their phones that identified their status—and if this universal testing were combined with the appropriate quarantine procedures, we might've known enough to decide about going to Passover celebrations or any of the other activities that we had quite casually performed before. But without that level of transparency and with the consequences of a bad decision being possible death for ourselves or for other people, what were we to do? If rational decision-making involves weighing probabilities and outcomes, during the early months of the COVID-19 pandemic, it was very difficult to be rational.

Figure 3.1 illustrates the problem. In many everyday decision-making situations, the rational choice falls into a rather narrow zone, and it's relatively easy to know what to do. You have a clear view of the oncoming SUV; you can judge the speed of traffic; you've been driving your car long enough to know its capabilities; and you decide whether to press on the gas. The Rational Choice Model works best when the utilities and probabilities of the various outcomes are known. There will always be some uncertainty, but the general shape of the problem is well drawn.

Unfortunately, in the early months of the SARS-CoV-2 epidemic, we had only the most basic public health knowledge. Few people completely ignored the situation, but for many, trying to thread the needle of doing enough but not too much did not seem like a great option. No matter where you landed in the "Rational Choice Zone" your decision was no better than a guess. There were those who valued their freedom enough that they were willing

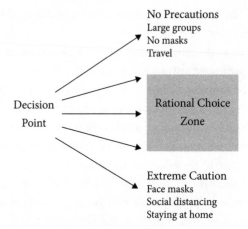

Figure 3.1 Illustration of a decision during the early months of the coronavirus pandemic. Somewhere hidden within the gray box is an efficient, rational level of caution that could not be known at the time but might be revealed in the future.

to take more risks, and there were many who could not stay home for financial reasons. But for those who were lucky enough to have a choice, a precautionary principle—a kind of "better safe than sorry" approach—was dominant. Until more was known about the virus and how to avoid it, many people concluded the best decision was to go far enough in the cautious direction to be fairly certain you were overdoing it.

On March 15, 2020, Dr. Anthony Fauci, the director of the National Institute of Allergy and Infectious Diseases, made an explicit appeal to this strategy. Appearing on *Meet the Press*, at a time when there were only three thousand cases of COVID-19 in the United States and sixty deaths, he said, "The golden rule that I say is, when you think you're doing too much, you are probably doing enough or not enough." When asked whether the nation should go into a fourteen-day shutdown (which, at the time, sounded severe), his answer was, "I think we should be overly aggressive and be criticized for overreacting."[8] In the days following, the overwhelming majority of states began issuing stay-at-home orders, some of which lasted for over two months before gradually being lifted.[9]

When Passover came, my friend was one of the many people who participated in their family seders at a distance via Zoom. Being together at the same table would have been much better, but it did not seem like the right decision. In 2020, many Jewish families substituted the usual motto, "Next year in Jerusalem," with the more modest wish, "Next year in person."

Health and Self-Control

In the early months of SARS-CoV-2, the true risk involved in many everyday decisions was unknown, and given the high stakes, many people chose to overcompensate. If any of the protective measures people took were unnecessary, it would only be revealed in hindsight when more was known. For various understandable reasons, some people may choose to take greater risks, but when a serious illness is poorly understood, being extremely cautious is not irrational.

But what about the health risks that are far better understood? In these cases, it is possible to be delusional—in either the overly optimistic or overly pessimistic direction—but whether such delusions are helpful or not depends on the context.

When it comes to health problems, we no longer have to consult a shaman or magician who will divine our futures from the flight of birds or the cracks in heated bones or turtle shells. Although cures for cancer and several other serious diseases still evade us, risk factors for many of the most serious causes of death have been identified, and it is clear that our behavior has a powerful influence on health. A 2018 World Health Organization report found that 71 percent of deaths worldwide were caused by noncommunicable diseases, many of which could have been prevented. For example, 54 percent of deaths were in just four disease categories—cardiovascular disease, diabetes, cancer, and chronic respiratory disease—all of which have substantial behavioral components.[10] A number of these diseases are influenced by diet, physical inactivity, and smoking. For example, diabetes, which is responsible for 3 percent of deaths both globally and in the United States, has increased dramatically in recent decades in parallel with rising rates of obesity. In 2014, 9 percent of the world population had elevated glucose levels.[11]

The answer to most of these premature deaths is simple: eat healthy foods in moderation, don't drink too much, get regular exercise, and avoid tobacco altogether. That doesn't sound difficult, but the world is full of temptation. Many of us fall prey to bad decisions in our youth and fatty foods, cocktails, and sloth as we grow older. We enjoy all of our indulgences, and some of us may even make a rational decision to trade health and longevity for the chance to burn the candle at both ends. Others make the equally rational choice to keep their eyes on prize of a long and healthy life. They read the latest science and follow their doctor's advice. But apart from all these rational people, there are many who suffer from delusions about their health and the kind of shape their bodies will be in as they get older.

Because tobacco use is associated with both heart disease and cancer—the two leading causes of death—young people's attitudes toward smoking have been widely studied,[12] and optimistic biases—the tendency to underestimate risks with respect to oneself—are common. The nature of the optimistic bias varies across studies, but the most consistent finding for smokers is that young people underestimate their likelihood of becoming addicted. For example, a study of Italian college students found that, when compared to nonsmokers and ex-smokers, current smokers were more likely to agree with the statement, "I could smoke for a few years and then quit if I wanted to."[13] Some longitudinal studies have asked adolescent smokers whether they would still be smoking five years later and then followed up to see what actually happened. In these cases, smokers greatly overestimated their likelihood of quitting. In one case, teens who at the beginning of the study only smoked one to six cigarettes per day, were more likely to have *increased* their smoking than to have quit five years later.[14] Similar results have been found for alcohol use. Young adult drinkers underestimate their chances of having alcohol-related diseases and of becoming addicted to alcohol.[15]

Although much of this research highlights the longer-term health consequences of smoking, drinking, and other risky behaviors, it is obvious that young people begin to smoke, in part, because they see some social advantage. For example, a 2004 study of northern California high school students found the usual optimistic biases: smokers and those who intended to start smoking were more confident in their ability to avoid addiction and smoking-related illnesses than nonsmokers. But high school smokers also believed they would receive several immediate benefits, including looking "cool," appearing more grown up, and being more popular.[16] Any behavior that is perceived to have immediate benefits combined with the possibility of long-delayed negative consequences creates a problem of self-control. This is why I try to keep ice cream out of the house.

According to an old joke, a mother walked into her son's room and caught him masturbating. The mother said, "You better stop doing that or you'll go blind!" The boy replied, "Can I do it until I need glasses?" Given that adolescents see smoking as a mix of benefits and risks, might they be making a conscious, well-reasoned trade-off? Perhaps these young smokers are not deluded at all. Until people like Kahneman and Tversky came along to suggest otherwise, economists operated under the assumption that we were all rational actors, and a number of them have tried to test this assumption in the context of addictive behaviors. University of Chicago economist Gary Becker famously expanded the reach of his discipline by applying it to new topics, and in 1988 he and Kevin Murphy proposed "A Rational Theory of Addiction," which asserted that people who use addictive substances do so with the goal of rationally maximizing utility, fully understanding the possibly of difficulties in the future.[17] For example, the youthful cigarette smoker may choose the benefits of smoking now, knowing that the costs of smoking will accumulate over time.

This kind of reasoning is not unlike the standard economic view of income and spending over the life cycle. According to the life-cycle hypothesis, people estimate their income over their entire lifetime and spread their spending evenly across the years.[18] This means that they often anticipate going into debt when they are young and just establishing themselves in the world and recouping that debt later when they hit their peak earning years. In a similar fashion, according to Becker and Murphy, smokers and those who engage in other forms of addictive behavior factor in the future costs of their addictions. Their circumstances may change, altering the smoker's calculus, and some may choose to quit. But according to this theory, people make sound decisions about whether or not to consume addictive substances.

As you might expect, Becker and Murphy's theory has drawn some criticism. Like many economists, they grant addicts—and indeed all of us—with too much clairvoyance about the future.[19] More recent research on self-control suggests that we are far more sensitive to the immediacy of a reward than the economists thought, and as a result we have inconsistent preferences. As we enter the restaurant, our spirit tells us we don't want to order dessert, but when we see the strawberry cheese cake laid out before us, the flesh is weak. One of the other basic assumptions of economics is that we can rank things by order of preference and, assuming we have full information about each item, our preference ordering should be stable and therefore rational. As a result, our desire should be the same when the cheesecake is distant as when it is up close. In hindsight, the economists seem like a remarkably naive bunch.

Contrary to the view that smokers see the future clearly and build it into their decision-making, there is substantial evidence that most come to regret their choice to begin using tobacco. A 2006 large-scale study of smokers from Australia, Canada, the United Kingdom, and the United States found that, across all four countries, approximately 90 percent of smokers agreed with the statement, "If you had to do it over again, you would not have started smoking."[20] Concern about future health problems and reduced quality of life were strongly related to smokers' degree of regret. These results have been consistent over decades of studies.[21]

When I was a child, my father hung a wooden contraption on the wall that dispensed packs of cigarettes. Printed on the dispenser was the following anonymous poem:

> Tobacco is a dirty weed.
> I like it.
> It satisfies no normal need.
> I like it.
> It makes you thin, it makes you lean.
> It takes the hair right off your bean.
> It's the worst damn stuff I've ever seen.
> I like it.

My father lived to be 83 years old, which was well beyond the life expectancy for a man born in 1926, but having smoked most of his life, he ended his days tethered to an oxygen tank. He often expressed regret about his smoking habit and quit several times, but like many smokers, he was a living example of the poem's ambivalence.

We all experience ambivalence about day-to-day decisions in situations like choosing the strawberry cheesecake over future health. That ambivalence raises additional questions about whether we are the rational maximizers economists think we are. One way to eliminate the contradiction in these self-control dilemmas might be to think about maximizing differently. As you go about making decisions throughout the day, you could say that, in any given moment, whatever you choose to do is what makes you the happiest in that instant, or else you wouldn't do it. You are a moment-to-moment maximizer, and your choice of the next cigarette, the next credit card purchase, the next glass of wine, or the next moment watching cat videos rather than exercising reveals your preference in that instant. But it can't be that simple. It is a curiosity of human nature that we are often of two minds, and when we are unhappy with the choices we make, it is often because we fail to be as forward-looking as we would like. True, there are times when we discover we have been *too* forward-looking and made bad choices about more immediate things. We may look back and say, "I wish I had spent more time with my kids when they were young," or "I wish I had learned to speak Spanish."

But in the area of health, the challenge is more often to avoid a small imme-diate pleasure in order to gain a much larger reward somewhere in the future. As Howard Rachlin makes clear in his book *The Science of Self-Control*, the problem is made more difficult because the immediate temptation is usually quite concrete—a slice of strawberry cheesecake right now—and it is pitted against the much more vague and distant concept of "future health."[22] But despite these challenges and occasional errors, if we are as rational and clear-eyed as Becker, Murphy, and similarly minded economists suggest, why is there so much anguish and regret?

One possible answer is that we are not as rational as classical economic theory suggests, and we have particular difficulty making good decisions when our immediate desires are in conflict with distant goals. This happens both on a global scale, such as our inability to reconcile the prospect of an uninhabitable planet in the future with our inclination to drive cars, eat red meat, and burn coal today, or it can be much more mundane, such as our desire to avoid cavities and gum disease in the future versus our reluctance to endure the immediate discomfort of flossing. There are rational strategies that we can employ to help us with all these challenges, but our immediate question is, do delusions help or hurt us in our efforts to maintain or regain good health?

The answer depends on the delusion and under what circumstances it is employed.

The Motivational Effects of the Status Quo

One of the underpinnings of Kahneman and Tversky's discovery of loss aver-sion was the importance of the status quo. When we think about wealth, hap-piness, or health, we tend to see it on a linear scale that begins at zero—the complete absence of the thing—and goes up from there. This is, after all, how we measure most things in the physical world. Kahneman and Tversky rec-ognized that, at the point of making a decision, the most important factor is where we stand before and after the choice. How will the outcome affect our current condition? Because they had very different levels of wealth, the implications of losing or gaining a million dollars for Robert Redford versus Demi Moore and Woody Harrelson were quite different. These effects of wealth were understood as part of classical economics, but Kahneman and Tversky went on to propose a more general theory of gains and losses that was capable of solving the puzzle of Samuelson's Bet. It is obvious why someone might refuse an even wager: heads you win $100, tails you lose $100. But loss aversion explains why even some bets that look quite favorable might not appeal to us. As Samuelson's colleague explained, we feel the losses much more than the gains.

The status quo also plays an important role in decisions related to our health. With luck, we find ourselves in generally good health—a kind of comfortable status quo. In this case, the main goal is to stay the course, reap improvements where we can, but at all costs avoid losses. Once we are sick or injured, the goals reverse. The new status quo is no longer our friend, and returning to our former state—reversing the loss—is our preoccupation. We go into "recovery" or "rehab" mode, and we often make great efforts to recoup our prior state as soon as possible. What we consider the status quo of good health gradually changes over the years. As we age, strength, endurance, and memory slowly decline, but if all goes well, these changes fall within normal expectations. Old people can't do all the things they did when they were younger, but healthy older people are capable of rich and fulfilling lives. However, whether we are young or old, the sudden loss of our expected level of health creates the motivation to regain it. We still struggle with the same problems of self-control, but not feeling the way you want and expect to feel at a given age creates the drive to get back to a more comfortable equilibrium. In a book called *The Uses of Delusion*, our challenge is to determine whether delusions—either optimistic or pessimistic ones—help or hurt our efforts to be healthy.

Optimism above and below the Status Quo Line

Earlier I mentioned that a classic 1988 article by psychologists Shelley Taylor and Jonathan Brown revealed that delusions can sometimes be better for us than clear-eyed realism.[23] Taylor was trained as a social psychologist, but starting in the 1970s she became an important figure in the relatively new field of health psychology, which sought to understand how psychology and behavior affect mental and physical health. Contrary to earlier views, Taylor and Brown suggested that maintaining a biased self-regard—supremely conscious of our strengths but relatively oblivious to our weaknesses—produced tangible benefits, including better mental health, lower stress, and greater ability to cope with ongoing challenges. One of the most important areas of Taylor's work involved cancer patients. In particular, Taylor and her colleagues found cancer patients who responded by adopting the somewhat magical belief that they had some control over their illness coped better and, in some cases, reported having discovered new purposes in their lives.[24] As we saw in the last chapter, a general tendency to puff yourself up often brings benefits, and even the annoyingly self-aggrandizing person is rewarded and does not suffer socially as much as we might imagine.

In the years since Taylor and Brown's article appeared, research has generally strengthened the conclusion that optimism leads to better adjustment, coping, and health. There is no evidence that a rosy outlook produces a direct magical effect on health, but it spurs positive forms of coping behavior. Psychologists divide the kinds of actions people take into *problem-focused* or *emotion-focused* activities. An optimistic attitude often leads to a productive response, but the kind of coping mechanism chosen depends on the challenge being faced. Some stressors or health conditions lend themselves to action. For example, recovery from injury or the stress of being in law school can be mitigated using practical problem-focused strategies, such as adhering to a physical therapy regimen or establishing a regular study routine. Other kinds of problems are either less amenable to modification or more emotional in nature. For example, dispositionally optimistic people who experience a traumatic event might seek out the social support of friends and family or look for spiritual guidance. Alternatively, they may reconceptualize tragedy as something positive. Generally speaking, people who are dispositionally pessimistic use other less, adaptive strategies. They deny their condition, they disengage, or they employ avoidant wishful thinking.[25]

Looking at all the research together, there is mounting evidence that optimism leads to better health outcomes and even reduced mortality. The findings are stronger when participants report how they feel as compared to studies assessing objective health measures, but in both cases, dispositional optimism is widely associated with better health.[26] However, our optimistic teenage smokers represent an important caveat. The overwhelming number of studies showing the positive effects of optimism have been conducted on people who were currently experiencing some stressor or disease condition—cardiac disease, law school enrollment, cancer diagnosis, HIV infection, or recovery from trauma or surgery. As a result, these findings could best be applied to situations in which the status quo of health and/or well-being was lost and the individual was motivated to regain a more comfortable point of stability. The people in these studies were akin to Woody Harrelson and Demi Moore, desperate to regain a sense of comfort and balance, and a natural optimism—even to the point of magical thinking—was a valuable resource. Earlier in the process, before the onset of disease or stressful circumstance, optimism can have very different implications.

Most young people are in their physical primes. They feel healthy and strong, and the possibility of future arthritis, heart disease, or diabetes rarely enters their minds. The average twenty-year-old feels invincible, and although they don't know it, the way they look and feel in their twenties will be the standard by which they measure the slow decline in the years ahead. As some older person once said, "Youth is wasted on the young."[27] Many things get better with age, but in general our bodies are not among them.

Before the fruits of modern medicine and epidemiology were widely available, the zone of rational health decisions was likely to include things we now consider superstitious and misinformed. Wearing a magical amulet to preserve health was a rational choice for fourth-century Europeans because they had no alternative, but today we have a wealth of relatively dependable information about what choices tend to produce a longer and more fruitful life. We have a narrower and more reliable zone of rationality. Unfortunately, when we are young, old age is far off in the future and many more immediate forces pull at us.

As we've seen, optimism is not a good quality in a teenage smoker—unless, of course, the teenager is one of the few rational addicts who has factored in later health problems and does not come to regret having started smoking. The young smoker is a particularly good example of conditions above the status quo line where optimism is not a benefit. Most teenage smokers in their prime are feeling just fine and experiencing the social benefits and aesthetic appeal of tobacco use. They many not even be addicted yet. This is a very comfortable status quo that provides little motivation for change. But given the widely understood long-term effects of smoking, optimism can lead to future health problems. The usual self-control problems combine with youthful invulnerability and overconfidence to provide little incentive to quit smoking. For many, the belief that they can smoke for a few years and quit is clearly not a helpful delusion.

Pessimism above and below the Status Quo Line

So, might there be useful pessimistic delusions? Pessimism is generally considered a bad thing. Realism is perfectly fine, although, as we have seen, sometimes not as good as holding a positive delusion. But there is little in the western world that encourages the adoption of pessimism, other than, perhaps, the usual hard knocks of life. For the most part, all the voices of modern life—self-help gurus, motivational speakers, coaches, teachers, and parents—strive to instill optimism and confidence: the world is your oyster. But there are some situations in which a little bit of crazy pessimism might come in handy.

As the previous section suggests, for the person below the status quo line—the person experiencing injury, illness, or trauma—pessimism makes matters worse. It promotes avoidance and denial and does not facilitate the return to a normal status quo of health and happiness. But what about the people above the status quo line when things are fine but the future is uncertain? In this case pessimism, particularly a form called *defensive* or *reflective pessimism*, can be valuable.[28] Defensive pessimism involves maintaining unrealistically low expectations despite a history of success.[29] People who adopt this strategy are more anxious than optimists, and they deliberately imagine worst-case scenarios in order to come up with strategies aimed at avoiding possible calamity. By planning for every possibility, they manage their anxieties and often end up performing quite well. When they face a new challenge, the pattern begins again, almost as if their recent success never happened, but for those who employ it, defensive pessimism works on several levels. Furthermore, preventing a defensive pessimist the chance to employ the strategy leads to poorer performance.[30]

Defensive pessimism is not for everyone, and it is not entirely clear what leads someone to adopt it as a strategy. People who are not temperamentally anxious are more likely to use an optimistic approach and avoid thinking about the possibility of failure. In the realm of physical health, optimism is probably a more widely applicable strategy, but in some situations—particularly when we are above the status quo line but the possibility of danger looms in the future—defensive pessimism is a valuable approach.

SARS-CoV-2 was not the first coronavirus epidemic. There were two previous cases in the twenty-first century: the SARS-CoV-1 epidemic of 2002–2004 and the Middle East respiratory syndrome (MERS) outbreak of

2012–2013, both caused by coronaviruses and both contained before reaching the level of a global pandemic. When COVID-19 arrived in 2019, the more effective response of Asian countries to this spreading virus was attributed in part to that region's prior experience with disease outbreaks. In China, Japan, and South Korea, wearing masks in public was already a cultural norm. In addition, a study of Singaporean people's response to the SARS-CoV-1 outbreak showed that defensive pessimists were more likely to take protective actions to avoid infection than people who were low on this dimension.[31] The researchers concluded that defensive pessimism could be an effective motivational response that would not produce a self-fulfilling prophecy of failure. To the contrary, it generated protective behavior. Similarly, a study of French-speaking Swiss citizens during the 2009 H1N1 influenza pandemic found that people who considered themselves less vulnerable to disease were less likely to use protective measures such as hand washing.[32]

In the early months of the COVID-19 epidemic, when little was known about how the virus behaved, many people followed Dr. Fauci's directions and assumed the role of a defensive pessimist. There was no shortage of anxiety to motivate people to think about every surface they touched and every encounter with people outside their homes. Many people continued to wear masks and gloves, and the stores quickly ran out of soap and hand sanitizer. However, as frustration built in the United States, some people began to reject the use of masks, a reaction that was not discouraged by President Trump, who was almost never seen wearing a mask in public. These different reactions were also anticipated by the Singapore study of the SARS-CoV-1 response. The researchers found that people who embraced the Chinese values of prudence, industry, and civic harmony were more likely to employ defensive pessimism, which in turn led to more diligent efforts to avoid infection.[33] Asian societies are considerably more collectivist than many countries in the west, and within the United States, mask-wearing soon became a political issue that split people into two groups: some placing greater value on civic-mindedness and others on individual freedom. Masks were said to be more protective of other people than oneself, and as a result the successful mitigation of spread depended upon a collective will to help one another.

Below the status quo line, when general well-being has been lost and we are in rehabilitation mode, there is no advantage to pessimism. A demoralized approach to the possibility of success and recovery saps motivation ("What's the point?") and makes success unlikely. In the domain of physical health, successful mitigation or improvement typically requires something of us. We must exercise, change our diet, take medications, visit the doctor, and do whatever the health professionals tell us. Pessimism tends to sap the will to do all these things and, as a result, can lead to a kind of negative self-fulfilling prophesy.

The overall picture of the role of positive and negative delusions in physical health is summarized in Figure 3.2. The top row represents those rare people—young or old—who are healthy and have consistently met all the commonly understood recommendations for healthy living. They are normal-weight nonsmokers who exercise regularly, eat a healthy, primarily vegetable-based diet, avoid drugs, and drink moderately or not at all. They use sunscreen whenever they are exposed to the sun, brush their teeth three times a day, and floss once a day. They get regular checkups and do whatever their doctor says. If these habits are well established, then whether these saintly individuals are optimistic or pessimistic will have little bearing on their physical health.

As we have seen, the addition of a looming threat changes the picture in important ways. Optimism is generally not a benefit in this case. The healthy teenage smoker, the sedentary beer and hamburger lover, or the confident uninfected person in a pandemic are not likely to take the actions that will avoid future health problems. These are the situations where the motivational anxiety of defensive pessimism, while perhaps not entirely pleasant in the moment, can get us to do what's necessary to achieve well-being in the long haul.

Once we are below the status quo line, optimism is our friend. We are looking to restore the status quo of health that we have become used to, and a bit of positive thinking goes a long way. Even when the odds are slim that

	Optimism	Pessimism
Healthy No Threat	?	?
Healthy Future Threat	Inaction/ Risk-taking	Protective Action
Ill or Injured	Rehabilitative Action	Inaction/ Acceptance

Figure 3.2 The effects of delusional optimism and pessimism under differing levels of physical health. The dark horizontal line separates positive status quo from negative.

we will get back to where we were, delusional optimism will keep us going to physical therapy, exercising, eating our low-salt post-coronary disease diet, and doing all the things that will get us as far as possible. Pessimism—or even realism—will not be as beneficial as a bright outlook.

Delusions and Psychological Health

Up to now we have focused on the motivational effects of optimistic and pessimistic delusions, the power they have to change our behavior and directly affect physical health, but these delusions also have important psychological implications. Unfortunately, in some cases the emotional and motivational effects of delusions are at odds with each other, creating a direct trade-off between psychological and physical health.

In addition to its motivational value, defensive pessimism is often employed to shield against bad news. Although I didn't know what to call it at the time, I used this strategy when I got my first full-time job teaching at a liberal arts college. The college was a beautiful but somewhat alien place. I'd come up through public schools and state universities, supporting myself with student work jobs and graduate teaching assistantships, and I was now at a landscaped New England college that I could never have afforded myself—a place where a large percentage of the students had come from boarding or private day schools and where many of the faculty had degrees from Ivy League universities. I wanted to stay as long as possible, but, according to the rules, if I didn't get tenure in my sixth year of teaching, my seventh year would be my last. Tenure meant job security, but it was hard to achieve. So, I told myself, *Don't get used to this place. You don't belong here. You may have to leave someday.*

I had rarely used this psychological strategy before. Graduate school was also supposed to be hard, but it wasn't that difficult for me. As I prepared for my comprehensive exams and my dissertation defense, I felt fairly confident that I would succeed. At the same time, I did not want to appear overconfident to my peers or professors, so whenever anyone asked me about my studies, I would adopt a concerned expression and say I was doing OK. But at my new job, it wasn't an act. It was do or die. So, I worked as hard as I could while steeling myself against the possibility of failure.

My defensive posture may have kept me anxious and motivated as I worked toward the goal of tenure, but I think my primary goal was to diminish the negative emotions an unsuccessful tenure case would bring. If I was denied tenure and had to leave the college, I could handle it better if I'd been expecting to fail all along. Six years would have been enough time to fully immerse myself in the pleasures of a great job, but doing so would have made the loss more painful. As it turned out, I was spared the experience of failure, but I discovered my defensive strategy had an unexpected downside. When I was awarded tenure, I was, of course, very happy, but for almost a year afterward, I found it difficult to shake the familiar feeling that I did not belong. I was denied a bit of enjoyment until I could relax and accept that I was a full member of the faculty. There was an unforeseen cost of my defensive posture, but given the high stakes situation, I doubt I could have approached it any other way.

Defensive pessimism often appears when a day of reckoning approaches. In the previous chapter, we saw that students often express confidence about their test performance until just before they are about to learn their grade. This is seen as a clear attempt to prepare oneself emotionally for the possibility of a bad outcome. Similarly, students sometimes use a self-handicapping strategy. They will go out the night before the exam rather than studying or getting rest so that, in the event of a bad outcome, they can say, "I was so hungover that morning!" By providing a different explanation for the failure, they can preserve some self-esteem and suggest that they are capable of doing better.[34]

As important as these days of decision can be, they are brief, whereas the defensive pessimism involved in preparing for a pandemic or lowering your long-term chances of cancer, heart disease, and/or diabetes may require a sustained effort of a year or a lifetime. Unfortunately, defensive pessimism provides much of its motivational benefit by being unpleasant. It is by definition an anxious state that is only somewhat alleviated by daily efforts to avoid the future loss of health. As a result, defensive pessimism is not a stance that provides immediate psychological benefit. Delusional optimism, on the other hand, if adopted in the correct quadrant of Figure 3.2, can provide both motivational and emotional benefits.

No matter how it is employed, optimism feels good. For those above the status quo line, whether there is a looming threat or not, being optimistic feels better than the alternative. Hopefulness is its own reward, and it insulates us from the anxiety that might otherwise be our fate. It is quite obvious why, at least in the West, there is a strong bias in favor of optimism. In contrast, when there are benefits to pessimism, few of them are felt in the moment.

Defensive pessimism provides the motivation to take protective action now and can mitigate any disappointments experienced in the future, but all this comes at the cost of some anxiety in the present. Nonetheless, if anxiety is unavoidable—for example, while living through a global pandemic—defensive pessimism can be a good way to deal with it.

Finally, optimism's greatest strength comes below the status quo line. The benefits of optimism are most obvious in those cases described by Taylor and Brown and the researchers that have come after them: people dealing with a cancer diagnosis, recovering from a heart attack, or rehabbing an injury.[35] When you are faced with a current health challenge, optimism provides the dual benefits of an immediate emotional lift and the motivational fuel to keep you going toward the goal of regaining your place above the status quo line. Furthermore, even when the optimism is delusional and unrealistic, the evidence suggests it brings tangible health benefits.

A few final words. I have been talking about optimism and defensive pessimism as though they were choices or strategies that can be employed, but as you can imagine, it is not as simple as that. Some people are dispositionally bright and sunny and others are Eeyores who always see the dark side of every situation, and we don't really know how people end up on one or the other end of that spectrum. We will come back to this issue in chapter 8, but for now we should acknowledge that neither positive nor negative delusions will be equally possible for everyone.

Finally, this chapter highlights both the psychological and health benefits of some delusions—irrational optimism and defensive pessimism. As we proceed through the rest of the chapters you will notice that each of the helpful delusions we cover will bring a mix of practical and psychological value. The emphasis will often be on the practical benefits because, as emotionally valuable as a delusion may be—in adapting to the loss of a loved one, for example—delusions that help us function in the world have added value.

4

Things Unseen

One for sorrow,
Two for joy,
Three for a girl,
Four for a boy,
Five for silver,
Six for gold,
Seven for a secret never to be told.

—Traditional nursery rhyme about magpies

During his years as a presidential candidate, Barack Obama had an Election Day superstition. In any hard-fought campaign, Election Day brings a strange stillness. After a blizzard of appearances, rallies, and bus rides, the candidate ritualistically shows up to vote in the morning and perhaps makes a few get-out-the-vote media appearances, but much of the day is spent in anxious anticipation of results that come many hours later. On the campaign trail, Obama played basketball with staffers as often as possible, and with the help of long-time aide Reggie Love, a former captain of the Duke University basketball team, Obama began a tradition of organizing a game on Election Day. The tradition became a superstition when they played on the day of the 2008 Iowa caucus, which Obama won, but failed to organize a game for the New Hampshire primary, which he lost to Hillary Clinton.[1] Obama, Love, and Michelle Obama's brother Craig Robinson played with staff members in Chicago on November 4, 2008. In that election, Obama beat the Republican candidate, Senator John McCain, by seven percentage points in the popular vote and ninety-seven electoral college votes to win his first term as president. In 2012, the Election Day game included Secretary of Education Arne Duncan and former Chicago Bulls players Scottie Pippen and Randy Brown. No official score was released, but pool reports indicated the President's team won by twenty points.[2] That evening, Obama beat Mitt Romney by four percentage points in the popular vote and 106 electoral college votes to win reelection for a second term.

Like political candidates on Election Day, athletes are often anxious on game day, and it is common for them to develop rituals to pass the time. The Baltimore Ravens place kicker, Justin Tucker, lays out his uniform, including his underwear, helmet, and cleats on the floor in front of his locker before he dresses for the game. It is a continuation of a practice used by his childhood idol Deion Sanders, but according to ESPN Tucker denies it's a superstition. " 'It's not a superstition, it's a ritual,' [he] said with a smile. 'I think I'm superstitious about calling things superstitious.' "[3]

These superstitions undoubtedly help treat the jitters when it is not possible to do anything more practical: when the campaign is over, and in the case of the athlete waiting to compete, when it's too late to exercise or practice. But there's a difference between these superstitions. After he executes his pre-game ritual, Tucker is engaged in a skilled activity, and there is a chance his superstition will inspire better kicking performance. Because there is no evidence of actual magic in the world (sorry about that), the effect would have to be psychological, but the possibility is there.

President Obama's superstition, on the other hand, has no chance of affecting the outcome of the election. Although it is clear that he felt better playing basketball than not, by the time the game started, all of his election-related skills had been deployed. As a result, his basketball superstition was akin to the bingo player who brings lucky trinkets to the game. The calling of letters and numbers is random, and the bingo player is a passive participant. To be more than merely psychologically useful, a superstition should lead to some tangible effect, which is only possible in a skilled activity.

First, we should probably acknowledge that there is a difference between the negative or taboo superstitions and those aimed at bringing good luck. Today, it is hard to see any benefit of the fear of the evil eye or the number thirteen. Life would be much simpler if no one had every taught us about these things. The unfortunate people who have been indoctrinated into believing fear-based superstitions are forced to deal with them whenever they pop up. In the UK, seeing a single magpie bird ("one for sorrow") is considered bad luck, and superstitious Brits who come across a lonely magpie employ a number of countermeasures to ward off danger. In many places in the West, people are haunted by the number thirteen. *I need to schedule a surgical procedure, but the next available appointment is on Friday the 13th.* For better or worse—and it is probably worse—the commercial world is often designed to reduce the frequency of these feared encounters. Most hotels in the United States do not have thirteenth floors—or, more accurately, they call it the fourteenth floor—and many airports skip over Gate 13. It is understandable that, in the past, people were searching for explanations for the bad things that happened in their lives, and so negative superstitions evolved to fill a gap in knowledge. But science encourages us to look elsewhere for explanations, and in my opinion most fear-based superstitions should be forgotten.

One possible exception is the belief in a certain kind of jinx. Psychologists Jane Risen and Thomas Gilovich conducted a series of experiments on tempting fate.[4] They had Cornell undergraduates read a scenario about a young man who had either done the reading for his college class or not. The participants were asked how likely it was the young man would be called on if the professor asked a question about the reading and no one volunteered an answer. When the young man had tempted fate by coming to class without doing the reading, participants predicted it was significantly more likely he would be called on by the professor. In another study, the scenario involved a student who'd applied to Stanford for graduate school but had not yet heard from the admissions office. Consistent with her nature, the student's mother sent him a Stanford t-shirt. Half the participants read a version of the scenario in which the young man wore the t-shirt the next day and the other half read a version in which the young man stuffed the t-shirt away in a drawer. Finally, both groups of participants were asked how likely it was that the young man would be accepted to Stanford. As expected, when the young man tempted fate by wearing the t-shirt, participants judged his chances of getting admitted to Stanford significantly lower than when he put the t-shirt way.

Normally, irrational fears are not very useful, but Risen and Gilovich suggest that our worries about tempting fate may have an adaptive value. Tempting fate involves taking an unnecessary risk that departs from your own typical behavior or from accepted norms of behavior. In addition, these are circumstances that—when they go wrong—often spark counterfactual thinking, imagining "what might have been."[5] If you leave the house without an umbrella when rain is predicted and get caught in a downpour, you are likely to kick yourself and feel regret.

Risen and Gilovich point out that societies all place constraints on actions that don't serve the needs of the group. Sometimes those constraints are formalized in laws, but often other kinds of control are used. The irrational belief that the universe will settle the score by punishing rash acts instills a more subtle form of social control, and social groups that encourage these fears may benefit from the strengthening of group values and cohesion. Some people may see this balancing effect in religious terms, with God punishing people who demonstrate hubris or pride, and others may simply believe that the cosmos has an interest in justice: *that's just the way things tend to work out.* According to Risen and Gilovich, a belief that the world or God will conspire to make you fail when you tempt fate—and the anticipation of feelings of regret—may be a hedge against boastful actions and unnecessary risk taking.

In general, the positive luck-enhancing superstitions are a more fertile ground for usefulness. When a superstition is deployed in preparation for some performance—an athletic competition, school exam, job interview, or business presentation—there is the possibility of a positive effect. For example, a superstition that involves wearing the same pair of socks throughout a tournament run, tying your shoes in a specific way, and bouncing the ball exactly five times before a first serve—all things Serena Williams reportedly does—could possibility put her in a psychological zone that enhances play.[6] This is not magic, but a productive delusion. Many observers consider Williams to be the best woman's tennis player of all time, so she has indeed been very successful. Could her superstitions be part of her secret?

Unfortunately, the evidence at the moment is murky. For many years, no one bothered to ask the question, Do superstitions have practical value? Most psychological research on the topic was aimed at describing the believers and identifying what personal characteristics and experiences led to belief in superstition. But in recent years, psychologists have begun to explore the practical implications of luck-enhancing superstitions. A big breakthrough came in 2010 when a group at the University of Cologne in Germany published a series of tests, the most famous of which came to be known as "the golf ball study."[7] It was a remarkably simple setup. Twenty-eight college students were recruited for the experiment, and each was individually brought to a room where their task was to putt a golf ball into a cup. They were given ten tries, and the cup was 100 cm (approximately 39 inches) away. For a random half of the students, the experimenter handed the participant the ball and said, "Here is your ball. So far it has turned out to be a lucky ball." The other half of the participants were in the control group and were simply told, "This is the ball everyone has used so far." Earlier the experimenters had determined that approximately 80 percent of the students in the study believed in luck. As predicted, the "lucky ball" group performed significantly better, with an average of 6.4 successful putts, compared to 4.8 for the control group.

The German golf ball study created quite a splash because it was the first to show evidence of a performance effect based in superstition, but eventually there were doubts. In recent decades, psychology has gone through a period of reexamination. Some classic experiments that had been cited in textbooks for years could not be reproduced when attempted by different researchers. Typically, science journals are more interested in publishing new findings, and there is a bias against going back to redo something that has already been published. Unfortunately, scientists discovered that this publishing bias and other weaknesses in the research process meant that a shockingly large number of classic studies could not be reproduced in other laboratories. Being able to replicate an effect is a hallmark of science. If researchers discover something exciting in their lab, but other researchers following the same procedures can't get it to happen, the finding is unreliable. The resulting "reproducibility crisis" in psychology has spurred a shift in emphasis toward opening up the research process and going back now and again to attempt to reproduce experiments under different conditions.

In part because of the excitement it created, the golf ball study became the focus of a replication attempt. The original study had only fourteen participants in each group, so, in an effort to strengthen the study, investigators at Dominican University in the United States conducted a replication with four times the original number of participants.[8] In addition, the authors communicated with the German researchers to make certain their procedures were as close as possible to the first study. Unfortunately, the results showed no difference between the lucky ball group and the control group, despite the American participants believing in luck at a level equivalent to the German participants. The Dominican researchers went on to try a second replication with a more salient lucky ball manipulation. In this case, participants drew their ball from a sack containing four plain golf balls and four marked with a green clover. If the participant selected a clover-marked ball, the experimenter said "Wow! You get to use the lucky ball!" Despite these efforts to fortify the lucky ball effect, the second study proved no better. Plain and lucky ball users putted with approximately equal accuracy.

As a result, we are left with a muddle. It certainly seems plausible that superstitions could have a practical effect for athletes, actors, job-seekers, and anyone else who is hoping to do well at a difficult task, but at the moment we are lacking clear evidence of such an effect, at least in the context of a lucky object enhancing performance. Belief in superstition is widespread, and many people report having trinkets, charms, or pieces of clothing that are lucky for them. So, it is likely that having and using these objects is suffi-ciently soothing to maintain their use. But at the moment, we lack clear proof that superstition's power goes beyond its emotional value to actually make success more likely.

Of Rituals and Incantations

Many of the superstitions that athletes employ, including Justin Tucker's ar-rangement of his uniform on the locker room floor, are rituals performed before the competition. Rituals of various types appear to be universal to human life, and ritual-like behavior is also common among nonhuman an-imals.[9] In recent years psychologists have turned their attention to the psy-chological effects of performing rituals, and unlike the spotty findings of the golf ball studies, rituals appear to have more consistent benefits. Previously it was known that athletes who used a pregame ritual performed better than those who do not, but these were correlational relationships.[10] It could very well be that whatever factors make you a good athlete also make you more likely to perform rituals without there being any direct relationship between the two. As a result, psychologists have begun to have people perform rituals in the lab to see what effects they have.

Some of these experiments have been rather creatively designed. For ex-ample, in order to study the effects of rituals on dealing with grief and loss, two Harvard Business School professors brought a group of people into a lab and told them that one person would win $200 and be able to leave immedi-ately.[11] Then, the experimenters conducted a lottery, sent the winner home with the cash, and collected data on the disappointed people left behind. In a study of the effects of rituals on public performances, participants arrived at the laboratory and discovered that, as part of their service, they would have to sing the song "Don't Stop Believing" by the '80s rock band Journey in front of a small audience of strangers.[12] Other participants in the same study were asked to solve math problems in a timed test.[13]

The results of all this research show that rituals are useful in a variety of contexts. They help people sing better in front of strangers, solve math problems more accurately, and cope with the disappointment of not win-ning $200. In addition, performing a ritual can help improve self-control of people who want to make healthier food choices and lose weight.[14] In typ-ical research fashion, the rituals employed in the laboratory were rather pared-down sequences. Here are the directions for the ritual used in the "Don't Stop Believing" study:

> Please do the following ritual: Draw a picture of how you are feeling right now. Sprinkle salt on your drawing. Count up to five out loud. Crinkle up your paper. Throw your paper in the trash.[15]

This sequence of activities is laden with a bit of symbolism. It is an emotional self-portrait sprinkled with salt (magic salt?) and thrown away. But it doesn't have any obvious connection to a common superstition or religious practice. The experimenters did label it a ritual, and in this case, that mattered. Participants who did exactly the same sequence when it was described as "random behaviors" did not reap the same benefit. But subsequent studies have shown that, even without labeling it a ritual, a sequence of actions that is ordered and repeated can have the same effect. For example, in one study, participants in the first group were asked to perform an ordered sequence of "gestures" twice in a row before making a decision requiring self-control, and those in the second group were asked to choose from a list of "gestures" and perform them in a random sequence just once. After both groups made their self-control decisions—choosing whether to go to a party with friends (a selfish choice) or to a fundraising event at a conflicting time (a prosocial choice)—they were asked if the sequence of actions felt like a ritual and, as we might expect, the people whose gestures were ordered and repeated said it felt more like a ritual. In addition, significantly more people in this group chose to attend the fundraising event (59 percent) than in the random gestures group (19 percent).[16]

So, it looks like we are on to something with rituals. They seem to do some good. But a few questions remain. What exactly is a ritual, and how do they help? And, now that we know they are helpful, are they delusions? Researchers in this field have identified three primary features of a ritual. First, rituals are rigidly ordered sequences of actions that are done the same way each time. Second, they have some symbolic meaning. Outside the laboratory, rituals are often an expression of the individual's religious faith. The Passover seder (seder means "order") is a ritual meal done the same way at the beginning of each Passover season. The Muslim practice of praying five times a day includes a repeated sequence of poses performed while facing toward Mecca, and the daily Christian ritual of the rosary is an ordered sequence of prayers that also involves a weekly cycle centered around the religious mysteries. But many common rituals have neither religious or superstitious meaning. Finally, when rituals are connected with a specific goal, the connection must be indirect. As a result, a basketball player who has a habit of practicing free throws before each game is not performing a ritual because practicing has a direct connection to performance. However, listening to a specific song in the car on the way to the arena or following a specified sequence in dressing for the game could constitute a ritual.

The mechanism by which rituals function is quite simple and is grounded in our need for control. The link between anxiety and control is one of the central pillars of human psychology. In most cases, experiencing a loss of control leads to anxiety. Alternatively, anxiety is often felt as a loss of control. The successful performance of a rigid sequence of actions restores a sense of order and mastery over the physical world.[17] In the "Don't Stop Believing" study, students who performed a ritual before singing were less anxious and had lower heart rates than those who did not. Participants in both the self-control and grief studies had a greater sense of control, which led to improved self-control choices and better coping with the loss of $200. These are precisely the kinds of indirect effects we were looking for in the golf ball study, but the evidence suggests rituals produce a much more reliable benefit than belief in lucky golf balls.

Which brings us to the final question. We now have great confidence that rituals are psychologically beneficial, but are they delusions? According to our rational choice standard, there are at least two ways rituals could be irrational. First, the practitioner could believe there is direct causal link between the ritual and the desired outcome. This form of epistemic irrationality violates the emerging definition of a ritual—that it *not* be directly connected to the goal—and makes the belief a superstition. If tennis star Rafael Nadal believes that his extensive rituals bring him luck—rituals that include always stepping on the court with his right foot, never stepping on any of the white lines between points, and endlessly adjusting the shoulders of his shirt before each serve—then he may be employing a useful delusion. Nadal's well-documented rituals look similar to those associated with obsessive compulsive disorder and are so time consuming that they frequently delay the progress of the match, but it is unclear what he believes about them.[18]

A second way of achieving a delusional ritual is to recruit an interceding actor. When people implore a deity, saint, or demon to help with the task at hand, their beliefs include supernatural elements that are not supported by evidence. As a result, a boxer may benefit from a delusion when, as part of a pre-bout prayer, he implores God to give his left hook the power to knock out his opponent. But, given that most researchers have studied very secular and nonsuperstitious forms of ritual, the data suggest that the reduced anxiety and increased sense of control result from the ritual itself, not from the attendant beliefs. Most rituals are probably infused with some incantatory symbolism that is fitting for the user, but it need not be superstitious. Indeed, surveys of people who have used personal rituals to get through difficult times suggest that very few of these rituals are overtly religious or superstitious. For example, one study found that 46 percent of respondents reported using a ritual in an anxiety-provoking situation. Of these ritual users, only 20 percent said their ritual had religious elements and 17 percent said it had superstitious elements.[19] Rituals of various forms are a popular way to deal with difficult situations, but it appears that many of them do not involve irrational beliefs. They are beneficial but not delusional. Nonetheless, if superstitious belief or religious faith is your gateway into the use of a ritual in difficult times, the ritual is likely to help.

Before leaving this topic, we should acknowledge that many common rituals are not individual acts. They are performed as part of a social group. We sing hymns in church and the national anthem before sporting events; teams pray together before games or perform a group cheer; and at the beginning of a shift, Walmart (previously Wal*mart) employees perform the following call and response cheer while clapping rhythmically:[20]

Leader	Associates
"Give Me a W!"	"W!"
"Give Me an A!"	"A!"
"Give Me an L!"	"L!"
"Give Me a Squiggly!"	"Squiggly!" (Everybody wiggles as if doing the twist.)
"Give Me an M!"	"M!"
"Give Me an A!"	"A!"
"Give Me an R!"	"R!"
"Give Me a T!"	"T!"
"What's that spell?"	"Wal-Mart!"
"What's that spell?"	"Wal-Mart!"
"Who's number one?"	"The Customer!"

Group rituals bond people together and provide proof of membership and belonging. Religious rituals are the most obvious example, but families often establish specific rituals that bind them together. Many of these group rituals are not scheduled in response to a current threat. They are part of the daily or annual cycle of the group. But when, as in the case of a team cheer or group prayer, they are performed just before a game or at some other challenging time, the existing evidence suggests that, in addition to their bonding function, they may help calm jangling nerves and provide a sense of empowerment.

Going on Faith

Rituals bring us to religion. The rational choice model is built upon the Cliffordian idea that "it is wrong always, everywhere, and for anyone, to believe anything upon insufficient evidence,"[21] and yet, by definition, a number of core religious beliefs are taken on faith, without evidence. As a result, actions guided by religious belief are possible candidates for the kind of delusional (or at least nonrational) benefits that William James might endorse.

Depending upon how you look at the data, religious belief is either a blessing or a curse. On a macro level, less religious countries and states within the United States are happier than more religious countries and states, but in a given location, people who are more religious are happier than less religious people. Greater religious engagement at the state level predicts shorter life expectancy and higher crime rates, but more religiously engaged individuals have longer life expectancies and are less prone to criminal behavior. Researchers call these findings the "religious engagement paradox,"[22] but religion is far from the only characteristic to show conflicting results from ten thousand feet versus on the ground. Low-income states and high-income individuals have voted Republican in recent elections, and liberal countries and conservative individuals report better well-being.[23] I will leave it to the sociologists and political scientists to sort out the macro-level findings, but at the individual level, religious belief seems to be associated with a number of positive effects. Of course, because we cannot bring people into the laboratory and randomly assign them to religious and nonreligious experimental conditions, most of the evidence about the psychology of religion is correlational, and as a result, we have questions about cause and effect relationships. Do happy people gather in houses of worship or do religious beliefs and activities foster happiness?

The research fairly consistently shows that, wherever you live, people who are more religious are happier than those who are less religious. But a closer look demystifies these findings a bit. Rather than degree of belief, the important variable appears to be the level of involvement with the group. For example, a 2016 survey of over fifty-six thousand Americans found that only 26 percent of people who never attended religious services reported being happy, and happiness rose consistently with more frequent attendance, peaking at 47 percent for people who attended services several times a week.[24]

The social effects of a religious community also play out in other areas. Many people think that religion is necessary for a moral life, and it is true that religious people give more to charity—including nonreligious charities—are more likely to volunteer, and make more blood donations than nonreligious people.[25] The belief that you must be religious to be moral may explain why surveys have consistently shown that US voters would prefer a Catholic, Jewish, or Muslim president over an atheist.[26] But as in the case of happiness, many of the moral benefits of religion come from active engagement with the group—not from belief. As political scientists Robert Putnam and David Campbell write in *American Grace: How Religion Divides and Unites Us*, "Once we know how observant a person is in terms of church attendance, nothing that we can discover about the content of her religious faith adds anything to our understanding or prediction of her good neighborliness."[27] Furthermore, there are negative effects of engagement with a religious congregation. In a remarkable study, researchers from the New School for Social Research and the University of British Columbia found that the frequency of attendance at mosque—not the degree of religious devotion—predicted support for suicide bombings of Israelis.[28] The researchers also surveyed Israeli Jews living in the West Bank and Gaza about their support for the 1994 suicide attack by Baruch Goldstein that killed 29 Muslims. When prompted to think about synagogue attendance, these Israelis were more likely to describe Goldstein as a hero than when prompted to think about prayer. Finally, in a follow-up study of Mexican Catholics, Russian Christian Orthodox, Israeli Jews, Indonesian Muslims, UK protestants, and Indian Hindus, the researchers measured the respondents' willingness to die for their god/beliefs and their support for the statement "I blame people of other religions for much of the trouble in this world."[29] When they combined the responses to these two questions to produce a measure of "parochial altruism," they found that, for each of these groups, attendance at services and not religious devotion predicted the level of parochial altruism.

All the major religions promote valuable moral lessons, and it is clear these lessons have an effect. The study of Israeli support for suicide bombings mentioned in the previous paragraph was a "priming" study, in which certain kinds of thoughts and memories are activated. Prior to asking the crucial question about the suicide bomber, participants were primed by asking them either about their synagogue attendance or about their frequency of prayer. Other studies show that by priming religious thoughts people can be motivated to be more generous. For example, when participants were asked to unscramble sentences that included religious words (e.g., spirit, divine, God) they subsequently offered more money to their opponents in a game that allowed them to keep all the money if they chose.[30] Other studies have found that subliminal flashing of religious words on a computer screen made people less likely to cheat.[31] These moral nudges are a good thing, but religious thoughts do not have a unique effect. For example, in the sentence unscrambling study, the researchers were able to inspire the same generous behavior in their participants by having them unscramble sentences that included secular words, such as civic, jury, court, police, and contract. Similarly, studies have shown that people are less likely to take coffee without paying when exposed to the image of a pair of watching eyes. It needn't be God watching over you to instill moral behavior, just the suggestion that somebody is watching.

We can now draw a number of conclusions about the value of these forms of magical or non-evidence-based thinking. First, superstitions are comforting in the moment, but may not have more practical value. You may feel better wearing your lucky socks to the final exam, but it's unclear whether they will help you ace the test. The evidence is stronger that rituals can reduce anxiety, stimulate a sense of control, and boost impromptu karaoke singing skills as well as pop math quiz scores, but the rituals don't need to be magical incantations to create their effect. Indeed, many people use rituals at difficult moments, and it appears that very few of them are superstitious or religious in nature. Finally, those who are active in their religious communities are happier and—in some contexts, at least—better people, but there is little evidence that these benefits come from their belief in God, saints, or other supernatural phenomena. Active membership in a community, be it a knitting club or a church, undoubtedly has benefits. If irrational beliefs inspire you to engage in a ritual or to get involved in a religious group, then you may benefit from a helpful delusion, but, unlike some of the other cases we will encounter, there are ways to derive these same benefits without delusion.

5

Soul Mates

Love is the enemy of sound judgment, and occasionally this is in service of the good.

— Tayari Jones, *An American Marriage*

Once, in the early intoxicating months of a romantic relationship, I was mansplaining something to my beloved, and on my way to a much more important point, I happened to say, "Of course, theoretically—given the many millions of people in the world—each of us might have fallen in love with any number of other people and been just as happy. . . . "

Big mistake.

I never got to the more important point. The reaction to my breezy comment was swift and intense. "No, no, no! That is not true! Don't say that!" Or words to that effect. My partner expressed the belief that we were uniquely matched soul mates, and she was deeply disappointed that I did not see things the same way. In most other respects, she was a very rational, scientifically minded person, but in this case, she seemed to believe that—by some miracle of chance or fate—we had each found the one person on the planet who was best suited to be with the other.

For my part, I was very much in love with this woman. Furthermore, although I am a very logically minded person, I consider myself a romantic. I am easily moved to tears by sentimental books and movies. I have strong responses to music, art, and theater, and I have forged deep relationships, many of which have lasted throughout my life. But what my beloved was saying in this case just didn't make sense to me. The idea that we were one-and-onlys was mathematically implausible.

Looking back, I wonder if, on some level, my partner understood that what she was saying couldn't be true, but she needed to believe—against logic—that we were soul mates. And she needed me to believe it, too. Despite all evidence to the contrary, she wanted us to share a conviction that our love was special, and she wanted us to confess our love to each other, almost in the manner of a vow.

As it turned out, there were no actual vows in that relationship. A couple of years later, the romance ended, and we went our separate ways. There were probably many reasons why things didn't work out for us, but I've wondered if that soul mate conversation revealed a crack in our bond that—combined with others—played some small role (possibly more than a small role) in our eventual demise.

The Promises We Make

Wedding vows can be a problem for someone who wants to be both rational and honest. Many Christian weddings still include a phrase promising love and fidelity "till death do us part." At the moment they make these declarations most couples are bathed in the warm glow of emotion, and they may really believe what they say. But many must also know that approximately 50 percent of marriages end in divorce.[1] In the United States in 2012, the median length of a first marriage that ended in divorce was 12.3 years.[2] True, all those Hollywood actors are pulling the average down, but there aren't enough of them to explain the overall trend.[3] Oscar Wilde famously said, "Marriage is the triumph of imagination over intelligence. Second marriage is the triumph of hope over experience." This is a cynical view, but not one unsupported by evidence. As you might expect, second and third marriages have even higher failure rates.

In contrast to the Christian custom, both Jewish and Islamic marriage practices often include some nod to the possibility of divorce. Traditional Jewish custom allows for a woman to divorce her husband only if he gives her permission in the form of a written document called a *get*. As a result, some modern conservative and reform *ketubot* (marriage contracts) include more equitable methods of accomplishing a divorce and providing for the support of the wife. Similarly, an Islamic marriage contract includes financial provisions for the wife in the event of divorce or the husband's death.[4] Traditionally, neither religion provided equal access to divorce for women, and as a result, Reform Judaism recognizes civil divorce as terminating a marriage.

But many Christians still make the till-death-do-us-part promise— or struggle with it. One possible solution was proposed by a Palm Beach attorney in a 2013 *Washington Post* opinion piece.[5] He suggested couples re-place wedlock with a "wedlease," an agreement to be married for a five- or ten-year period, renewable by mutual consent. Wedlessees would retain sep-arate property ownership and might offer a "security deposit" to be awarded to either party if the other leaves before the term of the wedlease has expired. Based on what I can glean from a Google search, the idea has yet to catch on.

In recent years, there has been some debate among philosophers about whether it is right to make promises when you know there is a chance you will not keep them, such as those in wedding vows or in resolutions to quit smoking, lose weight, or run a marathon. The problem with these promises is that it is difficult to make them and be both rational and sincere. If you promise to stop smoking, despite knowing there's a good chance you'll fail—perhaps you've tried and failed in the past—you risk being either insincere (because you have doubts) or irrational (because you are ignoring the evi-dence). In the case of the marriage vow, a truly honest and rational statement might omit a promise but express a sincere desire for a life-long bond and a commitment to try. *I really want this to work, and I promise to do my best.* But for many people, this will not sound very romantic. Merely opening the window of doubt will be a disappointment to couples who believe—or want to believe—they are soul mates.

The philosopher Berislav Marušić has argued that in many cases it is not irresponsible to make the wedding promise, even when there is objective ev-idence—such as the average divorce rate for your demographic—that points to the possibility of failure.[6] According to his view, even when the data show that many people like you break their promises and even if you haven't al-ways been faithful to partners in the past, you might still have reason to be-lieve you will be successful, despite the difficulties involved. Marušić suggests that, in situations like this, the project is not merely to predict your future behavior based on demographic data or even prior personal experience. Rather you should consider the reasons in favor of promising, and if they are sufficient, you simply decide to do it. If, after taking into account the possi-bility of failure, there are sufficient practical reasons for you to be faithful and true (e.g., you really love your partner, you believe your partner really loves you, and you want the relationship to last), then you can promise responsibly. Marušić's approach rests on the power of human agency and according to his view, if you decide to be true to your partner and believe that you will, you can promise to do so in good faith, without being either irrational or in-sincere. Furthermore, he suggests that, if you convince the person receiving your promise that you have taken into account the odds against success in coming to your decision, you provide reasons for your partner to trust you.

If Marušić's theory is valid for wedding vows, it goes against a common view of how love works. Many people have made promises at their wedding, believing in the moment that they were neither irrational nor dishonest and that they and their partners were soul mates, and yet at some future point, after the promises are a dim memory, their feelings change or are transferred to another person. Falling in or out of love is often considered to be an involuntary act. Furthermore, we are remarkably prone to falling in love with people who, sooner or later, we recognize are not right for us. The unlikely trio of Emily Dickinson, Woody Allen, and Selena Gomez—in somewhat different contexts—have all expressed variations on the theme, "the heart wants what it wants."[7] Rather than choosing to love someone, many people "fall" in love, are swept off their feet, or are in some other way buffeted by love rather than in charge of the enterprise. Sometimes people report feeling an immediate attraction. A 2007 study of 137 Dutch couples found that 43 percent reported they had fallen in love "at first sight."[8] Some of these memories may have been polished a bit to heighten the sense of destiny, but this kind of lighting strike is a very common way of talking about love. In his novel *The Only Story*, Julian Barnes writes, "Who can control how much they love? If you can control it, it isn't love. I don't know what you call it instead, but it isn't love."[9]

Contrary views have been expressed. In an emotional scene in the movie *Closer*, based on the play by Patrick Marber, Dan (played by Jude Law) confesses to his girlfriend Alice (Natalie Portman) that he has had an affair with Anna (Julia Roberts):

ALICE: "How? How does it work? How do you do this to someone?"
DAN: [shrugs]
ALICE: "Not good enough!" [Begins to pack up her things.]
DAN: "I fell in love with her, Alice!"
ALICE: "Oh, as if you had no choice? There's a moment. There's always a moment. 'I can do this. I can give in to this, or I can resist it.' And I don't know when your moment was, but I bet you there was one."

Clearly both people are biased in their assessments of the situation. Scorned lovers tend to emphasize the betrayer's freedom of choice, and betrayers tend to point to things beyond their control, as Dan does in this scene.

Nonetheless, many would take Alice's side. Had there been a wedding vow or some other promise between them, Alice would probably have been happier if Dan had adopted Marušić's view of promises.

For the moment, we can leave aside the question of whether or not we have control over the act of falling in or out of love. We will come back to that topic in chapter 9. But both these cases—the soul mate paradox and the wedding promise—demonstrate how lovers sometimes need to hear particular types of statements from their partners, statements that it could be argued are epistemically irrational. The mere suggestion that my lover and I were not uniquely destined to be with each other brought a strong reaction, and in the wedding ceremony case, any less than a promise to love "until death do us part" would be deeply disappointing to many a fiancé.

These problems might be resolved by simply deciding to lie. Lovers lie to each other all the time, and there is often a kind of mutual consent. In sonnet 138, the poet and his younger lover, Shakespeare's "dark lady," agree to be deceived:

> When my love swears that she is made of truth,
> I do believe her, though I know she lies,

The poet pretends to believe his lover despite knowing that she lies—both that she tells a falsehood and that she lies with other men—but there is a sense in which the poet deceives himself, as well. The poet is concerned that he's grown old, but chooses to believe her claim that he has not:

> Thus vainly thinking that she thinks me young,
> Although I know my years be past the best,

He sums up the situation in the final couplet, in which the word *lie* takes on both meanings:

> Therefore I'll lie with love, and love with me,
> Since that our faults in love thus smother'd be.

A lover's wish to be lied to is a common trope in popular music. For example, in the 1983 hit song "Tell Me a Lie," covered by Janie Fricke and others, a woman asks a married man to lie to her and say he loves her so that they can spend the night together.[10]

Couples often enter into a tacit agreement that they will sometimes lie to each other. There are the "white" lies that make us feel better. The classic examples are about one's appearance ("You look even more beautiful than the day I met you"), but of course they can be about almost anything. The philosopher Clancy Martin claims that lying to make your partner feel better is a valuable part of a healthy relationship and that unrealistic expectations about truthfulness are the enemy of love. "If you want to have love in your life, you'd better be prepared to tell some lies and to believe some lies."[11] He points out that the philosopher Immanuel Kant, who said it was never acceptable to lie, was a life-long bachelor.

But are all these lies and irrational statements useful? Are they even irrational? As we saw in chapter 2, liars are far from deluded. Lies may be immoral, but they're not necessarily irrational. Liars know the truth and strive to obscure it. They are engaged in a utilitarian enterprise that any classical economist would understand. The liar calculates the marginal return on lying to be sufficient to compensate for the risk of detection. In the case of sonnet 138, both parties seem to have a clear understanding of the truth and the purposes of the lies. For the poet, the lies are more comforting than the truth, and because it is likely the dark lady knows he doesn't really believe her, she is acting rationally, too. Similarly, the singer in "Tell Me a Lie" sees her situation quite clearly but needs the reassurance of the lie. I suspect something similar was going on in my soul mate example. It is quite possible my beloved knew what I was saying was true, but she needed me to believe the lie. Part of the weakness of our relationship may have come from what Clancy Martin would call my unrealistic expectations about truthfulness.

The wedding vow example is slightly more complicated. In this case, the situation is clearly designed as a hedge against future weakness of will. Although Catholics still forbid divorce under most circumstances, many of the religious prohibitions have fallen away in modern times.[12] But the wedding ceremony is often a social event, conducted in front of witnesses. I was surprised to learn that, in my state of Connecticut, a wedding can legally consist of just the couple and an officiant. Running along the seashore early one morning, I stumbled upon just such a ceremony consisting of a man, a woman, and a minister. But most weddings are larger, and it is not uncommon for hundreds of people to witness the couple's vows to one another. Although I am not aware of any empirical data on the topic, promises made in front of a community of people are probably a little more embarrassing to break. Obviously, it is not enough to do the trick in many cases. I once incurred a substantial expense to attend the large and elaborate first wedding of a relative, only to learn that the couple had split a year later. I wondered if they'd managed to pay the wedding bills before the divorce bills arrived. But it is clear that the public nature of the wedding ceremony is meant to give the couple a sense that the community is invested in their success. It's also true that, like your intended, most wedding guests would not be entirely satisfied with a promise to merely do your best. So, like Clifford's ship owner who is not certain about the seaworthiness of his vessel, the person with doubts about their ability to remain true is under great pressure to push those doubts aside. The desire to please both your partner and the assembled group provides a powerful incentive to suppress any thoughts of failure.

The ship owner and the wedding participant might be aided in their task by cognitive dissonance. The discomfort created by the conflict between their beliefs and their actions might be resolved by changing their beliefs. As described by Clifford, the ship owner seems to deliberately push any doubts about the seaworthiness of his vessel out of his mind, but he is a fictional character invented by Clifford to make a point. In the case of marriage vows, it is likely that many participants change their beliefs over time. Anticipating the kinds of pledges they will need to make and the importance of these declarations for their intended, they may carve out some exception to the probability of failure and convince themselves that they will love and cherish their spouses until parted by death.

So let's assume that, by whatever means, both my former partner and the average wedding couple actually believed what they were saying, and let's further stipulate that the statements are objectively irrational. Although there may be some religious people who, for example, believe in the Jewish concept of *bashert*—that their match is predestined and ideal—the rest of us might agree that, as a mathematical fact, it is highly unlikely for two people to happen to find in each other their unique soul mates. Further, we might agree that it is irrational to promise to do a very important and difficult thing when the odds of success are far from a lock. Even if there is a good chance of success, due to your demographic group, it is not clear that a promise is rational.

If we agree that these people are deluded, are their delusions helpful? Science has not addressed these exact cases, but the evidence we have suggests that they might be positive delusions. If either the soul mate concept or the wedding promise is expressed with apparent sincerity, they may be reflected back by the other member of the couple in a kind of positive feedback loop, strengthening the relationship. These beliefs might create a kind of self-fulfilling prophecy. This is not unlike the doctor who promises a course of treatment will have a positive effect, thereby creating expectations in the patient that result in a positive placebo effect. It's not clear how strong the effect would be. Many relationships still fail, but these beliefs may have some practical value.

Falling in love is neither rational nor irrational, but it does help the species survive. In Charles Baxter's novel *The Feast of Love*, the girlfriend of the very romantic main character says, "all this love business is just nature's way of getting more babies into the world. The rest of it is just all this romance non-sense." Of course, in an evolutionary sense, love does make sense, because keeping an infant human alive requires a substantial commitment of time and labor. It helps to have backup. But how do positive delusions help foster romantic relationships?

Delusional Dating

Even before you get the opportunity to commit yourself to a partner, self-delusions can help you find one. Just as it does in other social and career settings, overconfidence can pay off on the romantic playing field. A number of studies show that confident people are judged more attractive than their less confident competitors. For example, in one study, researchers created a speed-dating event in which heterosexual college student men had a series of four-minute conversations with heterosexual women from a different university. The women found the men who were more confident more attractive and were significantly more likely to say they would want to see them again.[13] But confidence can be a double-edged sword.

A number of studies have identified overconfident people using the Overclaiming Questionnaire (OCQ), which asks about your familiarity with topics in ten knowledge areas that sound a bit like *Jeopardy!* categories: historical names and events, fine arts, language, books and poems, authors and characters, social science and law, physical sciences, life sciences, popular culture, and current consumer products.[14] For each item, participants are asked to rate their familiarity on a seven-point scale, from 1 "never heard of it" to 7 "know it very well." Scattered among the questions are thirty items that do not exist. For example, the physical science section asks about some real things (e.g., "Manhattan Project" and "plate tectonics"), but it also asks about "cholarine" and "plates of parallax." Overconfidence is determined by adding up the degree of confidence respondents have in their knowledge of these bogus items.

The OCQ has been used in a number of contexts, and people who score high on it show a mixed bag of characteristics. They have higher self-esteem and better "ego-resilience," meaning that they are able to deal more effectively with everyday challenges, but they are also higher on measures of narcissism.[15]

A group of researchers from Australia and the United States created a mock dating study, in which male and female participants took the OCQ and then were asked to write a short dating profile for themselves.[16] These dating profiles were given to a new set of participants in accordance with their sexual preference (male profiles for gay men, female profiles for lesbians, male profiles for heterosexual females, etc.), and the second group was asked to rate the personalities that came through in the dating profiles.

The results were somewhat equivocal for the overconfident high scorers on the OCQ who claimed to know a lot about plates of parallax and other nonexistent things. As we might expect, males and females who were overconfident on the OCQ came across as more confident in their profiles, but these overconfident people were also seen as more arrogant, a characteristic that the potential mates did not find appealing. As a result, any benefit that overconfident people might have gained by projecting confidence was wiped out by their arrogance.

All was not lost, however. In a subsequent set of studies, the researchers assessed the effect of overconfidence on a person's willingness to compete for the attention of a potential mate in a hypothetical dating situation.[17] Participants were given the dating profile of a competitor and then allowed to choose between competing for a desired mate or opting for a less competitive social experience that would not include the person they were most interested in. There were two findings. First, as one might expect, participants who were overconfident were more likely to choose to compete for the desired mate. On the other hand, when the dating profile of a participant's rival had been written by someone who was overconfident as measured by the OCQ, participants perceived this person as being difficult and were more likely to choose the less competitive social situation. So, according to these studies, overconfidence does not make you a more attractive mate, but it may help clear out some of your competition in the dating world.

Some of the same researchers subsequently did a longitudinal study of boys at a private school in Australia that revealed some social benefits of overconfidence.[18] At the beginning of the study, the researchers determined levels of overconfidence by comparing the boys' own ratings of their abilities in sport and intelligence with objective measures of performance in these two areas. They also assessed each boy's popularity by asking them to come up with a list of their ten best friends at school. The number of times a boy's name came up on the best friends lists was taken as an indicator of his popularity. The results showed that overconfidence in both intelligence and sport led to better mental health and that overconfidence in sport but not intelligence led to greater popularity over time. It is not clear that greater popularity among other teenaged boys at school would translate into better dating success, but it probably wouldn't hurt. Thus, this study provides another example of social benefits accruing to people who have an inflated view of themselves.

Two recent studies by different sets of researchers have attempted to determine whether self-deception could have a positive effect on success in acquiring sexual partners.[19] Both studies used male and female heterosexual college students and both used a questionnaire that measured the extent to which participants deceived themselves about their positive qualities. For example, in one item participants were asked to agree or disagree with the statement "I always know why I like things." Given that there is always some ambiguity about why we like things, strong agreement with this item is considered delusional. The result of both studies found that participants who were deluded about how great they were reported having more sexual partners, but in one of those frustrating things that happens in science, one study found the effect only in men and the other only in women. The different results may have been caused by the somewhat different methodologies used, but science waits for a clearer understanding of how self-deception about how wonderful you are affects sexual success.

Finally, it is a common observation that heterosexual men overestimate the degree to which women want to have sex with them. In the current coffeehouse culture, this trend has inspired many personal advice essays with titles such as "No, Your Barista Is Not Flirting with You." To the extent that men are deluded in this way, it would encourage them to pursue partners despite relatively low odds of success. This will undoubtedly end badly in many cases—when, for instance, the barista rebuffs your advances—but in the long run the benefits of this misperception may outweigh the costs.[20]

Deluded in Love

So, self-delusion might help you find a mate, but perhaps the more important question is whether there are delusions that are of value once you've found your person and are in an ongoing relationship. Today many more people are opting to remain single than in earlier decades,[21] but marriage and other long-term relationships remain very popular. In 2012, I conducted a study called "Looking Back on Life" that suggested that marriage and family remained important goals.[22] In an online survey, I gave 475 American adults a list of ten possible life accomplishments (e.g., fulfilling marriage or love relationship, successful family, being very well-off financially, being a good person, etc.), and asked them to imagine they were approaching the end of their lives and that only one of the ten accomplishments could be true for them. Which would they choose? By far the most desired accomplishment was "have a successful family" and "fulfilling marriage or love relationship" was second (see Table 5.1).[23]

Results vary across the world, but studies generally show that people are made happier by entering into a partnered relationship—especially women—and that partnered people are happier than nonpartnered.[24] On average, married people are happier than nonmarried people throughout their relationship, but after the wedding, things often go downhill. Sex, one

Table 5.1 The "Looking Back on Life" Study

%	Single Life Accomplishment
31.6	Have a successful family
15.4	Fulfilling marriage or love relationship
14.9	Be a good person
14.3	Have an exciting life
10.5	Be very well off financially
5.9	Helped others in need
3.4	Accomplished in the arts
2.3	Important science discovery
1.5	Be an authority in a field
0.2	Be famous

Respondents were asked to imagine they are approaching the end of their lives and that only one of the listed life accomplishment could be true of them. Results are for 475 US adults (Vyse, 2012).

of the inherent benefits of a long-term relationship, tends to drop off in frequency over time, as does marital satisfaction, and despite how much my survey participants valued having a family as an accomplishment, having children—particularly more than one—tends to drive marital satisfaction down.[25] Be careful what you wish for. Happiness hits bottom when children are teenagers but recovers substantially when the children leave home. An empty nest is a happy nest.[26]

Despite the continued attraction of married life, a happy relationship remains a challenging goal to achieve and maintain. As part of his project to apply the tools of economics to other topics, Gary Becker theorized a kind of marriage marketplace of potential mates lining up their lists of preferences and striking deals that maximized their relationship utility.[27] He proposed this view long before the advent of Tinder, Grinder, eHarmony, or Match.com, when looking for love began to resemble picking out new living room furniture.

Other writers have applied this kind of economic analysis to life within marriage, suggesting that relationships survive as long as the benefits outweigh the costs, and it is clear that many people in partnered relationships see things this way. Psychologist Bernard Murstein studied couples with varying degrees of what he called "exchange orientation," which was characterized by a tit-for-tat approach to duties and privileges.[28] People who were high on exchange orientation were more likely to endorse statements, such as "If I do dishes three times a week, I expect my spouse to do them three times a week." Contrary to classical economic theory, which might predict that the invisible hand of the relationship marketplace would have marital partners striking deals that satisfy them both, Murstein found that exchange-oriented couples had less satisfying relationships.

In another example of my romantic mistakes, my former wife and I kept separate financial accounts and tried to divvy up chores and bills equitably. Bernard Murstein was my department colleague at the time, and he warned me that this approach did not bode well for us as a couple. My wife and I lasted 20 years before going our separate ways—surpassing the average length of a first marriage that ends in divorce—but in hindsight our seemingly fair-minded, tit-for-tat approach to daily tasks and expenses did not build a sense of trust. Or, perhaps, it was inspired by a lack of trust. In any case, our rational approach to marriage may not have been a strength.

In *Passions within Reason: The Strategic Role of the Emotions*, economist Robert Frank points out that a relationship based on simple market decisions is not very strong.[29] At the beginning the couple might be happy, but as things change, someone more attractive or with more assets might pass by. There are transaction costs in jumping from one partner to another, but in many cases a strictly consumerist calculation would support leaving the old for the new. On the other hand, being irrationally (or nonrationally) in love with your spouse—having a selfless love that is not tit-for-tat and, as a result, does not fit the standard economic self-interest view—has a stabilizing effect. For example, many people who are genuinely in love feel guilty if they betray their partners—even when they have done nothing wrong. One of the more appealing descriptions of this phenomenon was offered by humor writer David Sedaris while describing his relationship with his partner, Hugh, in an NPR interview.

> I mean, sometimes in a dream, I'll have sex with somebody else. And then even in my dream, I think, oh, no, I know I'm going to have to tell Hugh. I can't keep it a secret from him. My relationship's over. And I'm asleep. I can't even cheat on Hugh in my sleep.[30]

Obviously, some people are able to overcome their qualms and have affairs, but many of us are adequately socialized to feel guilt and anxiety whenever temptation knocks. We may not feel as guilty as Sedaris—feeling bad about having illicit sex during a dream—but, for many, these feelings, combined with worries about getting caught, are sufficient to keep them from renting a hotel room after a business lunch. The result is the imposition of greater costs for infidelity and more stable relationships.

A 2000 study of college students asked them to rate twenty-three potential qualities they would want in a partner.[31] The number one rated quality was "honest/dependable," and this characteristic was judged particularly important to a long-term relationship in comparison to a casual sexual encounter. Yet, as we have seen, Shakespeare, various country music singers, and the philosopher Clancy Martin all point to the need for some dishonesty if a relationship is to work for both members. Despite the college students' stated desire for honesty, some lying in service to the cause of maintaining a loving relationship—and not merely to cover one's tracks after going for drinks after work rather than coming straight home—is probably good for a relationship. Your results may vary. But, as I've suggested, lies are not delusions.

Some people do have delusions within and about their relationships. For example, some believe they are unique soul mates and that no other match could be as satisfying. Would it have helped if I'd believed, like my partner claimed to, that we were uniquely matched? Sadly, there is some evidence it might have. Honesty and trust are important qualities in a romantic relationship, but complete clear-eyed realism may not be a friend to love. Some couples do idealize each other, and there is overwhelming evidence that this is better for their relationships than a more honest view. We might predict that overly idealizing your partner at the beginning of a relationship is a setup for disappointment, but that appears not to be the case.

It is a bit of a scientific challenge to measure the distance between an objective assessment of a person and an idealized one, but researchers have come up with a few ways to approximate the level of unrealistic idealization. First, members of a relationship are asked to rate their partners on several dimensions and then rate an ideal partner on the same dimensions. The closer these two descriptions come together the more likely the rater is idealizing the partner. Of course, it could be that the partner being rated is objectively perfect, so a second method of dealing with this problem is to have the partner rate themselves. Prior research has shown that self-ratings tend to be grounded in reality, and as a result when a person rates their partner close to how they rate an ideal partner and somewhat distant from what the partner rates themself, this pattern of results suggests unrealistic idealization. Finally, in some cases, researchers have asked couples to nominate a friend who could provide an external assessment of each member of the pair.

A number of studies have looked at the effects of unrealistic idealization of partners and most have shown long-term positive effects on marriage. For example, one study led by Sandra Murray of the University of Buffalo followed 222 childless newlywed couples over a three-year period.[32] As expected, the newlyweds' marital satisfaction declined over time, but when the couples were separated out by whether or not they unrealistically idealized their partner, the researchers found that those who idealized their partners at the beginning of their marriages maintained a significantly higher level of satisfaction throughout the period of the study. A number of other researchers have shown similar results. For example, a 2006 study that followed 168 newlywed couples over thirteen years concluded that "marital love is less likely to decline when partners enter marriage with idealized images of one another."[33]

Additional research by Sandra Murray and colleagues sheds light on the nature of these idealized relationships. In a study of 105 married couples, Murray and her colleagues found that the happiest relationships involved people who egocentrically saw themselves in their partners.[34] They believed their partner was a kindred spirit who was more similar to them than was objectively the case. Murray suggests that this inflated sense of coherence leads the couple to believe they are soul mates who have a unique understanding of each other. Again, truth and reality are not the best foundation for love and happiness.

Of course, one might imagine that when couples idealize themselves, their relationships are no different from the nonidealizers. They simply overlook all the flaws and conflicts. But according to Sandra Murray and colleagues, this is not the case.[35] Longitudinal studies suggest that people who idealize themselves and their partners actually build relationships that are more satisfying. Rather than looking at themselves through rose colored glasses, these couples are prescient. They create the better relationships they believe they have.

Although, as you might expect, many studies show a relationship between marital satisfaction and the likelihood of divorce,[36] so far studies of idealization within couples have not found a relationship with divorce. Researchers hypothesize that, although these happy delusions influence marital satisfaction, their effect is overwhelmed by other, more powerful factors that lead to divorce.[37] As a result, maintaining a positive delusion about your partner may make for a happier relationship, but it's no protection against breakup.

How to Become Deluded?

So, there are clear benefits of both self-deception during the dating period and an unrealistic idealization of your relationship once you are paired up. But how do you become one of these overconfident or romantically idealistic people? In my own case, despite wanting to express my great affection for my partner, I would have to have been a very different person to accept the notion of one-and-onlys. I had a basic understanding of math and human psychology and was not capable of just putting those factors aside. In my marriage, I clearly chose to keep separate bank accounts and divvy up chores. As far as I recall, neither of us seriously considered using a different system. Similarly, many people are quite comfortable with promising to love their spouse "until death do us part," but others are uncomfortable making that vow. They may be very much in love and looking forward to being married, but they cannot not in good conscience promise something that has a substantial chance of not happening.

How do you become a person without doubts rather than a person with doubts who doesn't feel comfortable glossing over them? Alternatively, how do you become a person with an idealized rather than realistic view of your partner? These questions may as yet be unanswerable, but I will try to pick away at them in chapter 10.

6

The Living Dead

Let me not to the marriage of true minds
Admit impediments. Love is not love
Which alters when it alteration finds,
Or bends with the remover to remove.
O no! it is an ever-fixed mark
That looks on tempests and is never shaken;
It is the star to every wand'ring bark,
Whose worth's unknown, although his height be taken.
Love's not Time's fool, though rosy lips and cheeks
Within his bending sickle's compass come;
Love alters not with his brief hours and weeks,
But bears it out even to the edge of doom.
If this be error and upon me prov'd,
I never writ, nor no man ever lov'd.

—William Shakespeare, Sonnet 116

Although it might seem out of character for a rough-hewn Vietnam War veteran, my friend Susan's husband was a skilled artist. In the months after his death, she had several of his works framed and gave them to his friends. Today on my living room wall is a small, abstract drawing depicting twenty-five numbered circles, like billiard balls, arranged in a perfect square—five rows of five. The piece conveys order and almost frantic disorder. The numbers appear in a random pattern, and they and their penciled circles have been deliberately smudged. Five circles have been painted yellow, providing the only color in this foggy black and white piece, but I have never discovered why these numbers in particular were singled out.

Within a year or so, Susan appeared to have made a reasonable transition. We stopped hovering over her, and despite our early success at getting her drunk, going out drinking did not suit her as a regular activity. She returned to her previous life of work and church. I heard she remarried.

Joan Didion also made a kind of transition. On Christmas Day, a year after her husband's death, she visited the Cathedral of St. John the Divine and hung a flowered lei on a brass rod that held the marble name plate to the family burial vault. As she left the cathedral, a thought came to her:

> I know why we try to keep the dead alive: we try to keep them alive in order to keep them with us. I also know that if we are to live ourselves there comes a point at which we must relinquish the dead, let them go, keep them dead.[1]

For Didion, flowered leis were a reminder of a happy time in Hawaii, but she recalled that leis soon turn brown. As she approached the end of *The Year of Magical Thinking,* she wrote, "The lei I left at St. John the Divine would have gone brown by now."[2]

In the United States, the American Psychiatric Association (APA) is the self-proclaimed guardian of the border between normal and abnormal behavior—mental health and mental illness—and common grief has been a highly controversial petitioner at that border. Over the years, APA's *Diagnostic and Statistical Manual of Mental Disorders* (DSM) has gone through several revisions, and new diagnoses have been added. The current 2013 edition of the manual, *DSM-5,* is a doorstop that weighs in at just under a thousand pages. In all the previous editions of the manual, grief was excluded from the possible causes of depression on the grounds that including it would medicalize a normal feature of life and possibly lead to the overprescription of antidepressant medications. But for the first time, with the publication of the fifth edition of the *DSM,* bereavement was included as a possible contributor to depression. According to the APA, depression can be caused by many factors working together and to exclude its diagnosis during grief was potentially harmful to the patient.[3] So now, if the right conditions are met, your psychiatrist can give your grief a billable code (296.21 if your episode is mild and 296.22 if it is moderate)[4] and send you home with a prescription.

But for most people who experience a loss, this is not an important question. The sudden death of a spouse or a child can be a devastating life event, but the kinds of experiences my friend Susan and Joan Didion had do not require a clinical diagnosis. It is not clear that either of them was treated for depression.[5] Nonetheless, their nagging sense that their husbands might come back is not unusual.

If a psychologist or psychiatrist were to label this phenomenon, they might say Susan and Joan were in *denial.* The idea that denial is a stage in the process of mourning is most strongly associated with Elizabeth Kubler-Ross, the Swiss-American psychiatrist whose 1969 classic *On Death and Dying* proposed a five-stage system of grieving: denial, anger, bargaining, depression, and acceptance.[6] According to Kubler-Ross, the stages were typical of all mourners, and they must all be experienced or "worked through" before arriving at acceptance.

The idea that grief should be work was introduced much earlier. In 1917, Sigmund Freud published an article, "Mourning and Melancholia," in which he used the phrase "the work of mourning."[7] In his view, the bereaved person had to go through a process of remembering and ultimately disconnecting from the lost person. New bonds of affection could not be established until the bereaved person had severed their emotional bonds with the deceased. This notion of grief work soon became part of the orthodox view of the bereavement process, and stage theories eventually emerged. Before Kubler-Ross, the famous British infant attachment theorist John Bowlby proposed his own stage theory of grief.[8] Interestingly, neither Bowlby nor Kubler-Ross had formulated their theories based on observations of grieving people. Bowlby had assumed the process of disengagement was similar to that of infants he observed after separation from their mothers. Kubler-Ross devised her theory from observations of terminally ill medical patients dealing with the news of their diagnosis. Both of these situations are quite different from an adult adjusting to the loss of a loved one,[9] and neither stage theories nor the concept of grief work are endorsed by most modern bereavement researchers.

Contrary to the earlier theories, grief is thought to be a highly individualized process. The majority of people are quite resilient, and the kind of grief work advocated by Freud and Kubler-Ross is thought to be counterproductive.[10] Rather than forcing a deliberate closure or letting go, there is a growing recognition that distraction and avoiding thoughts of the loss can ease the initial emotional shock. In addition, rather than breaking all emotional ties, a kind of continuing bond with the deceased can often be helpful. Death ends a life but not necessarily a relationship. For some people this may involve imagining the loved one in heaven, but for others it may simply mean weaving the deceased person into their lives through simple acts of remembrance, such as visiting the grave or establishing an ongoing method of honoring the loved one. In Susan's case, she distributed his artwork, and as a result her husband has been a small part of my life and several others over the intervening decades. Joan Didion wrote a book about her relationship with her husband and her first year without him. Sadly, just twenty months after her husband's death and two months before *The Year of Magical Thinking* was published, Didion's only child, Quintana Roo Dunne Michael died. She memorialized this relationship in her next book, *Blue Nights*.[11]

But what about the delusions exhibited by Susan and Joan Didion? Were they helpful? It is not uncommon for the bereaved to see, hear, feel the presence of—or even carry on conversations with—the deceased love one. It's also common to catch sight of a stranger on the street and momentarily think they are your departed wife or friend. People have these experiences whether they believe in an afterlife or not. But Susan and Joan did not have these kinds of visions. Instead, they had a kind of double consciousness. Neither was confused about their husbands' deaths. If you asked them, they would say that their spouses were dead. But at the same time, they had a nagging belief that what they knew to be true might not be true. This is a common experience when the relationship is very close and the loss is sudden. In the early stages of grief some people may even search for the loved one. Many of us remember the first anguished days after the collapse of the World Trade Center towers on September 11, 2001. In part because there were no physical bodies to be recovered, people posted pictures of their loved ones asking "Have you seen my husband?" But even after a conventional funeral and cremation or burial, spouses often continue to disbelieve, at least on some level.

The death of a loved one is often met with an initial period of disbelief, and research shows that approximately half of all bereaved people report feeling the presence of the deceased person.[12] In reality, the numbers are undoubtedly higher because talking to or feeling the presence of a dead person is not an easy thing to admit in western cultures. People worry they'll be considered crazy. In Asia, where ancestor worship is common and elaborate rituals in honor of the dead are maintained, the culture supports a continuing relationship with the dead. Chinese people frequently make offerings to the dead and conduct other rituals in an effort to honor and ensure the happiness of their departed ancestors.[13]

These two women seemed to be aware of holding two conflicting ideas in their heads at one time. Their husbands were dead but their husbands were coming back—dead, yet maybe still alive. This condition bears a resemblance to the participants in Seymour Epstein's red and white jelly bean experiment who know in the System Two part of their brains that the smaller bowl has the better chance of success at the same time that the System One part of their brains is unavoidably attracted to the larger bowl with its greater number of red beans. In the case of Susan and Joan, the rational side of their brains understands their husbands' fates. The intuitive quick-acting, emotional side thinks "he's just going to walk through a door." It was clear that Susan understood this was an irrational idea. The fact that she mentioned it to me suggested that she understood it was an odd belief. Nonetheless, this was a confusing feature of her grieving in those early days.

Does this kind of delusion help? I don't think science has yet produced a definitive answer, but it appears to be a common response to a sudden truth that is too difficult to fully accept. In addition, the current practice of grief counselors is not to confront these irrational thoughts. According to two well-known grief researchers, the role of the therapist is to exhibit "respectful attention, reassurance, and unconditional regard."[14] There is a bit more research on people who experience the loved one as a continuing presence—either by seeing, hearing, feeling, or talking to them. In the early days of bereavement research, these experiences were usually considered evidence of "complicated grief" and an undesirable continued attachment to the lost person. But the modern view suggests a much more nuanced approach. For example, a recent study of elderly Danish people who had lost a spouse found that 52 percent reported having some kind of continuing experiences of the presence of their spouses.[15] Furthermore, 62 percent of those who had these encounters experienced them as positive. Only 7 percent said the presence of their deceased spouse was negative. As one might expect, widows and widowers who had longer marriages were more likely to have these experiences.

Perhaps the clearest thing that can be said about continuing experiences with lost loved ones is that they can be either pleasant and meaningful or troubling, and the nature of these experiences often depends on the bereaved's relationship with the loved one when they were alive. Researchers in the United Kingdom interviewed seventeen people who had continuing experiences of presence between one and eleven years after the death of a relative, family friend, or partner.[16] In the majority of cases, the experiences involved hearing the loved one's voice or merely having a feeling of their presence. Based on the interviews, the researchers categorized the nature of these experiences and found that twelve out of the seventeen participants described encounters that were helpful in solving some current problem. For example, a young man trying to help his grief-stricken grandfather with a dishwasher that wasn't working properly heard his grandmother's voice telling him where to look for the solution. Other participants felt that they received encouragement with a difficult task. Some of the bereaved also had encounters that helped resolve unfinished business with the deceased. For example, one woman had a difficult experience when her boyfriend hid his terminal illness from her and abruptly ended their relationship. They later partially reconciled, but hearing his voice after his death helped to maintain their reconciliation.

There were people who reported unpleasant interactions with their deceased relatives, such as a daughter who heard her father's critical voice, but the researchers categorized this episode and other similar ones as continuations of a troubled relationship. In addition, in some cases, feeling the presence of the deceased left the bereaved person feeling more alone. So, although the majority of experiences were positive, some were not, and the length and nature of the relationship with the loved one before their death were related to the nature of the experiences of a continued relationship after death. Finally, when the experiences of presence after death are positive and meaningful, it is hard to imagine any reason to object. As one bereavement researcher put it, "rather than 'saying goodbye' or seeking closure, there exists the possibility of the deceased being both present and absent."[17] For many bereaved people, that possibility is a reality that adds comfort and meaning to their lives.

Dead people do not speak nor do they appear in doorways. They have no need for the shoes they once wore. It is irrational to believe that the dead can be with us again in any place other than our memories and imaginations. Yet many people have continuing experiences that seem real to them. Furthermore, the majority of these experiences are welcome. Today, counselors often express the view that treatment strategies should be aimed at assisting people with troubled relationships with the deceased. Grief is highly individual, and treatment should be tailored to the individual's needs. There is less data regarding the more immediate traumatic response seen by Susan and Joan Didion but it seems likely that the belief their husbands would return was an initial reaction to sudden death that helped ease them gradually toward acceptance. Most of those who have more long-lasting relationships with their lost loved ones welcome their continuing presence. They seem to have found a way to hold on to a bond interrupted by death.

British novelist Julian Barnes, whose wife of thirty years died of a brain tumor in 2008, wrote in his own grief memoir that he often considered suicide and had even planned how he would do it—a glass of wine, the bathtub, and a Japanese carving knife. But he was saved by an extremely active relationship with his wife after her death:

This is what those who haven't crossed the tropic of grief often fail to understand: the fact that someone is dead may mean that they are not alive, but it doesn't mean that they do not exist.[18]

Barnes talked to his wife regularly after her death and heard her voice talking back, which he said, "calms me and gives me courage."[19] In a very real sense, his life depended on this continuing relationship with his wife: "If I have survived what is now four years of her absence, it is because I have had four years of her presence."[20]

7

Bedtime Stories

In any case, however, I believe that the Roman Emperor was in the wrong in ordering one of his subjects to be executed because the latter had dreamt that he had killed the Emperor. He should first of all have endeavoured to discover the significance of the man's dreams; most probably it was not what it seemed to be.

—Sigmund Freud, *The Interpretation of Dreams*

In November, 1872, an assistant curator at the British Museum was pouring over hunks of stone speckled with chicken scratches.[1] The young curator was born to unskilled laborer parents, which meant that he could not attend high school, much less college. But his father apprenticed him to a printing firm in London, where he soon excelled at engraving banknotes. The young apprentice was fascinated with Mesopotamian history, and on his lunch hours he walked to the museum where he began to study the pieces of clay tablets in the collection. Learning on his own, he mastered the cuneiform markings of Akkadian, the language spoken in Mesopotamia from the third millennium BCE to approximately eight hundred BCE, and the staff of the museum soon recognized that the engraver had a remarkable talent for deciphering the stone scribblings. They offered him a position at the museum, and soon this self-taught son of laborers had surpassed his Cambridge-educated colleagues.

On the fateful day in 1872, the young curator, George Smith, translated a section of tablet (see Figure 7.1) that described a flood—a great deluge—and he became so excited that he started to dance and remove his clothes. It is not clear how far he got with that project, but it is easy to understand his excitement. Much of the motivation for studying ancient Babylonian history was to test the validity of the Bible. Could the events described in the Book of Genesis be true? Or might they reflect some foundational legends shared by various cultures? The tablet Smith translated was from an archeological site

Figure 7.1　Tablet 11, the flood tablet, of the Epic of Gilgamesh, which is held by the British Museum.
Source: Wikimedia

near the city of Mosul in what is now Iraq, and his delight stemmed from the recognition that the flood he had uncovered was much like Noah's flood. As excited as he was at that moment, the full significance of his revelation would become clear later: he had discovered the eleventh tablet of the twelve-tablet *Epic of Gilgamesh*, one of the oldest known works of literature. The copy he translated was written in the seventh century BCE, but the events it related were thought to be as old as two millennia BCE. This heroic story of King

Gilgamesh and his challenges had been lost to history for over two thousand years, and George Smith, the son of laborers, was the first person to read it and translate it for the world.

The Epic of Gilgamesh is spread out across twelve tablets, each with six columns of cuneiform Akkadian script. It is assumed that many copies of the poem were made, and over the years since Smith's first discovery, additional pieces have been found, some in other languages, that restore missing segments of the story. As recently as 2014, two scholars of Babylonian literature published a translation of a newly discovered piece of tablet 5.[2] In addition to the flood tablet discovered by George Smith, *The Epic of Gilgamesh* includes a scene similar to the Garden of Eden from Genesis, with man created from soil, and other biblical parallels. At the beginning of the story, the central hero Gilgamesh is a seer king, who is oppressing his people. Out of concern for the citizens, the gods create a double for Gilgamesh—Enkidu the fighter, who dwells among the animals in the wild. The two heroes fight but eventually become friends, and Gilgamesh goes on to face a number of challenges.

At several points in the action of this ancient story characters have dreams. On tablet 1, Gilgamesh has a dream about a star in the sky that falls on him and is too heavy for him to lift. Eventually "like a wife" he loved, caressed, and embraced the star. Gilgamesh's mother, the wise goddess Ninsun, interprets her son's dream for him. According to Ninsun this dream foretells the arrival of a companion who will be strong and "his friend's savior" (meaning Gilgamesh's savior).[3] On tablet 1 column 5, Ninsun urges Gilgamesh to go find this companion, who is, of course, Enkidu. On tablet 4, Gilgamesh and Enkidu travel over a series of mountains on their way to do battle with Humbaba, the guardian of Forest of Cedars. At several points in the journey, Gilgamesh camps on the side of a mountain and performs a ritual in an effort to bring on a dream: "O mountain, bring me a dream, so I see a good sign."[4] In each case, Gilgamesh is confused by his dream, but Enkidu provides an encouraging interpretation.

In the ancient Middle East—not only in Babylon, but among the Hittites and Egyptians—dreams often had a number of functions. Dreams might contain messages from the gods, reflect the dreamer's mental state, or depict future events.[5] As interpreted by his mother, Gilgamesh's dreams from tablet 1 foretold the future. Approximately twelve hundred years after the earliest written versions of Gilgamesh, the Greek poet Homer described several message dreams. In Book 2 of the *Iliad*, Zeus sends a "murderous dream" to Agamemnon. The dream takes the shape of Nestor, an elder whom Agamemnon respected, and Nestor speaks to the sleeping Agamemnon, urging him to take up arms against the city of Troy.[6] Similarly, in Book 4 of the *Odyssey*, the goddess Athena sends a phantom in the form of Penelope's sister to Odysseus' house. The phantom enters Penelope's room passing through the "doorbolt slit" and speaks reassuringly to Odysseus' sleeping wife.[7]

Ninsun's interpretations of Gilgamesh's dreams would have been familiar to contemporary readers of the epic. In both Mesopotamia and Egypt, priests and other wise people offered readings of dreams. The ancient world was a dangerous place, and many forms of divination and fortune telling were a regular part of everyday life. Almost any random process—the flight of flocks of birds (augury), the galloping of herds of horses, the patterns of oil drops on water, or the chaotic content of dreams (oneiromancy)—were interpreted by professionals who claimed they could uncover prophetic messages. Dream books listed the meanings of various dream events and what they fore-told for the future.[8] One of the most famous of these was the five-volume *Oneirocritica* (*Interpretation of Dreams*) by the Greek diviner Artemidorus of Daldis, who consulted with many diviners in his research for the book.[9] Despite persistent popular notions about dreams, the Roman writer Cicero dismissed the idea that dreams could predict the future or bring messages from the gods. He pointed to the obviously chaotic nature of the images we see during sleep.

It's easy to understand why people might search for meaning in these crazy nocturnal movies that often feature the dreamer as a main character. When I was eight or nine, I had a Master bicycle lock, but eventually I forgot the combination. As I rode around my neighborhood, the lock would jangle against the bike frame in a taunting reminder that it was uselessly stuck there forever. One night, in a dream, I watched myself complete the three-number combination, and when I awoke, I ran directly to my bicycle and success-fully opened the lock. As magical as this event seemed at the time, it wasn't a prophecy. Memories fade, but they can be triggered by context. I knew the combination once, and I apparently remembered it in my dream. Pretty cool, but not magic.

Dreams have mystified us for millennia. Today, dream interpretation is far less popular than in earlier eras, but if it survives at all, some of the credit must go to the father of psychoanalysis, Sigmund Freud. Both Freud and his intellectual descendant Carl Jung praised Artemidorus' book on dream interpretation.[10] Freud worked in a socially repressive Victorian era, and his psychological theory suggested that much of what drives behavior stems from unconscious motivations. At the turn of the twentieth century, he published *The Interpretation of Dreams*, which proposed that, rather than foretelling the future or delivering messages from the gods, dreams were a window into our hidden motivations. The stories that played out in our heads at night were expressions of wish fulfillment.[11] Because the clues to the unconscious were garbled, patients needed a guide to reveal the meanings of dreams and, as a result, dream analysis became a standard feature of psychoanalysis. Jung also believed that dreams were a window into the unconscious and that current questions or difficulties were often the subject of the dream:

> It is said that the bridegroom never dreams of the bride. That is because he has her in reality; only later, when there is trouble, does he dream of her— and then she is generally the wife.[12]

Sleep is a little like death. Everyone goes there, but it is difficult to get reliable reports back about what it's like. Both involve a loss of consciousness, and unless we go off into the weeds of paranormal phenomenon, being able to carry on a conversation generally requires that you be conscious. In the case of sleep, memories of our dreams tend to fade very quickly. By the time I've had my first cup of coffee, I'd be hard pressed to tell you what I'd dreamed that night. Only the most vivid parts of our dreams remain with us in the waking world, and they seem to fade from memory more quickly than the real events of our conscious lives. Because sleep occurs on the other side of the borders of consciousness, it has been quite difficult to study. Our sleeping bodies give off some signals that are detectable by laboratory equipment, and sleep researchers have been known to wake up dreaming experimental subjects to ask them what was going on just before they awoke—a technique that produces more detailed reports of dreams but must be very annoying for the sleeper. In my view, people who are willing to submit to this kind of abuse for the sake of science deserve praise far beyond the modest amounts they are paid for their service.

Even the simplest question about sleep—why do we do it—remains something of a puzzle. One researcher recently called it "the greatest biologic mystery of all times."[13] Several plausible theories have been proposed. Perhaps the most obvious involves its restorative function.

Rather than being a consistent state, sleep has a kind of "architecture" that typically involves alternating between two primary forms of sleep several times during the course of the night. These changes can be detected by the use of an electroencephalograph (EEG) machine that records the electrical waves produced by the brain. At the beginning of the night we fall rapidly into a deep slow wave or nonrapid eye movement (NREM) sleep which might last for an hour or so until we begin to show the quicker EEG waves of rapid eye movement (REM) sleep—so called because during this period the sleeper's eyes move back and forth beneath the lids. Throughout the night we cycle back and forth between NREM and REM approximately every ninety minutes but most NREM sleep occurs at the beginning of the night and most REM at the end.

The restorative theory is supported by a number of common effects. After strong physical exertion, we tend to spend more time in deep NREM sleep, and when awakened during a period of NREM sleep we feel groggy and tired. This is not the case for REM sleep, a stage that produces a more rapid EEG pattern that is much closer to a waking EEG. Although people function surprisingly well on very little sleep, excessive sleep deprivation produces mental confusion and poor functioning. After building up a sleep deficit over several days, when given the chance, people will sleep longer than usual— however, they rarely sleep as long as would be required to replace all the lost sleep. Sleep deprivation is also associated with poorer immune function, and prolonged sleep deprivation in rats can cause death.[14]

One of the simplest and most common explanations for sleep is that the world is dangerous at night. We are vulnerable when we sleep, but we are also ill-suited to moving about in the dark. According to self-preservation theory, humans and other diurnal animals avoid danger by remaining in one place when it is dark. The reverse is true for nocturnal species that are vulnerable during the day (cockroaches and mice) or have sensory capabilities adapted for predation in darkness (badgers, foxes, and owls).

The various theories of sleep are not mutually exclusive, and researchers continue to debate their relative merits. But, if possible, there is even more confusion about the function of dreams. We dream in both NREM and REM periods, but dreaming during the slower wave NREM period is more like thinking. It typically has no visual component and as a result the content is not as crazy. Nonetheless, this thinking-dreaming can carry emotion, and when a person is anxious about something, NREM sleep may involve nervous rumination about some object of worry. REM sleep is associated with the vivid, movie-like dreams that are more familiar to us. During this period of the night, we undergo a kind of paralysis that keeps us from physically acting out our dreams, and a number of sleep disorders are associated with the misalignment of this paralysis. For example, the comedian Mike Birbiglia suffers from a sleep disorder in which the paralysis of REM does not occur. Untreated, he sleep walks regularly, and in his Off-Broadway one-man show, he described an incident in which—while asleep—he jumped through a second-floor window of a motel wearing only a pair of underpants.[15] He now controls his sleep disorder with medication and by sleeping in a sleeping bag.

Another theory of sleep suggests it's a time when neurons and synapses are stimulated to promote brain health. Synapses, the tiny connections between different neurons in the brain, need to be stimulated in order to maintain function, and not all synapses are fired during the day. Further support for this hypothesis can be seen in the sleep patterns of babies. A newborn infant whose brain is growing rapidly reverses the usual adult sleep totals with eight hours of wakefulness and sixteen of sleep, but, as all parents know, babies can pop in or out of sleep at various times during the day. It can take a long time before the new human settles into the pattern of a single bout of sleep at night—the beginning of a much happier period for the parents. Babies also show a greater priority for REM sleep. Unlike adults, they go into REM first and spend equal amounts of time in REM and NREM. As the child ages, the amount of REM diminishes, hitting adult levels of approximately 20 to 25 percent of sleep time at about ten years old. Taken together these observations suggest that sleep is important to building healthy neurons and making new synaptic connections.

Some of the strongest research findings suggests that sleep—particularly REM sleep, but not exclusively REM sleep—helps lock in what we have learned during the day. For example, when laboratory participants are asked to do a perceptual task—picking out a line at an odd angle among a field of many similar lines—performance improved after a normal night's sleep. In a famous study, a group of researchers brought participants into a lab to learn a similar perceptual skill (see Figure 7.2), but in this case, the researchers had their learners sleep that evening with EEG devices on their heads so their progress through the stages of sleep could be monitored.[16] As uncomfortable as it must have been to sleep with wires attached to their heads, the researchers proceeded to make matters worse by waking the participants up whenever they went into REM sleep. The result was that these participants had an *almost* normal night of rest but with greatly reduced REM periods. On other occasions the researchers poked the participants when they went into deep NREM sleep. Remarkably, the researchers found the normal

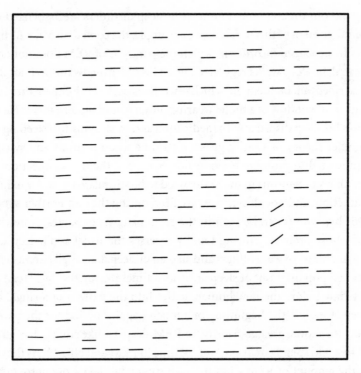

Figure 7.2 A stimulus array similar to that used in the Karni et al. (2000) REM sleep study. The participant's task was to identify the shape of the target texture which varied in orientation from the horizontal background texture (the three diagonal lines in the lower right quadrant).

improvement in performance for participants whose NREM sleep had been limited. They did just as well as they would have following a normal night's sleep. But when REM sleep was limited, the usual overnight improvement in performance was erased. It was as though the participants had never practiced the task before and had to start fresh on the second day. The researchers concluded that REM sleep was particularly useful in consolidating what had been learned in the perceptual task. However, once the skill was fully learned, disruption of REM sleep—while undoubtedly unpleasant—did not affect performance.

This kind of consolidation of learning during sleep has been confirmed in many other studies with different kinds of learning tasks. There are some limitations and conflicting evidence. For example, not all memories are solidified in the same way, and the sleep effect appears to be greater for *procedural* memories, such as how to perform a kind of calculation, than for *declarative* memory, such as memorizing the chemicals of the periodic table of elements. In addition, some antidepressant drugs wipe out most or all of REM sleep, and yet there are no reports of widespread memory problems among users. It is possible that, for these individuals, other stages take over the consolidation function, but some things remain unclear. However, the majority scientific opinion holds that for most of us REM sleep is important for locking down new material that is being learned.[17]

But what of the dreams themselves that arise so vividly in REM sleep? Of all our irrational thought, dreams account for some of our most frequent and profound irrationalities. While we are dreaming we feel emotions and witness bizarreness and lunacy with great clarity. We can fly, cars can drive underground, people from our past pop up from nowhere, and people we have never met behave like they are close friends. We are captive audiences for our dreams as they are going on, and we cannot help but be impressed by things that never happen in the waking world but are commonplace during sleep.

Given the dramatic and confusing nature of dreams, it is understandable that people have assigned them deep significance and strived to uncover what that significance might be. Although ancient Assyrians, Egyptians, Greeks, and Romans believed dreams were the grist of prophesy, modern science rejects that notion. Whether we use dreams, Tarot cards, astrology, or palm readings, there is no evidence that anyone can foretell the future. Similarly, although many psychoanalysts still believe dreams are a window into the unconscious and continue to analyze their clients' dreams, behavioral science has rejected most of Freud's psychological theories as untestable and has discarded the notion that dreams are a key to hidden psychological knowledge.

We do many things without conscious awareness. Anyone who has ever had a regular commute has had the experience of arriving safely at their work parking space without having any memory of all the small decisions and actions taken to get them there. But Freud's idea of unconscious drives—the three competing forces of Id, Ego, and Superego—are not measurable or testable. They are more metaphor than scientific fact. As a result, modern dream research does not see hidden unconscious drives in the crazy dramas we play out at night.

Under some circumstances, science does see meaning in dreams. The organ most closely associated with learning and memory is the *hippocampus*, so named due to its physical resemblance to a seahorse (from the Greek *hippos* "horse" and *kampos* "sea monster," although I've never really seen the similarity). The hippocampus is in the center of the brain underneath the large mantle of cortex and is part of a group of structures called the *limbic system*. Several of the other structures of the limbic system are involved in the expression of emotion, which makes sense because, although we are rarely aware of it, learning, memory, and emotion are closely related.

We are still largely in the dark about the purpose of dreams, but nightmares provide a hint to their function. When the experience of dreaming goes badly enough, we may remember it as unpleasant experience after waking. Indeed, nightmares can frighten us to the point of waking up in the middle of the night. Sleep researchers think they know a few things about these scarier dreams. First, nightmares happen during the more vivid dreaming of REM sleep. Second, they are a common symptom of psychopathology, but they are also a very common experience in healthy people. Eighty-five percent of adults report having at least one nightmare in the previous year[18] and 2 to 6 percent report weekly nightmares. We also know that nightmares can be triggered by trauma. In a classic study, people who experienced the 1989 San Francisco earthquake reported more nightmares than those who did not, and the number of nightmares experienced was directly related to distance from the earthquake.[19]

Taken together, these studies and others like them suggest our nightmares are related to the amount of stress and anxiety we carry around during the day. If you are going through a difficult period due to a recent trauma or to stress about your health, finances, or relationships, disturbing, anxious dreams are more likely to occur. Furthermore, a recent theory suggests that these unsettling dreams are a feature, not a bug. It has long been understood that fear can be diminished by repeated exposure to the thing that scares us— as long as this is done under safe conditions. People who have a debilitating fear of dogs are asked to quietly imagine encountering a beagle while comfortably seated in a therapist's office. After adjusting to the idea of dogs, the therapist might gradually introduce actual contact with a dog. In contrast, avoiding the feared object or activity tends to maintain the phobia.

It is difficult to know for certain, but according to one theory, part of the reason our dreams are so emotionally charged is to help us manage fear.[20] Emotions play a greater role in learning and cognition than we recognize. Traditionally we have considered head and heart to be different realms. But the anatomy of the limbic system at the center of our brains shows us that emotion and learning are connected, and in the case of learning to fear things, that connection is quite clear. According to this fear extinction theory, natural selection has given us nightmares as a way to unlearn—or, at least, adapt to—the things that scare us or make us anxious in the waking world.

Other proposals for the function of dreams include mood regulation and preparation for threats we may encounter while awake. Importantly, these theories are backed up by research and are not mutually exclusive with the more widely endorsed theories of memory consolidation and coping with fear.[21] For anyone looking for a rich area of study, the world of sleep and dreaming is fertile ground. Much of what happens to our bodies at night remains a mystery, but based on the evidence so far, it is likely that sleep has many functions.

Dreams are irrational, but not completely irrational. They often have a kind of plot, and many of the characters we meet in our dreams are recognizable. But dreams take us through the looking glass to a fantasy land where the usual laws of time and space do not always apply. Crazy things happen, and somehow they feel real. Only upon waking is the truth revealed, and then our dreams quickly fade.

The human effort to make sense of these nocturnal dramas has come full circle. *The Epic of Gilgamesh* shows us how, at the birth of civilization, dreams were considered the keys to valuable and prophetic knowledge. In the early days of modern psychology, Freud saw a different kind of key in dreams—one that revealed the unconscious drives of his Victorian clients. Some psychoanalysts still hold to that view today. But, in the latter half of the twentieth century, as scientific methods of studying the brain emerged, dreams were demoted. For a time, the conventional view was that the brain needed to do various forms of maintenance during the night and that dreams were just a side effect of a nocturnal repair process. Because our brains never turn off completely, our perceptual and memory systems tried to knit together some kind of story from the electrical signals generated during this period of maintenance, but the dreams had no inherent function of their own.[22] The dominant theory of memory consolidation during sleep is completely compatible with this rather modest view of dreams.

Dreams are a kind of delusion. In their description of characteristics of dreaming, researchers Allan Hobson and Robert McCarley wrote that dreams include "a delusional acceptance of these phenomena as 'real' at the time that they occur."[23] But are dreams helpful delusions? Most of the positive delusions that we encounter in this book follow a relatively direct causal line (see the "Waking World" of Figure 7.3) Exposure to the world leads to the formation of beliefs that subsequently guide our actions. If the beliefs are irrational and yet they lead to some kind of advantageous behavior, then we have a positive delusion.

If dreams are a side effect of physiological restoration or the process of embedding memories, then they are delusions that signal something productive is going on (see the "Basic View" of Figure 7.3). Dreams are not helpful in themselves, but the processes that evoke them are. However, we now have growing evidence that dreams may have value in their own right. Studies have shown that the amount and quality of REM sleep is positively related to recovery from depression and other emotional problems. In addition, there is a growing body of support for the idea that the actual content of dreams prepares us for threats and helps us manage our fears (see the "Emerging View" of Figure 7.3). The science of sleeping and dreaming is still in its infancy—or perhaps early childhood—but these newer lines of research may serve to resurrect the value of dreams and pull something of value out of the crazy fantasies we dive into each night.

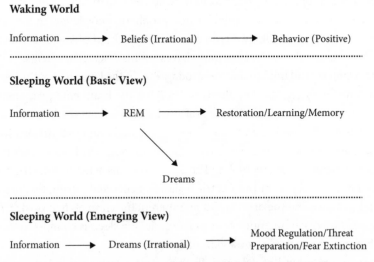

Figure 7.3 Positive delusions in the waking and sleeping world. In the waking world, irrational beliefs (epistemic irrationality) can sometimes lead to productive behavior. According to the basic view, REM sleep is important to learning and memory consolidation, and dreams are a side effect of these activities. In the emerging view, the irrational content of the dreams is a necessary part of their role in mood regulation and adaptation to threats.

George Smith, the talented student of Mesopotamian history and culture, pursued his life's work to the very end. The Gilgamesh tablets Smith translated had come from the Royal Library of Ashurbanipal, the last of the Assyrian Kings. The library was filled with stone tablets, and Smith made several trips to the excavation site near Mosul in search of additional pieces of the epic. On his third trip, financed by the British Museum, the area around the site was under threat of both plague and cholera, and the heat was so intense that it was difficult to dig. Smith was in ill health and decided to head home. Early into the trip back, he died at the age of thirty-six, in Aleppo—probably from dysentery—leaving behind a wife and six children. Smith's salary at the British Museum had always been modest—he would have earned more had he stayed on as an engraver—but due to his discovery of *The Epic of Gilgamesh*, he was something of a hero in London. Newspaper accounts of his death and the dire circumstance of his family led to the awarding of a tiny government pension—£150 per year—to his wife.[24]

8

The Gangster Within

The reactions of the human machine are loosely linked behaviour systems, participating in the common delusion of being the self.[1]
—H. G. Wells, "The Illusion of Personality"

I have a clear memory of the day she was arrested. I was visiting with a friend in the student activities office of the university where I was a graduate student. It was September of 1975, long before the advent of cable news or the Internet. Our only way of getting news was broadcast television, radio, and newspapers. Another student opened the office door, stuck his head in, and said, "They've found Patty Hearst." As clear as the memory seems, it has probably morphed and transformed over time, but I have it nonetheless.

Patricia Hearst came from great privilege. She was the granddaughter of William Randolf Hearst, the newspaper magnate who was the model for Orson Wells' *Citizen Kane*. Her father Randolf Hearst was chairman of the executive committee of the Hearst Corporation and publisher of the San Francisco *Examiner* newspaper. Patricia was heir to one of the largest fortunes in the country, and on February 4, 1974, while a sophomore at the University of California, she was kidnapped from her Berkeley apartment by a small radical group calling themselves the Symbionese Liberation Army.

Soon after her capture, Patricia became a different person. Two months after the kidnapping, she announced on an audiotape that she had joined her kidnappers as a member of the SLA and was adopting a *nom de guerre*, Tania, a name used by an East German woman who fought alongside Ché Guevara in Bolivia.[2] Two weeks later, on April 15—tax day—Tania and four of her comrades conducted an armed robbery of a Hibernia Bank in the Sunset District of San Francisco. According to plan, Patricia took a position in full view of the security cameras, brandishing an automatic rifle and shouting at the customers to lie down on the floor while the other SLA members gathered up the cash. "First person puts up his head," she said, "I'll blow his motherfucking head off."[3]

A month later, Patricia would participate in a shoot-out at Mel's Sporting Goods in Inglewood, California. Left alone in a Volkswagen van while Bill and Emily Harris, two of her SLA comrades, went into the store, she noticed them in a scuffle with store employees in the parking lot. Bill Harris had been accused of shoplifting. Patricia picked up a machine gun, stuck it out the window of the van, and began shooting in the direction of the store. She emptied the clip, picked up another automatic weapon, and resumed shooting. Miraculously no one was hurt, but she provided enough cover for the three to escape.

The Patty Hearst kidnapping was national news for months, and as soon as the pictures of a clearly recognizable Hearst participating in an armed bank heist appeared (see Figure 8.1), she was elevated to a kind of hero status among the campus radical crowd. The iconic Tania poster, showing Hearst in military garb, posed in front of the SLA symbol of a seven-headed cobra, machine gun at the ready, became a popular dorm room decoration.

Figure 8.1 Assault rifles in hand, SLA members Tania (Patricia Hearst) and Donald DeFreeze robbing the Hibernia Bank in San Francisco on April 15, 1974.
Source: Wikimedia.

Hearst and several SLA members were fugitives for over a year, participating in a number of bombings and bank robberies, but on September 18, 1975, the FBI found Patricia and another SLA member in an apartment in San Francisco. News of her capture spread quickly, and when she arrived at police headquarters, she raised a revolutionary fist to the gathering crowd. During the booking process, she gave her occupation as "urban guerilla."

But soon after her arrest, Patricia transitioned back into her heiress role. During her first week in jail, she wrote letters to her SLA boyfriend, proclaiming how deeply she missed him, and continued to use radical SLA rhetoric and portray herself as a "revolutionary feminist," all of which created problems for the legal defense that was eventually mounted. But as soon as she was in custody, the many advantages of wealth returned to her side. Her parents hired a legal team that included the most famous lawyer in the world, F. Lee Bailey.

By the time her bank robbery trial began, Patricia had recovered the appearance of a young lady of wealth, well-dressed, neatly coiffed, and demure—nothing like the revolutionary giving a fist salute when she was arrested in September of 1975. Bailey's defense was based on the premise that Patricia had been "brainwashed" by her captors. She had been blindfolded and confined to a closet for the first month of her captivity while being bombarded with revolutionary propaganda. In addition, she claimed to have been raped by one of the SLA members.

The jury didn't buy it. There was substantial evidence that her relationships with SLA men were consensual and, in at least one case, very deeply felt. Furthermore, there were many opportunities to safely escape her SLA comrades, but instead she chose to stay and keep fighting. At the Mel's shootout, she was left alone in a van with the keys in the ignition, but rather than drive herself to the nearest police station and turn herself in, she picked up a machine gun and started shooting up the store. The jury deliberated for a single day before finding her guilty of armed bank robbery and use of firearms in the commission of a felony.

After her conviction, in a dramatic case of unequal justice, Patricia was allowed to go free while awaiting appeal under elaborate bail conditions only a very wealthy family could have met. When the appeal failed and she returned to jail, the Hearst family launched a vigorous and ultimately successful campaign to have Patricia pardoned. In January of 1979, Jimmy Carter commuted Patricia's sentence, and on his last day in office, President Bill Clinton issued her a full pardon. She is the only person to have her sentence commuted by one president and be pardoned by another. The only bank robbers luckier than Patricia Hearst are the ones who got away.

After her release, Hearst married her police bodyguard, wrote a book about her experiences, made many media appearances, and had a modest acting career in television and movies, including appearances in several films by director John Waters. A life-long dog lover, Hearst has had multiple winning entries at the Westminster Kennel Club Dog Show.[4] Despite spending over a year on the lam with a group of revolutionary terrorists, Patricia appears to have almost fully rehabilitated her public image. In the words of legal journalist Dahlia Lithwick, Hearst's brainwashing defense "ultimately succeeded—not in any court of law, but in the court of public opinion."[5]

So, what do we make of the Patricia Hearst story? There is a strong suggestion that she was two people. Before and after her SLA period, she was an heiress, living a rare and comfortable life—the last person you would expect to become a gangster. But, despite her successful public relations campaign, many who followed the case believed that when she was Patricia, she was Patricia, and when she was Tania, she was Tania. Of course, Tania would never have emerged had Patricia not been kidnapped and held hostage, but at some point, relatively early in the process, she began to bond with her captors and adopt their political views. As shocking as this metamorphosis was, in hindsight, there were hints of a rebelliousness that made Patricia ripe for recruitment. At the time she was kidnapped, she was only nineteen years old. Two years earlier, she had begun a relationship with a high school teacher and then, instead of attending Stanford as her parents wanted, she followed her boyfriend to Berkeley when he entered graduate school. By the time of the kidnapping, she was a college sophomore who was not getting along with her mother and was growing dissatisfied with her former high school teacher boyfriend.

Brainwashing was always a dubious idea. It first appeared in the Cold War Era as an explanation for the behavior of American prisoners of war who showed sympathy for the views of their captors, and it was used as a plot device in thrillers such as *The Manchurian Candidate*. A related idea, "Stockholm syndrome," in which prisoners are said to identify with their captors, was also introduced in the early 1970s.[6] Hearst's brainwashing claim gained substantial credibility in 1978, when nine hundred members of the People's Temple religious group led by Jim Jones killed themselves at his direction in a mass suicide event in Guyana. As concerns about new religious groups—cults—grew in the 1970s and 80s, brainwashing and "Stockholm syndrome" became popular legal defenses for members of these groups who had committed crimes. A few conditions listed in the American Psychiatric Association's *Diagnostic and Statistical Manual* support a kind of mutual psychosis—a *folie à deux*—and during this period of cult anxiety, psychiatrists and psychologists often gave testimony supporting a "not guilty due to brainwashing" defense. Nonetheless, as in the Hearst trial, juries have generally not been persuaded.[7]

It is difficult to arrive at an objective understanding of wrongdoing because our moral judgments get in the way. For example, few people would blame the person who takes credit for a transformation in the opposite direction—from bad to good. Reformed sinners and bank robbers who become upright citizens are praised for turning their lives around and held up as examples, even if—perhaps, especially if—the accomplishment comes after going into military service or having a religious conversion. Few would call it brainwashing as long as it led to a positive outcome, but if you join a less mainstream religious or political group and do something wrong, brainwashing becomes an attractive explanation.

This biased view is reflected in a similar phenomenon called the "side-effect effect." In a classic experiment, two groups of people were asked to evaluate written scenarios differing by a single word.[8] In the version given to one group, the CEO of a company is told about a new program that would increase profits, but would also harm the environment. The CEO says, "I don't care about that, I just want to maximize profits. Let's go ahead with the program." In the version seen by another group of people, the word *harm* was replaced with *help* (i.e., "the program will help the environment"). Again, the CEO says, "I don't care about that. I just want to maximize profits. Let's go ahead with the program." In both cases, the predicted effect occurs: the environment is harmed in the harm version and helped in the help version. Finally, after reading the scenario, participants were asked "Did the CEO intentionally [harm/help] the environment?" When participants read the *harm* version, most said, yes, the CEO had intentionally harmed the environment. However, when participants saw the *help* version, most said, no, the CEO did not intentionally help the environment. The business program was exactly the same in both cases, but the moral valence of the side effect—helping versus harming—greatly influenced how intentional it was judged to be. Of course, in the courtroom, judgments of intent are very important. The person who knowingly and intentionally produces harm is held responsible and judged more harshly than the person who harms unintentionally.

Psychology's simpler explanation for the Patricia Hearst paradox is that people adapt to their social environments. In his book about the case, writer Jeffrey Toobin concluded that both after her kidnap and after her arrest, Patty Hearst had responded rationally to her surroundings. While she was in jail, F. Lee Bailey separated Patricia from her former SLA comrades and kept her in the company of her parents, attorneys, and pre-SLA friends. Once arrested, it became clear she was in serious legal jeopardy, and her parents were the ones who could help her. According to Toobin, "Patricia was always a rational actor—with the SLA and now with her lawyers. Even in chaotic surroundings, she knew where her best interests lay."[9]

This view doesn't account for the many times she could have escaped the SLA—which would also have been a rational act for anyone hoping to avoid harm—but Patricia was kidnapped in the heady, countercultural era of the early 1970s. It's likely the political message of the SLA appealed to Patricia's rebellious spirit, and after becoming Tania, her commitment to the cause and her new social relationships were enough to sustain her on a violent revolutionary path that did not end until the FBI caught up with her.

The Making of I

We take for granted that we are us. Stuart and Sally and Nate and Joan are all meaningful concepts that describe recognizable individuals with predictable personalities. This consistency contributes to the sense of who we are, but it also has important social significance. We place great value in our judgments of others in order to know how to interact with them. Whenever we agree to any ongoing social relationship—marriage, a business partnership, or merely friendship—we make a moral assessment.[10] Before the deal is struck, we need to know that we can trust that person and have a sense of how they will behave in the future. Without a belief in this kind of stability, it would be hard for our highly social species to succeed.

Most of us think we know our authentic identities, and the people we've spent time with know us, too. If asked, a relative or friend would probably be able to provide a recognizable description of the kind of person you are. Furthermore, if that description were sealed in an envelope and opened ten years from now, it might still sound a lot like you. As a result, it is hard not to believe we have traits or characteristics that, if not unique to us, are at least typical of us—a personality that is something of a constant. Yet, whenever there is a horrific murder, it's a cliché of local news coverage to have a neighbor or friend say, "He seemed like just a regular guy." Although the conventional view is that we each have a basic essence—a core that reveals our character—psychologists have questioned this assumption for decades. Is our sense of personal identity a delusion?

One of the most prestigious behavioral science research publications is the *Journal of Personality and Social Psychology*. Another well-regarded journal bears the name *Personality and Social Psychology Bulletin*. Personality psychology and social psychology are actually two distinct areas of study that are frequently at odds with each other, and yet they are often put together in this way. What they have in common is the goal of describing the behavior of typical people: all of us who fall into the category of standard issue, non-mentally ill folks. But, in general, personality and social psychology take very different approaches to the project of revealing our basic nature.

It is impossible to accurately summarize a field as old and broad as personality psychology, but, in general, personality researchers have supported the view that character is stable. The Greek physician Galen (129–c. 200 CE) proposed a system of personality types based in four temperaments—sanguine, choleric, melancholic, and phlegmatic—a theory that remained popular for centuries. Beginning in the late nineteenth century, Sigmund Freud, Carl Jung, Erik Erikson, and Abraham Maslow would propose more elaborate theories, but they did little to alter the conventional view that normally functioning adults have relatively consistent personalities.

In the late nineteenth and early twentieth century, psychology became much more quantitative, and the application of statistical methods to the measurement of human characteristics led to rapid advances in the study of personality. Rather than trying to identify qualitatively different personality types, the focus moved to the identification of traits or dispositions that separated one person from another. Beginning in the late nineteenth century, much of the motivation for this work came from the eugenics movement, a twisted outgrowth of Darwin's theory of natural selection whose proponents—many of them highly educated British men—thought they could do humanity a favor by culling out the weaker stock. Eugenics quickly focused on the most controversial of all traits, intelligence, and the methods that could be used to measure it. Many of the basic statistical methods taught in college classes today were first introduced by British eugenicists, including Francis Galton, Darwin's half cousin, (mean, standard deviation, correlation), Karl Pearson (correlation), Ronald Fisher (analysis of variance), and

Charles Spearman (correlation and factor analysis).[11] Factor analysis became particularly important in the effort to find a measure of general intelligence because it purported to reveal the common core (or factor) underlying a group of separate tests. Americans Raymond Cattell and Louis Thurstone, among others, made important contributions to the development of factor analysis and the field that came to be known as "psychometrics."[12]

Explicit appeals to eugenics and social Darwinism gradually went out of favor, particularly after World War II, due to their association with Nazism. Intelligence is still a topic of academic study, but it has largely split off as an independent area, distinct from the more general topic of personality. Nonetheless, the psychometric methods developed by eugenicists are employed in the effort to summarize human personality as a collection of traits. For the last few decades, the most popular trait approach has been the five factor theory, which suggests that people can be described by how they line up on five core dimensions: openness to experience, conscientiousness, extroversion, agreeableness, and neuroticism (acronym = OCEAN). After filling out a standardized questionnaire, a profile can be created for each person showing whether they are high or low on each of the five basic traits. In addition, prominent five factor researchers have gone to some lengths to show that your profile remains fairly constant over your lifespan, and some suggest that this stability of personality may have genetic roots.

Social psychology evolved under very different circumstances. Rather than focusing on essences buried within the person, a group of researchers recognized that humans are an intensely social species and that much of what we do is in reaction to the people around us. More than any other field of psychology, the course of social psychology has been strongly influenced by history. A number of the foundational researchers were born in Europe and emigrated to the United States to escape persecution. Others were first generation Jewish-Americans whose research was shaped by the horrors of the Holocaust.

Solomon Asch was born in Russian Poland in 1907 and emigrated with his parents to the Lower East Side of Manhattan at the age of thirteen. He attended New York public schools and City College, followed by graduate study in psychology at Columbia University. Asch was strongly influenced by the German school of gestalt psychology, which studied visual perception and was associated with the phrase, "The whole is greater than the sum of its parts." Both in Europe and the United States, gestalt psychology was an important force in the burgeoning fields of cognition and social behavior. Asch did research on a variety of topics, including how people form impressions of other people and the role of a speaker's prestige in swaying an audience, but he is most often remembered for his experiments on independence and conformity.[13]

In the classic Asch experiment, a group of six to ten college students were recruited for what appeared to be a simple visual perception task. They were presented with a poster with three lines of different lengths and a comparison line that always matched one of the three choices (see Figure 8.2). In a kind of multiple-choice test, each person in turn said which line they thought matched the comparison line. Everything went well for a while, and then after several trials using different sets of lines, the first person on the next trial picked a line that was obviously wrong—either too short or two long. To make matters worse, the next few people said they agreed with the erroneous choice. Unbeknownst to the one true participant, all the other people in the room were employed by the experimenter and were answering according to a script. Typically, the true participants in the experiment found themselves facing a group of four to seven people who were all supporting an obviously wrong choice.

When people performed this task alone, almost no errors ever happened, which demonstrated that the participant's job should not have been very difficult. But when faced with a unanimous group supporting an obviously wrong answer, Asch found that only a quarter of the unsuspecting

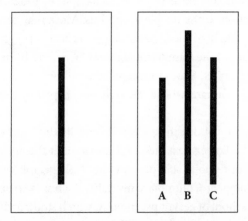

Figure 8.2 The Asch perception task. The participant's job was to identify which of the three choices on the right matched the length of the example line on the left.

participants were willing to consistently go against the group and give the correct answer.[14] The median number of errors out of twelve crucial trials was 5.5. This is by no means complete surrender to the group, but the results were surprising enough that they have been described in most introductory psychology textbooks ever since.

In the mid-1950s, as Asch's conformity studies were beginning to appear, he spent a year at Harvard as a visiting scholar, and a young graduate student named Stanley Milgram was assigned to be his teaching assistant. Milgram was born in the Bronx, New York to Jewish parents who had emigrated to the United States during World War I. Members of his extended family were in peril in Europe during World War II and, following the war, relatives who had escaped the concentration camps but still bore numbers tattooed on their bodies briefly stayed with his family.[15] Nazism and the Holocaust were on Milgram's mind as he began his research career, and before long a new understanding of the Holocaust began to take hold.

In 1960, Adolf Eichmann, a primary organizer of the Nazi program to deport and exterminate Jews, was captured in Argentina and taken to Israel. The German philosopher Hannah Arendt, who herself had escaped to the United States, wrote an account of the war crimes trial of Adolf Eichmann for the *New Yorker* magazine that was released subsequently as a book, *Eichmann in Jerusalem: A Report on the Banality of Evil*. Although many people found it difficult to accept, Arendt came to the conclusion that Eichmann did not harbor an unusual hatred of Jews or suffer from mental illness. Instead, he was a bureaucrat following orders whose primary weakness was an inability to think for himself. According to Arendt, Eichmann was "terribly and terrifyingly normal."[16]

Had Arendt concluded that Eichmann was a psychopath, the story might have ended there, but the trial offered the much more unsettling idea that evil was banal—that average people were capable of carrying out unspeakable acts in an orderly fashion, thinking that they were doing good. In early 1960, Milgram was at Princeton University, where he was working for Asch, and he was trying to figure out how to take Asch's research a step further to study obedience rather than mere conformity. The Holocaust was a motivation for this research path, and at some point in 1960—possibly in May, when Israeli agents captured Eichmann—Milgram figured out how to have an authority figure command the participant to do something cruel.[17] The result was the now famous (and somewhat infamous) Milgram obedience studies.

Milgram performed many variations of his obedience studies, but the classic one involved two people who were recruited by a newspaper advertisement for an experiment on learning. Straws were drawn to determine who would be the "learner" and who the "teacher," but in fact the learner was a trained actor working for Milgram and the drawing of straws was rigged so that the true participant was always the teacher. The experimenter, who wore a lab coat, explained that this was a study of the effect of punishment on learning. The teacher's job would be to read questions over an intercom to the learner, who would be in the next room. The teacher sat in front of an intimidating looking device with a long series of switches. The experimenter explained that the switches were used to deliver brief shocks to the learner and the voltage increased from left to right from 15 volts to 450 volts. The switches beyond 360 volts were labeled, "Danger severe shock," and the last few switches were simply marked "XXX." The teacher's job was to read multiple-choice questions to the learner and give him a shock whenever the answer was wrong. Furthermore, with each successive wrong answer the teacher was to move to the next highest voltage switch. To give the situation a sense of reality, the teacher was given a sample shock to feel what the learner would be getting. Finally, before disappearing into his booth, the learner managed to mention that he had a heart condition.

Once the experiment began, it followed a set pattern. The learner got some answers wrong, and the teacher kept moving up the line to stronger and stronger shocks. Eventually, the learner could be heard complaining in the next room, screaming after each shock and begging to stop the experiment. If the teacher kept going, eventually the learner stopped responding altogether, and the experimenter explained that, because not answering was counted as an error, the teacher must continue to administer shocks. If the participant hesitated or objected at any point, the experimenter urged him to keep going, saying "The experiment requires that you continue," and eventually, "You have no other choice, you must go on."

Milgram described the experiment to a group of psychiatrists, and asked them how far they thought the participants would go before quitting the experiment. They predicted that the overwhelming majority of people would quit by the tenth switch, 150 volts, and that only one out of a thousand people would keep shocking to the very end. The actual results could not have been more different. Sixty-five percent of participants went all the way to the end, and all of the participants went beyond 300 volts.[18]

Hannah Arendt had said "the trouble with Eichmann was precisely that so many were like him,"[19] and Milgram's research showed that she was right. In his 1974 book, *Obedience to Authority: An Experimental View,* Milgram made a direct connection between his findings and Hannah Arendt's conclusions in *Eichmann in Jerusalem*: "This is, perhaps, the most fundamental lesson of our study: ordinary people, simply doing their jobs, and without any particular hostility on their part, can become agents in a terrible destructive process."[20]

When these studies appeared, they provoked strong reactions. Several researchers raised ethical concerns about Milgram's methods because many of the participants showed signs of strain as they gave increasing levels of shock. Other commenters criticized the findings in much the same way that Hannah Arendt was attacked for her conclusions in *Eichmann in Jerusalem*. In part due to changing ethical standards for research, the experiments were not replicated for many years, which left open the possibility that people would not behave the same way today. But in 2009, Santa Clara University social psychologist Jerry Burger ran a modified version of the experiment and found comparable levels of obedience.[21] In addition, Burger found that women and men did not differ in their level of obedience.

In the following years several other social psychology experiments provided additional examples of the power of the environment to control human behavior. In the early hours of March 13, 1964, as she made her way home from her bartending job, Kitty Genovese was brutally murdered in the Kew Gardens neighborhood of Queens, New York. According to a newspaper report, thirty-eight people in nearby apartments witnessed the murder in progress and did nothing. Although subsequent investigations cast doubt on the number of witnesses and showed that, contrary to the newspaper report, two people did call the police and that a 70-year-old woman went down to the street and cradled Genovese's body until the police arrived,[22] the highly publicized event inspired psychologists Bibb Latané and John Darley to run a series of studies of bystander intervention in New York City, using Columbia and New York University students, either as unsuspecting participants or as actors carrying out the studies. Some of these experiments were conducted in real-life settings, such as New York City subway cars and sidewalks.[23] Latané and Darley's most important finding became known as the *bystander effect*, which suggested that the likelihood of a person helping someone in need is inversely proportional to the number of people nearby. Thus, if you are alone when someone next to you stumbles and falls, you are very likely to help out, but if we add three or four other people to the scene, the chances that you (or one of the others) will help drops drastically. The feeling that you have a responsibility to act is diffused among all those present.

Finally, Philip Zimbardo's famous 1971 Stanford prison experiment appeared to show that merely adopting the role of a guard could lead to brutal behavior. Zimbardo created a simulated prison and advertised for volunteers in the Palo Alto area. After giving the respondents a screening to eliminate anyone who might be psychologically unfit, he randomly assigned half of the participants to be guards and half to be inmates. According to legend, the guards freely exercised their power and began to devise their own methods of degrading and controlling the prisoners. Many were clearly enjoying being a guard. In response to this treatment, several of the inmates began to show signs of mental breakdown, and Zimbardo was forced to shut down the experiment. The original plan had been to run the study for two weeks, but it ended after only six days. Decades later, Zimbardo would become an expert witness on behalf of one of the US soldiers involved in the abuse of Iraqi detainees at Abu Graib prison, an episode he recounted in his book *The Lucifer Effect: Understanding How Good People Turn Evil.*[24]

Zimbardo's Stanford prison experiment was more of a demonstration project than a controlled investigation, and more recent research has provided a more nuanced picture of the bystander effect. For example, when bystanders recognize that a victim is in danger or when bystanders know each other, they are more likely to act.[25] Nonetheless, taken as a whole, these social psychology studies—and many others—represent a substantial challenge to the dominant message of personality psychology. The work of Asch, Milgram, Latané, Darley, and Zimbardo all points to the power of the situation. Placed in the right—or more accurately, wrong—environment, many people of good character can be convinced to lie, give strong electrical shocks to people with heart conditions, not help a person in need, and, perhaps, become violent revolutionaries and genocidal murderers. All of which is a reminder that, to a much larger extent than we appreciate, our being good or bad people is a product of luck.

The conflicting views of personality researchers and social psychologists were made explicit in 1968 when psychologist Walter Mischel—who would become famous for his marshmallow studies of children's self-control—published the book *Personality and Assessment*, which launched what came to be known as the "person-situation debate."[26] Mischel and others pointed out that many of the traits that personality theorists claimed were consistent within a person showed wide variation across settings. For example, in a classic study, Theodore Newcomb measured the extraversion or introversion of fifty-one boys at summer camp in twenty-one different settings.[27] He found the relationship between a boy's level of extraversion in one setting was unrelated to his extraversion in another. Knowing how he behaved in setting A told you nothing about how he would behave in setting B. This and many other studies that looked at behavior across different environments found very little trait consistency, which meant that traits might not be as important as previously thought.

We sometimes get a glimpse of this inconsistency in everyday life. We often get to know people in particular environments, giving us little sense of how they might behave in other circumstances. In my college teaching days, I spent most of my time in the company of students and other professors, but one year I agreed to fill in as a low-level dean and worked more closely with many non-teaching staff members. As I got to know them better, the staff told me about the difficult professors they sometimes had to deal with. A few of the names were not a surprise to me because they were people who just seemed to be cranky most of the time, but several of the troublesome faculty they identified were a shock. Colleagues who had been unfailingly polite and charming to me had well-known reputations for chewing off the heads of staff members. People avoided them as much as possible. Although it was a small college with little of the hierarchical structure of many larger organizations, some faculty felt they could drop the façade of cordiality with staff and reserve their good manners for people with PhDs.

The person-situation debate continues to this day with some people firmly committed to the trait personality camp and others to the situationist social psychology camp. Still others have found a kind of Goldilocks middle ground in an "interactionist" position that cedes some ground to dispositions while recognizing the substantial power of context.[28]

Despite the consistency of traits that personality psychologists have been able show with paper and pencil tests taken at different points in time, there remains the nagging problem of the unmeasured environment. When a person sits down to fill out a personality inventory, what context are they thinking about? When measures of their traits are found to be stable over time, is there any assessment of how their social environments and living arrangements have remained the same or varied over the same period? It is always easier to track down the person and give them a questionnaire than it is to follow the person around and measure the kinds of experiences they've had throughout the years. Although the personality psychologist's dispositional view comes naturally to us, Milgram's research and the other situationist experiments of the 1960s and 70s continue to be some of the most powerful and philosophically challenging studies in the history of psychology, and they test our conventional notions of selfhood.

The Moral Core of Personality

There is a growing recognition that we believe in a consistent self because we need to. For many of us, the alternative is unacceptable. People who say their vows and make the commitment to be married to one another make certain assumptions. Most recognize that circumstances will change and new experiences will come along, but they believe the core of their spouse's personality will hold steady. A permanent physical injury would be difficult to deal with, but Jamie would still be Jamie. Even in cases of dementia, many people say that they still can detect their loved one's unique personality showing through[29]—although this is not always the case. I once heard of a woman who had a long combative relationship with her mother, but as the older woman's Alzheimer's disease progressed, her personality changed and she became very sweet—leaving the younger woman somewhat confused and frustrated. The daughter had been carrying around years of animus, but confronted with this softened version of her mother, she didn't know what to do with it. Nonetheless, this is a rare event that further dramatizes how much we expect personalities to remain consistent over time.

The classic experiments of the situationists differ in another important way from the approach taken by the trait psychologists. When we look at Milgram's obedient teachers, Latané and Darley's passive bystanders, or Zimbardo's cruel guards, it is obvious what a good person should do in these situations. Social psychology of the 1960s and 70s was aimed at identifying the psychological forces that influence moral behavior. In contrast, the trait theories dominant in personality psychology tell us little about whether someone is good or bad. You could be a very conscientious embezzler or an extroverted bully. The relative absence of moral content in trait psychology is not an accident. It dates back to beginnings of the field. In the 1930s, Gordon Allport, a foundational trait theorist, suggested that the dispositions measured by personality psychologists should be free of "preconceived moral significance,"[30] and in the intervening years, psychologists have generally followed Allport's lead. But does a person's profile of traits tell us what we really want to know about a them? The five factor trait theory may reveal whether someone is a good fit for a particular type of job or is a compatible prospective mate, but there is a growing understanding that moral qualities are central to our notions of personality.

When a person enters or leaves your life, their character is at the forefront. We are a highly interdependent species, and as we negotiate the social world, moral qualities are fundamental. At first meeting, our primary concern is often whether this new person can be trusted. In ancient times, the questions were more basic. *Are you friend or foe? If I share my food with you with you now, can I trust you will do the same for me later?* But today, our social circles of family, friends, and work all involve people we have learned to trust with some things and not others, or not at all.

Our final assessments of people also trend toward these basic qualities. I have been to many funerals, and regardless of the person's accomplishments, at the end of life, it is often their moral character that matters most. *She was a good person. Someone you could trust. Would do anything for you.* This observation is also borne out by the results of my "Looking Back on Life" study described in chapter 5. In general, when imagining the ends of their lives, people wanted morally weighted accomplishments more than individual achievements. Having a successful family, having a fulfilling marriage, and being a good person rose to the top of the list, and being well-off financially or being successful in the arts or sciences ranked lower.

Similarly, between the beginnings and ends of our time with other people, it is the moral fluctuations that matter most. I sometimes play a simple game with friends. Picking two people who are not officially linked in marriage or a romantic relationship but whom I know to be very close, I turn to one of them and say, "If Joe were to commit a cold-blooded murder, would you visit him in jail?" The answer the person gives says something about the way they think about friendship, but the case of cold-blooded murder is a strong test because it is one of the most morally repugnant and concerning acts one could imagine. In contrast, changes on the morally neutral trait scales used by psychologists to measure personality wouldn't provide the same kind of test. For example, the question, "If Joe suddenly became very introverted (or extraverted) would you still be his friend?" does not create the same kind of dilemma.

Psychologist Nina Strohminger recounted a story about a friend whose wife's personality was beginning to morph, and although he was not overly concerned, he wondered what the future would bring. Stohminger asked the friend what change would make his wife unrecognizable. He replied, "If she stopped being kind, I would leave her immediately."[31] Similarly, in those instances when we are moved to request a different kind of behavior from someone, the desired change often has a moral component. If Joe did become more introverted, it would be an interesting transformation to observe, but unless his introversion had some additional implications, the change would be morally neutral. In contrast, a husband or wife might reasonably urge their spouse to become more open to new experiences (in keeping with the openness dimension of the five factor model), in an effort to keep the relationship fulfilling for both members. In this case, despite being directed at a neutral trait, the request has moral weight.[32]

Furthermore, a number of psychologists and philosophers suggest that we construct a personality—a narrative of the person—both for ourselves and for others because we need predictability. Human behavior is very complicated. We all have varying genetic gifts, learning experiences, and situational demands, and by constructing moral profiles of the people around us we are better able to navigate the social environment and get our needs met.

Memory plays an important role in this process. Over time, we construct personalities for people so that we can sort them out and know whom to avoid, whom to praise, and whom to hold responsible. The staff members at my college had a different moral profile for some of my faculty colleagues and used that information in planning their encounters. Philosopher John Locke believed that memory was central to identity and to moral responsibility. According to this view, if a person had committed a crime in the past, but due to "abnormal amnesia"—meaning more than simple forgetting—no longer remembered what they had done, they should not be punished. According to Locke, the continuity of self had been broken by the absence of memory.[33]

Something very close to this principle was tested in the American justice system in the 2018 Supreme Court case *Madison v. Alabama*. Vernon Madison was convicted of murdering a Mobile, Alabama police officer in 1985, but while on death row he suffered a series of strokes that destroyed much of his memory and rendered him unable to walk unassisted. Importantly, he claimed to have no memory of the crime. The 5-3 decision written by Justice Elena Kagan, narrowly separated from Locke,[34] suggested that the Eighth Amendment prohibition of cruel and unusual punishment allowed the punishment of some defendants who could not remember their crimes, but the law prohibited the execution of defendants who didn't understand why they were being singled out for punishment. The case was sent back down to the lower court to sort out,[35] and Mr. Madison succumbed to his deteriorating condition before the state court acted.[36]

The transplanted brain is one of the most enduring tropes of horror literature and film, beginning at least with Mary Shelley's classic novel *Frankenstein* and passing through the many *Frankenstein* film adaptations, as well as *Donovan's Brain* (1953), *The Brain that Would Not Die* (1962), *The Man With Two Brains* (1983), and *Get Out* (2017). The traditional plot involves a mad scientist whose meddling upsets the natural order by conducting the forbidden experiment. The subtitle of Shelley's novel was *The New Prometheus* and, as in the Prometheus legend, most brain transplant stories don't end well.

Philosophers and psychologists have also been fascinated with the transplanted brain scenario, because it is useful in testing common notions of personality and self. Locke proposed a case in which the brain (soul) of a prince was transplanted into the body of a cobbler and suggested that the person went with the soul and not the body.[37] For example, if your brain were transplanted into a new body, complete with your character and all your memories, would this new person be you? Would this reconstituted person retain or assume your identity?[38] Many people would say yes.

Following up on this question, Strohminger and philosopher Shaun Nichols conducted a series of studies aimed at identifying the essential nature of identity. In one case, they described a fellow named Jim who gets into a car accident and needs a brain transplant. Participants in different groups were told either that Jim was psychologically identical after the surgery or that he suffered from one of four specific deficits: visual agnosia (unable to recognize some objects), apathy, amnesia, or loss of moral conscience. Participants were then asked to rate the degree to which "he was still Jim." The loss of moral conscience was judged to make the biggest difference. The immoral version of post-operative Jim was rated significantly less Jim-like than any of the other versions.

So, at the beginning, end, and all points between, the moral character of the people around us is very important, and as a result, we keep tabs on their personalities and the degree to which they can be relied upon. But it is important to make one caveat. We encounter people in different ways, and we don't need the same things from everyone. In some cases, we simply need predictability, and moral considerations are less important. How would one even know if their doctor is a cruel parent or difficult employer. All any patient can or needs to know is how the doctor behaves within the office. In his book *On Truth*, philosopher Harry Frankfurt asserted that it was possible to live with and benefit from people who lie and show other kinds of fraudulent behavior: "It only means we have to be careful."[39] (This viewpoint suggests to me that Frankfurt might visit a murderous friend in jail.) It is simpler to negotiate the social world if we can count on people to have consistent personalities, but change happens, whether we like it or not. Couples depend on each other to avoid sexual relationships with other people, and if it becomes known that one person succumbed to situational demands and violated that trust, the other partner must incorporate this fact into their view of the relationship. Without the delusion of a coherent personality, we might be less surprised when uncharacteristic behavior emerges, but the rest of the time would be much more labor intensive and emotionally demanding as we tried to judge from moment-to-moment how people will act.

The Constructed Self

I can hear your objections. At this point you might be saying: *So even if I accept that situations can—in the extreme case—turn a Patricia into a Tania, and if I further accept that the sense of identity is a moral necessity because we need to know who is friend and who is foe, it still feels like I have a self. I have a sense of identity that follows me around each day, and it feels like me. If I am deluded about all of that, how is the trick done? Where does this feeling come from?*

You may feel like the philosopher René Descartes, who famously asserted, *cogito ergo sum*. The original French phrase was *je pense, donc je suis*, and both are translated as, "I think, therefore I am."[40] Everything else in the world may be an illusion, but of one thing you are sure. Because you can think, you know you exist.

The self that existed in Descartes' world was a self having the immediate sensation of thought. In his book, *A Treatise of Human Nature*, published in 1740, the Scottish Enlightenment philosopher David Hume proposed a *bundle theory* that can be seen as an extension of Descartes. Hume suggested that in each moment we experience a number of separate emotions, sensations, and perceptions that human imagination bundles together into a continuous string.

For Hume, perception is central to our sense of self. He said that whenever he made a deliberate effort to detect himself, "I stumble upon some particular perception or other, of heat or cold, light or shade, love or hatred, pain or pleasure."[41] He said he could not separate his sense of self from these distinct perceptual experiences and that in those cases when he perceived nothing at all, such as when he was in a sound sleep, "I am insensible to *myself* and may truly be said not to exist."

According to Hume the experience of a continuous self is a creation of our imagination. In one example, he described a man hearing a series of noises that are "frequently interrupted and renew'd." They are distinct sounds that may resemble each other, but are not a single sound. Nonetheless, the man hearing them considers each of them part of the same noise. They have little in common except a common source, and by inferring a common source—which in actual practice, sometimes turns out not to be the case—the man perceives all the sounds as part of the same noise. According to Hume, in a similar fashion our feelings and internal experiences—though actually distinct—are bundled together to make a coherent sense of self.

A more modern view of this process is offered by developmental psychologist Alison Gopnik, who suggested that autobiographical memory—what psychologists call *episodic memory*—is at the core of our sense of self. Episodic memory is our memory for the things that we have done and experienced. We know that it is distinct from *semantic memory*—memory for the kinds of things we learn in school, such as the names of state capitals or the French word for "book"—in part because of patients who've lost their episodic memory due to brain injury.[42] The most famous of case of memory loss was Henry Molaison (identified as H. M. prior to his death), who, in an effort to control severe epileptic seizures, had an experimental form of brain surgery when he was twenty-seven years old.[43] The procedure cured his epilepsy but rendered him unable to create new episodic memories. Similar to Lenny, the main character in the 2000 movie *Memento*, Molaison reintroduced himself to his doctor each day he saw her because he assumed it was their first meeting. Although his memory for events prior to the surgery remained intact, he lost the ability to create new semantic and episodic memories. Nonetheless, what psychologist's call *procedural memory* was not impaired. For example, researchers gave Molaison a mirror tracing task to learn over the course of several days. Molaison was required to use a pencil to trace around a star-shaped drawing while looking at his hand in a mirror, which reversed his movements. Mirror tracing is a difficult skill for anyone to master, but despite his other deficits, Molaison showed improved tracing across days. Each day spent practicing was new to him—he would begin the task not realizing he'd done it before—but his brain retained what he had learned on the previous days. Molaison had substantial deficits in episodic and semantic memory, but his procedural memory was fine. Unfortunately for Molaison, semantic and especially episodic memories are the conscious forms of memory that allow us to construct our autobiographies and our sense of self.

People with other forms of brain dysfunction show a separation of episodic and semantic memory. Researchers have studied many children with neurological damage caused by injury or brain tumors, and in some cases they are able to learn and perform well in school but have problems grounding their knowledge in the story of their lives.[44] They can learn something new and correctly report it, but later on they are unable to tell you where or how they learned it. In some cases, they are even unclear about whether they were taught the information or merely imagined it.

Gopnik describes the development of the sense of self in young children as a process that includes acquiring the ability to form autobiographical memories.[45] At the age of one year, children are unable to use a mirror and recognize what they are seeing as themselves. When a sticker is surreptitiously placed on their foreheads and they look into a mirror, they perceive the image as a different baby and gesture toward the sticker in the mirror. But by the age of two, children seeing themselves in a mirror with a sticker on their foreheads will touch their heads in recognition that the image in the mirror is them. This is the classic mirror test of self-awareness, and in addition to young humans, several animal species can pass it. Similarly, three-year-old children can correctly report *whether* they have seen something before, but not *when*. In one study, children were shown one picture on one day and another on the next. Later, three-year-olds were very accurate about whether they'd seen the picture before but could not say when. In contrast, six-year-old children were are able to say when they saw the picture with the same level of accuracy as adults.

According to Gopnik (and others), this ability to create an autobiographical memory, a narrative stream of our lives, provides the backbone of our sense of self. What Hume called imagination gives us the ability to see connections between the past and the present and to project out a future before us. Rather than experiencing the events of our lives as Humean discrete perceptions, we see them as linked, building one upon the other. It is sometimes—but not always—true that, when B follows A, it is because A caused B, and we make that inference all the time. Indeed, our survival as a species is due in part to our great ability to see these predictable patterns and use them to our benefit. As a result, it is understandable that we should see the moments of our lives as a long chain of interlocking events, rather than just a series of discrete perceptions. The psychological contributions of auto-biographical memory and imagination bring a kind of unearned coherence to our conception of self.

Many scholars of both Hume and Buddhism have noted that Hume's position, sometimes called his "no-self theory," bears a close resemblance to Buddhist ideas of identity.[46] According to Buddhist tradition, there is no coherent self that is consistent over time. Instead we experience fleeting individual sensations. Buddhist thought also acknowledges the separation between the true condition of an absent self and the conventional way we talk about the self. Enlightened beings know that there are two forms of speech, one conventional and one ultimate. When we use words such as "myself" or "I" we are not referring to something real but merely applying a grammatical convenience. The enlightened person never confuses this with ultimate speech that reflects the truth of human existence. According to Buddhism, meditation is the means of ridding oneself of the delusion of self. During meditation we lose our sense of a continuous identity and become aware of the fleetingness of sensation and emotion. Coming to terms with the absence of self also allows for the elimination of the self-oriented emotions of pride, humility, embarrassment, and envy.

Alison Gopnik, who herself supports a modern version of Hume's no-self theory, began to wonder whether Hume could have been directly influenced by Buddhist philosophy, and she took on a detective mission to determine whether this kind of direct influence was possible.[47] On the surface, the chances seemed quite slim. Hume wrote *A Treatise of Human Nature* in the late 1730s, at which time, Buddhism was all but unknown in the West. However, Gopnik knew that Hume wrote parts of *A Treatise* during 1735–1737 while living in the town of La Flèche in western France, not far from the Royal College of La Flèche. She discovered that during that period there was a Jesuit scholar at the Royal College who had direct exposure to Buddhist thought during a missionary trip to Siam, as well as indirect exposure through discussions with other Jesuits who had spent time in the East. Although she found no tangible proof—Hume was an unknown twenty-year-old at the time and no one collected his letters—Gopnik concluded that it was quite possible Hume learned about Buddhism in conversation with scholars at the Royal College.

The philosophies of Buddhism and Hume assert that our sense of a continuous self is a kind of perceptual illusion created by separate but similar sensations in the course of time, and contemporary psychologists suggest the illusion is forged of a need for predictability, especially about moral behavior. But this is not the only way our psychology is shaped by social and moral forces.

When she became Tania, Patty Hearst made a dramatic change of direction. She went from a rebellious but typical heiress to an urban guerilla who participated in armed robberies, shoot-outs, and bombings. She and her SLA comrades thought they were engaged in a highly moral battle, but once she was captured and reverted to the heiress role, she was judged by a different set of standards. The campaign that was mounted in her defense proposed that she'd been Patricia all along but that her captors had coerced and brainwashed her. She did not freely choose to engage in bank robberies and shoot-outs, and as a result, she was not responsible. The competing needs of the community to find justice and a resolution to the SLA saga required that Patricia's actions be a choice. Praise and responsibility can only be assigned to freely chosen acts. As it turned out, the jury was not persuaded by the brainwashing defense, and concluded that Patricia had choices.

It is to this question that we turn next. Did Patty have a choice? Do any of us have a choice?

9

The Mind's Best Trick

"You sound to me as though you don't believe in free will," said Billy Pilgrim.

"If I hadn't spent so much time studying Earthlings," said the Tralfamadorian, "I wouldn't have any idea what was meant by 'free will.' I've visited thirty-one inhabited planets in the universe, and I have studied reports on one hundred more. Only on Earth is there any talk of free will."

—Kurt Vonnegut,
*Slaughterhouse-Five**

I've saved the best delusion for last—a delusion so powerful that it may be difficult to believe it is a delusion at all. Consider the following cases drawn from actual events.

Case 1

It's a Saturday afternoon, and a man is visiting a toy store with his family. While his children peruse the aisles, he sidles up to a video game and begins to manipulate the joystick. He quickly becomes absorbed in guiding a monkey over the screen as it jumps over barrels and avoids other obstacles, then suddenly the words "Start Game" pop up on the screen. For several minutes, the man had assumed the game was already underway and that he was playing it, but now he sees his mistake. The game was in demo mode and the monkey was following a pre-recorded path across the screen. Although

* Excerpt from *Slaughterhouse-Five: A Novel* by Kurt Vonnegut, copyright © 1968, 1969 and copyright renewed © 1996, 1997 by Kurt Vonnegut, Jr. Used by permission of Dell Publishing, an imprint of Random House, a division of Penguin Random House LLC. All rights reserved.

the man believed he was making the monkey jump and move, his manipulation of the joystick had been completely irrelevant. It wasn't him.[1]

Case 2

Beginning in the early 1990s, a group of educators began to promote a new theory of autism. They suggested that many autistic children and adults suffered from a physical disorder and not a cognitive one. According to this view, a large group of people with autism had normal cognitive and language ability but were unable to express themselves because they lacked the necessary physical movements to do so. They were trapped inside their bodies. To address this problem, a prompting technique called facilitated communication was introduced: a helper (the facilitator) would gently steady the learner's arm or sleeve as they used a finger to type on a keyboard. The results were astonishing. Many young people who previously had been unable to communicate began to perform at normal grade level and, in some cases, to write poetry and novels. Facilitated communication had unlocked the potential inside these people, and the technique spread rapidly. Schools bought keyboard communicators for all their students and trained their teachers and staff to serve as facilitators. Parents learned to use the technique at home. Facilitated communication was so successful that its proponents claimed the old theories of autism needed to be discarded. Inside these broken bodies were thinking, feeling people who desperately needed to be set free.

By 1992, the O. D. Heck Developmental Center in Schenectady, New York had trained staff on all three shifts to use facilitated communication with their autistic clients, and the effects were so remarkable that the staff became deeply committed to the technique. Teachers used their own money to buy keyboard devices for their students, and they established rewarding friendships with people they now saw as their intellectual equals. But because the facilitators were holding the arms of their clients as they typed, some psychologists at O. D. Heck became concerned that the facilitators—and not the clients—might be the true authors of the words on the keyboards. Eventually, the psychologists decided to perform a simple double-blind test. A client and a facilitator would sit together at one end of a long table. A divider was placed down the center of the table so that pictures could be shown to the client and facilitator separately, without the other seeing, and the clients were asked to type the name of the object they saw in the picture. The trick was that on some trials the client and facilitator were shown the same picture; on others they saw different pictures. If the client was actually doing the typing, that shouldn't have mattered. The typed answers should conform to what the client—and not the facilitator—saw.

The results of the test were shocking. There was not a single correct answer. Using many different clients and facilitators there were a total of 180 trials when the two pictures were different, making it possible for the client to demonstrate independent communication. Not a single answer on those trials was correct. When the pictures were different, the answer typed was what the facilitator saw, not the client. The same lack of positive findings has been found in virtually all of the subsequent double-blind tests of facilitated communication.[2] The answers were only correct when the facilitator and the client saw the same picture. It was clear the facilitators were doing the typing.

Once the O. D. Heck staff were shown the data from the test, they were—in their own words—"devastated." They had no idea that they were the ones spelling out the words on the keyboard. It had been entirely unconscious, and the news was hard to accept. Many of the staff believed so strongly in facilitated communication that, when they realized it wasn't true, they went through a process of mourning. One staff member said, "It was like taking your best friend and going out and their being hit by a car." One speech pathologist said it took months before she could talk about the episode without crying. Eventually, life at the O. D. Heck Center went back to the way it had been before facilitated communication.

These two cases are different in a number of ways. Most importantly, Case 1 is a relatively trivial episode, and Case 2 has serious implications for the education of people with autism. But the two are similar in one important way: both involve confusions of cause and effect. Furthermore, the confusions are not about some event out in the natural world, such as whether that sound you hear in the basement is caused by an animal or by a malfunctioning furnace. In both cases, people were confused about whether they were causing something to happen. The man in the toy store believed he was making the monkey move when he wasn't, and the teachers at the O. D. Heck Center believed they were not doing the typing when they were.

These examples get at one of the core problems that has plagued philosophers and psychologists for millennia. In most situations we have the clear impression that we are in charge of our own actions. I think about a word, and I move my fingers on the keyboard to make it appear. You open the refrigerator door, choose what you want to eat, and reach for it. In all these situations we have the distinct impression that we are in charge. We are the deciders, and we are the doers. But since philosophy's beginnings, people have had doubts. Are we really in charge? And recent psychological research has only amplified those doubts.

Does Free Will Make Sense?

First let's take a look at the universe as a whole. Pull back the camera, take a Tralfamadorian view, and think about our Milky Way Galaxy, which is tossed in there among all the zillions of other galaxies in space, and somewhere inside the Milky Way Galaxy is our familiar sun with eight planets spinning around it. Somewhere on the pale blue third planet is you, holding this book. When we think about almost all of the universe we have no problem with determinism—with accepting that it is all just a matter of chemistry and physics. As Galaxy X goes streaming out into space carrying with it all its millions of stars, planets, asteroids, and space junk, we don't imagine that it got curious about what's going on over in some far-off corner of the universe and decided to go check it out. Similarly, we don't assume that the planet Mercury spins around the Sun in a close orbit because it has a peculiar affinity for temperatures that are 800 Fahrenheit during the day and -280 Fahrenheit at night. Closer to home, when it rains, we don't assume the clouds decided your lawn needed watering. If there is a devastating flood, some people claim God is punishing us for some sin we have committed. In these extreme cases, there is an understandable desire to assign some kind of meaning to otherwise brutal and arbitrary calamities, but science does not make room for supernatural explanations. The inorganic world is as mechanistic as billiard balls on a pool table, and most of the time we have no problem understanding it that way.

Crossing the line into the organic world, we still have little difficulty with most species. The weeds don't grow in your garden out of a malicious effort to frustrate you and use up your time. Even in the animal world, it is hard to see free will at play in the behavior of most species. Only in Disney movies do forest creatures seem to dance and sing as a free expression of some internal desire. More complex species—dolphins, chimpanzees, dogs, and cats—are more difficult cases. It is much easier to imagine that these animals have feelings and consciousness, a sense of self, and perhaps even free will. But most people would agree that, somewhere between earthworms and humans, a line can clearly be drawn. If there is intension, choice, and personal will, it exists in a relatively small number of larger brained species. Furthermore, when placed in the context of the whole known universe these few species are all tucked away on one blue rock in our solar system. As Vonnegut's Tralfamadorian suggests, there may be—or may have been—other sentient beings like us elsewhere in the universe. It is almost a mathematical certainty. But apart from our small colony, all of the universe seems to follow rigid physical rules—billions of galaxies, stars, and planets, and even the great majority of happenings on our own little planet. The problem of free will rests on the questions, *Are we part of that great expanse of the universe, or are we somehow different? Do we operate by the normal rules of nature, or are the rules different for us?*

Throughout history, when people have tried to explain the workings of the human body, they've made analogies to whatever was the most advanced form of technology at the time. When I was growing up in the 1960s, the standard landline telephone was a great symbol of modern engineering, and at school my teachers showed educational films produced by the Bell Laboratories that portrayed the human brain as a telephone switchboard.[3] Now that we have computers, the brain can be compared to a computer motherboard—or two of them—as I did in chapter 1.

Perhaps one of the most famous technological analogies was employed by the French philosopher René Descartes. In the Europe of Descartes' seventeenth century, automata—clockwork and pneumatic devices—produced the illusion of animate movement. The most impressive of these were large statue-like automata in the gardens of the wealthy that depicted entire scenes of moving animals and people (see Figure 9.1).[4] In some cases, there were hidden panels in the ground or in the steps approaching the figures that, when stepped on, tripped valves setting the figures in motion or releasing sprays of water.

Inspired by these mechanical entertainments, Descartes proposed that the bodies of humans and animals were akin to machines. Humans were distinct from animals in having a nonmaterial soul. The idea of a soul, apart from the body, was not new. Aristotle had proposed it much earlier, as had many other philosophers. But because he went into much more detail about the body and soul, Descartes is given credit for advancing early psychology. For example, based on his understanding of automata, he proposed a theory of reflexes that involved sense information flowing

Figure 9.1 A mechanical grotto designed by French hydraulic engineer Salomon de Caus, published in his 1615 work *Les raisons des forces mouvantes*.
Source: Internet Archive.

from the extremities to the brain, much like the pneumatic tubes of the automata (see Figure 9.2). In addition, he somewhat audaciously proposed that the pineal gland, deep within the brain, was the seat of the soul and the place where all thoughts were formed.[5]

Descartes' dualism—the idea of a human mind separate from the machine-like body—is still with us today. Our understanding of the body's machinery is far better than that of Descartes. For example, we now know that most reflexes are far simpler than Descartes imagined, with messages from your burning foot going no further than the spinal cord—not all the way up to the brain—before heading back to your leg muscles. We also know that the pineal gland in the brain produces the hormone melatonin, which regulates the circadian rhythms of sleep and wakefulness. Furthermore, neuroscientists have begun to make some progress in understanding the nature of consciousness by using brain-imaging techniques, such as functional magnetic resonance imaging (fMRI), to see what areas of the brain are operating when people engage in various mental activities. But we have made almost no progress on the central question of consciousness.

Figure 9.2 Illustration of a reflex from Descartes, *Traite de l'homme* (1664).
Source: Wikimedia.

Science continues to struggle with three enormously difficult problems:

1. The origin of the universe: How did something come from nothing?
2. The origin of life: How did life emerge from raw elements?
3. The origin and nature of human consciousness: Where does it come from? What's it about?

Scientists don't usually think about their work in competitive terms, but if asked to score these three hard problems, many would say that we've made more progress toward understanding the first two than the last one. We still stand on the edges of a great canyon of ignorance. On one side of the canyon are the many advances of physiology, medicine, and neuroscience that reveal the human body to be a gloriously complicated collection of tissues, fluids, and electrochemical sparks. It is a machine far more complicated and daz-zling than Descartes imagined, but unfortunately the part of the body most closely related to consciousness—the brain—is particularly difficult to study. There are many things you can do to the human body without killing it or drastically altering its capabilities, but cutting into a living brain is not one of them. For many years, researchers like the nineteenth-century French physician Paul Broca were forced to locate patients who appeared to be suffering from some disability and wait for them to die. He would observe them carefully in life and then, after removing their brains in autopsy, try to find evidence of the damage that might explain the patient's malady. Broca is most famous for discovering a speech problem—now called Broca's aphasia—that is characterized by normal understanding of language but a profound inability to produce the movements required for speech. Broca's aphasia is caused by damage to an area of the temporal lobe on the left side of the brain's outer layer.

In those early days of neuroscience, this slow and rather primitive process revealed some basic information about the functions of the brain. As in the case of Henry Molaison, even today damaged brains can sometimes help us understand memory and other mental functions. But there are many layers to this most complicated of organs, and its connections are often diffuse. Some operations are spread out among many different areas of the brain, making it difficult to get very far by studying random patches of tissue damage. In recent decades, some scientists have studied the brains of rats and mice, and others have invented a growing armament of scanners that make it possible to safely observe living human brains. All of these new technologies have helped us narrow the canyon of things we don't understand, but there is still a substantial void.

So far this canyon of ignorance, with science on one side and our private sensation of consciousness on the other—is unbridgeable. Researchers have offered various theories, but it remains largely a mystery how three pounds of wet neurons between our ears can give rise to the imagination of an Albert Einstein, a J. K. Rowling, or, for that matter, a René Descartes. Until scientists devise clever experiments that reveal how the clouds of thought and sensation emerge from the axons and dendrites of our cerebral cortexes—how the ghost gets into the machine—they will not be able to reach out to us across this gap in our understanding. And into that gap, among other things, falls any hope of a scientific understanding of our sense of conscious will.

What Camus called our ridiculous reason allows us to ponder many things: *What is the meaning of life? Is my lover true to me? What are the Red Sox' chances of winning the World Series?* When we use our reason to choose a course of action, we think first, and then we do. You think about how good a peanut butter and jelly sandwich would taste, and you go to the kitchen and make one. You think about going to exercise at the gym, and you decide it's too much of a hassle right now. You can go tomorrow. Some actions are more or less automatic, and we need not engage the heavy machinery. When you feel an itch, you just scratch. But when it comes to more deliberate actions requiring planning, we have a sense of thinking, of deciding, of making a choice. Some of this feeling comes naturally because one precedes the other. System Two may be slow in comparison to System One, but it is usually quick in comparison to physical movement. We will have more to say about the timing of these events later, but for now this is just the way it feels.

Those who want to argue in favor of a true conscious will, generally understand they face a number of challenges:

1. *The continuity of nature problem.* As we have seen, only the tiniest speck of the universe (us), seems to defy the natural, deterministic order of things. If humans are fickle beings with the ability to do or not do things, then we must carve out some kind of exception for this special species—and perhaps a few others. Why would that be the case? It seems odd, perhaps a bit deistic or egoistic, to suggest, as Camus does, that humans are separated from nature in this way. Not *of* this world, but somehow *in* it.

2. *The nonmaterial mind-body problem.* If our consciousness or soul is not part of our machinery, as Descartes and others have suggested, then how can a nonmaterial thing hovering above or within our body somehow move it? Is there a magic force field that emanates from an invisible gauzy brain? To many this seems like an unlikely bit of hocus-pocus.

3. *The prime mover problem.* This is the mental equivalent of the "If God made the world, who made God?" question. If there is a mind full of thoughts that cause our actions, where did our mind come from? The idea that the mind simply pops into existence without any prior cause creating or acting upon it seems like another bit of hocus-pocus, an appeal to supernatural forces.

Traditional Views of Intentional Action

The idea that people act freely upon the world has been part of our common understanding for a very long time. In Book III of his *Nichomachian Ethics*, Aristotle provides a lengthy analysis of the differences between actions that are "counter-voluntary," voluntary, or made "by decision."[6] According to Aristotle, counter-voluntary action happens by force or ignorance and evokes sympathy or pity in the observer. If a gangster kidnapped your family and threatened to kill them unless you steal money from your employer, complying would be a counter-voluntary action by force. Counter-voluntary action by ignorance is something you do voluntarily but produces a regrettable effect, such as attacking your son because you mistake him for an intruder. Similarly, in Aristotle's view, acts done in anger are counter-voluntary.

In contrast, voluntary behavior has its origin within the person and is neither ignorant nor driven by strong emotion. In Aristotle's view, animals and children are capable of voluntary action, but not decision. Furthermore, impulsive action is voluntary but does not involve decision in Aristotle's sense. Only mature adults who act after reasoned deliberation are capable of voluntary action with decision.

During the European Middle Ages, the conflict was between the idea of human freedom and the belief that God was all knowing. How could free will be reconciled with a religious form of determinism? Among other things, human choice was the justification for the final judgment of salvation or damnation, and yet God could see into the future and, presumably, know whether you would end up saint or sinner.[7] The doctrinal solutions to this dilemma were often a form of religious *compatibilism*.

Compatibilism is another form of Goldilocks solution that suggests that free action is not incompatible with determinism. Typically, we think of freedom and determinism as mutually exclusive categories. Either the world—including us—is constructed of chemical billiard balls bouncing through space, or there is some kind of nonmaterial ghost in our heads making decisions. Both things can't be true. But compatibilists argue that in a deterministic world people can still have choices—instances in which more than one action is possible.

Saint Augustine, writing in the late fourth and early fifth centuries CE had no doubt that humans had free will and that God was all knowing, but he suggested that God's omniscience included knowing how we would choose—a solution that seems to remove some power from God and reduce him to a predictor rather than a determiner of events.[8] The thirteenth-century Christian scholar Thomas Aquinas offered his own compatibilist view, writing that God was the first mover of all things, including human voluntary action, but God's all-knowing vantage point was eternal, not grounded in time, like ours. For Aquinas, this provided a solution to the conundrum that, according to Christian belief, all events on Earth are the result of God's will, but humans could still exert their own wills.

By the sixteenth century, the dilemma for European philosophers was reconciling human will with scientific—rather than religious—determinism, and the Enlightenment philosophers all struggled with this problem in their own ways. For his part, Descartes proposed a thoroughly dualist view, holding that the mind was unique to humans and apart from the body but somehow in control of it. From the vantage point of modern science, this is an unworkable solution to the mind-body problem because something separate from the body cannot logically move it. Descartes' dualism relies on magical forces.

In the traditional battle between passion and reason, Hume famously said, "Reason is, and ought only to be the slave of the passions, and can never pretend to any other office than to serve and obey them."[9] Reason and will are and should be driven by our passions. Taking an opposing view, Immanuel Kant suggested that humanity's unique capacity for reason made it possible to overcome our natural passions. Both men accepted that we are part of a deterministic natural world but each in his own way made an exception that allowed for choice. Hume's view of the natural world, including human action, was thoroughly deterministic, based in what he called a causal "necessity," but he also proposed that causal necessity could arise within a person in the form of spontaneity. Thus, he attempted to find a form of will that was compatible with the necessity of nature. He also suggested that ascribing some power to internal human necessity was important because the absence of will would be "entirely destructive to all laws divine and human."[10] In observing someone else, our moral judgment is based on inferences about the motives—internal causes—behind their actions. Kant's view was closer to Descartes' dualistic view. He argued that reason was a unique human ability with the power to direct our will and overcome passions.

Today the overwhelming number of professional philosophers consider themselves compatibilists, acknowledging the deterministic nature of the universe but holding that human choice is compatible with determinism. A 2009 survey of 931 philosophy faculty members found that 59 percent were compatibilists, and the remainder were fairly evenly distributed between the three remaining groups: *libertarians*, who believed we have free will apart from nature, *hard determinists*, who believe in a completely naturalistic world and the absence of free will, and those who chose "other."[11]

Setting philosophers (and many scientists) aside, almost everybody else is a libertarian free-willer, believing that much of the world is as deterministic as billiard balls, but human decision-making is not. Belief in human freedom is a deeply embedded cultural norm, and although most of the research on this topic has been done in Western countries, the existing cross-cultural evidence suggests it may be a universal and resilient norm.[12] A number of studies have asked participants to imagine that scientists have determined the neurological factors that cause a certain kind of behavior, and even when described in highly mechanistic and deterministic terms, people still report that the individuals described would have free will and be morally responsible for their actions.[13]

Nonetheless, people's intuitions about will and intent are not monolithic. We attribute different degrees of intention to different actions. To assess "folk concepts" of free will, philosophers Bertram Malle and Joshua Knobe surveyed a group of introductory psychology students about a hypothetical person, Anne, performing various actions.[14] A partial listing of their results is shown in Figure 9.3. As might be expected, actions that are typically considered to be less under voluntary control (sweating, having cravings, yawning) were rated low on intention. Actions that were judged higher in intention fell into one of two categories: behaviors that might attract negative moral judgment (interrupting, driving too fast, and stealing) or actions that seem more arbitrary (watering plants).

At its core, the existence of human free will is a metaphysical question—a question about the shape of reality. Either we have it, or we don't. Although

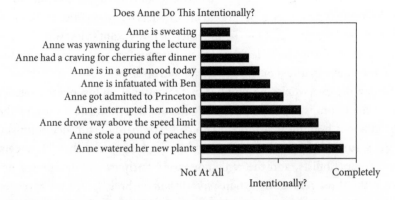

Figure 9.3 Folk judgments of the intentionality of various actions.
Data selected from Malle and Knobe (1997), table 2.

the nature of consciousness—including conscious will—remains one of the hard problems and is not likely to be convincingly solved for some time, theoretically this question should have a factual answer. Yes, no, or some blend of yes and no. But, as we have seen, our views of freedom and determinism are very difficult to extract from the need to assign praise or condemnation. From the beginning, it has been hard to separate the factual question of free will from its moral or religious implications. Belief in divine judgment required that Christians be free to choose good or evil, and secular society has reserved the assignment of praise and blame for voluntary acts. Many common legal systems include the concept of *mens rea* or guilty mind. This is not a requirement that the perpetrator *feel* guilt. Rather it requires that the criminal act was done intentionally. It is not enough to have killed someone. The worst punishments are reserved for people who have killed on purpose or "with malice of forethought." As a result, much effort goes into determining the defendant's mental state. If the jury had believed that Patricia Hearst was compelled to rob banks and did not genuinely intend to do so, she might have avoided punishment. The importance of intention is instilled at our parents' knees. We quickly learn that a harsher punishment is on the way if we did the thing "on purpose." The first exclamation after a young child breaks a dish or makes a mess is likely to be, "I didn't mean to!"

But, as we have seen, we are not objective judges of intention and will. In the last chapter we heard the case of the corporate CEO whose new program either harmed or helped the environment. Observers found the exact same action far more intentional when it produced harm rather than helping. Similarly, in the list of Anne's actions from the study by Malle and Knobe, her less admirable acts (e.g., stealing peaches) were judged more intentional than neutral or positive acts (e.g., getting into Princeton). The nineteenth-century German philosopher Friedrich Nietzsche was a free-will skeptic who wrote:

> Today we no longer have any pity for the concept of "free will": we know only too well what it really is—the foulest of all theologians' artifices, aimed at making mankind "responsible" in their sense. . . . Wherever responsibilities are sought, it is usually the instinct of wanting to judge and punish which is at work.[15]

It is now becoming clear that Nietzsche was right. When making judgments of intention, we do so in a backwards—or upside down—fashion. Ideally, when trying to assign moral blame or praise, we should first determine whether the act was intentional, and then assess its moral weight, in a kind of bottom-up process. However, there is growing research evidence that we approach this question in the opposite direction. We first determine whether we think the act is blameworthy, and then we assign intention to it. Our moral judgment drives our perception of the facts.

One example of this morally driven judgment comes from a set of studies that looked at allowing something to happen versus making something happen.[16] In one study, participants were asked to rate themselves on a scale from "strongly pro-life" to "strongly pro-choice."[17] Then, they read a scenario about a young woman, Sarah, who was two months pregnant and learned from her doctor that the fetus she was carrying had a rare vitamin B6 deficiency. If nothing was done, the fetus would die within a month, but if Sarah ate a special diet, the fetus would develop normally. Sarah had been worrying about the financial and emotional burden of having a child, and after thinking about it, she decided she would prefer not to carry the pregnancy to term. As a result, she didn't change her diet and, as predicted, the fetus died one month later.

After reading this story, the participants in the study were asked whether it was more appropriate to say Sarah *allowed* the fetus to die or *made* the fetus die. As you might expect, pro-life respondents were more likely to say Sarah made the fetus die. In addition, those who credited Sarah with greater agency in the death of the fetus more strongly endorsed the view that not changing her diet was morally wrong.

Hearing about a case of wrongdoing can even affect your general view of free will versus determinism. In another study, one group of people read a story about someone breaking into the home of a special education teacher and taking some of his valuables. Another group read a similar story that was more morally neutral. In this case, some aluminum cans were taken from the recycling bin at the end of a teacher's driveway. After reading the story, both groups filled out a questionnaire about their general views of free will. In this case, the people who saw the more serious theft version of the scenario expressed greater belief in free will—in general—than those who saw the recycling bin version. Naturally, the more serious theft version evoked a stronger desire to punish the perpetrator. Finally, the researchers found that the clearest indicator of the participants' free-will belief was not which of the two versions they read but the strength of their desire to punish the perpetrator. As Nietzsche might have predicted, when people have an inclination to punish, they believe more strongly in free will. Given that free will should be a factual question—it is either true or false—this is the opposite of the way things should work.

The Free-Will Delusion

Again, I can hear your objections:

> OK, so we might have some biases in our view of intention, will, and moral responsibility, and it may not make logical sense that our thinking, deciding, and choosing are somehow separate from the mechanics of our bodies and the rest of the universe. But I really do FEEL like I am deciding and choosing. In my head, I have this sensation of weighing options before I act. How can that be a delusion?

As we have seen, our senses are not always honest reporters of things as they are. The two examples at the beginning of this chapter were the appetizers for this section on the free-will delusion, but they don't reveal how we come to mistake cause and effect relationships involving our own actions. Fortunately, research conducted over the last few decades has peeled away much of the mystery of this delusion. The evidence comes from two areas: brain research showing what happens when we form an intention to act and psychological research showing how easily and under what circumstances we can be deceived about what we are and are not doing.

Libet's Experiment

Benjamin Libet caused quite a fuss.[18] He was born in Chicago in 1916 to Ukrainian Jewish immigrant parents who did not speak English in the home, and as a result, he learned the local language on the streets of Chicago's west side. The son of a tailor, Libet earned a scholarship to the University of Chicago, where he received his doctorate in physiology at the age of twenty-three.[19]

In the early 1980s, Libet began a series of studies of the brain activity that accompanies voluntary actions. In what later became known as the Libet Experiment, participants were brought into a laboratory where they were tested individually while wired up to an electroencephalogram (EEG) machine that measure brain activity.[20] They sat in a comfortable chair and were asked to look at a screen that showed a clock-like dial with a marker that spun around the perimeter every 2.5 seconds. Over a series of trials the participants were asked to make a motor movement—flicking a finger or a wrist—voluntarily and spontaneously, when the spirit moved them and without any preplanning. In addition, the participant was asked to note the position of the spinning marker on the clock dial at the moment they felt the urge to make the flicking motion.

Previous research had shown that voluntary motions, such as flicking a finger, are preceded by a build-up of a negative electrical charge in the brain called a *readiness potential*. Using the participants' EEG signals and the clock-dial procedure, Libet measured the time between the build-up of the readiness potential and the conscious urge to move, and what he found has been debated ever since. In several experiments, Libet discovered that the readiness potential begins to build up approximately a third of a second before the person has a conscious urge to move. When making a completely spontaneous flicking motion, your brain begins to prepare for the motion *before* you are aware of an urge to flick.

Many people interpreted Libet's results as support for a deterministic view of human behavior. If the brain begins the action before we have the idea to act, the idea can't be the cause. Causes move forward in time, not backward. Libet's results suggested that human action is caused by upstream forces on the body—our genetic inheritance, our cumulative history of experiences, and the immediate setting—and that the feeling of conscious intention is an additional effect of those forces rather than the cause of our actions.

Separating the Feeling from the Action

Harvard psychologist Daniel Wegner, who died in 2013, had a legendary wit. He was not a raconteur or joke teller but he made funny remarks.[21] He was partial to Hawaiian shirts and had an extensive collection of Groucho Marx nose-and-glasses sets. His wife described him as a "hysterically funny guy,"[22] and his impishness often came through in his writing. He once started a sentence, "To be fair . . ." and then started the next sentence, "Going back to being unfair . . . ."[23]

A talent for humor requires intelligence and creativity, qualities that served Wegner well in his scientific career. He became famous for his 1989

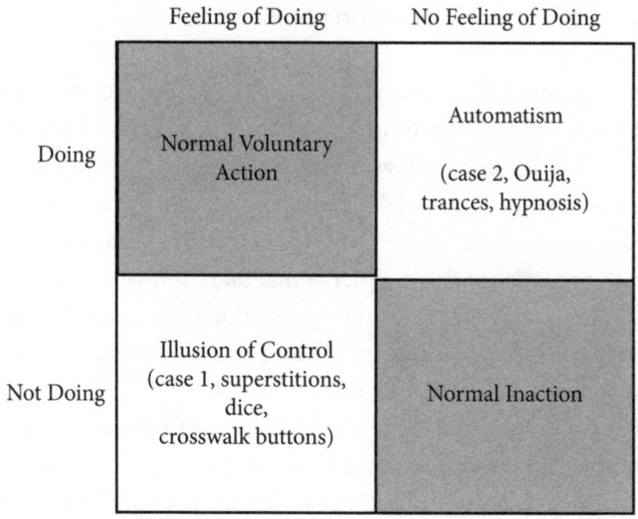

	Feeling of Doing	No Feeling of Doing
Doing	Normal Voluntary Action	Automatism (case 2, Ouija, trances, hypnosis)
Not Doing	Illusion of Control (case 1, superstitions, dice, crosswalk buttons)	Normal Inaction

Figure 9.4 Possible relationships of the feeling of doing to the act of doing.

book *White Bears and Other Unwanted Thoughts: Suppression, Obsession, and the Psychology of Mental Control*.[24] The white bear of the title is drawn from a story about the young Leo Tolstoy, who was challenged to stand in a corner until he had stopped thinking about a white bear. Tolstoy remained there for a long time.

Given the simple task of not thinking about something, we generally fail miserably. In Wegner's research studies, people who are asked not to think about a white bear often reported that they could think of nothing else. This is a trivial example, but there are many times in our lives when we would like to suppress certain thoughts—of an ex-lover, of an embarrassing episode, or an impending medical procedure—and we find it a hard to do so. When trying to suppress unwanted thoughts, people who are remarkably competent in other areas of their lives often demonstrate a dramatic lack of control.

Later in his career, Wegner turned to the psychology of agency and will. He recognized that—in many more instances than we are aware—we don't cause things we think we do, and we do cause things we think we don't. The situation is presented in Figure 9.4.[25] What we consider the normal state of affairs appears on the gray diagonal. We feel like we are doing something, and we are actually doing it. On other occasions, we have no feeling of doing, and indeed we are not. But there are far more instances that fit on the white diagonal than we realize.

Delusions of Action

Figure 9.4 is adapted from Daniel Wegner's book, *The Illusion of Conscious Will*, and Case 1 at the beginning this chapter was drawn from an experience he had while visiting a toy store with his children.[26] For several minutes, Wegner was under the impression he was playing a video game, when, in fact, the jumping monkey was under the control of a pre-game demo program. Although the premise of this chapter is that *all* of our sense of control is an illusion—or in our terms, a delusion—psychologists would call Wegner's toy store experience an *illusion of control* because it is clear there is no connection between the act and the outcome.

Other illusions of control come when we are confronted with random and coincidental events. A very common everyday situation is when we press buttons. In 2004, the *New York Times* reported that over 75 percent of the 3,250 crosswalk buttons at intersections in the city had been disconnected due to the computerization of traffic lights, and most of the nonfunctioning buttons were left in place to save the cost of removal.[27] It is impossible to calculate how many millions of presses have been made to inoperable crosswalk buttons by unsuspecting pedestrians, but for those not in on the secret, button pressing is maintained by the intermittent schedule of reinforcement produced when a press is occasionally followed by the lighting of the "Walk" sign. In those cases, we step off the curb thinking we've changed the light when we haven't. Elevators are another example. In many cases the "close-door" buttons in the United States have been deactivated to comply with the Americans with Disabilities Act, which requires that doors stay open long enough for people with mobility challenges to get through. As a result, pressing the close-door button on an elevator will often produce a false sense of power over the door.

The illusion of control is common in many situations where control is impossible. Dice players employ a number of superstitions, such as blowing on the dice for luck, as well as tossing them hard in the hope of a high number and softly for low one.[28] In chapter 2, we heard about the study of dice rolling and psychokinesis. Simply being the active participant who got to roll the die created an illusion of greater control. It is likely that many everyday superstitions, such as the wearing of lucky underwear and the use of rabbits' feet, are maintained by the illusion of control.[29]

As you press the crosswalk or elevator button, there is a bit of psychology that helps you think you've done something. When we act upon the world, the effects of those actions are often seen right away. As I type on this key-board, the letters on the screen seem to appear instantaneously, which helps to convince me that I am the one doing the writing and not a piece of nefar-ious software that has infected my computer. However, when the effects of our actions are delayed, the sense of agency starts to break down. Given the long delay involved, anthropologists have spent some time trying to deter-mine when humans first understood that sex caused pregnancy.[30]

Researchers studying our sense of voluntary action have discovered that the opposite effect also happens. When we feel like we made something happen, we perceive the effect as happening sooner. This finding has been shown in experiments with people making the same action, voluntarily and involuntarily. For example, in one study, participants pressed a key on a com-puter keyboard that was followed by a tone at delays varying between one thousandth of a second and a full second.[31] The participant's job was to press the key and then estimate the length of the delay to the tone. Crucially, in one condition, the participants pressed the key themselves, and in another, the participants pressed the key involuntarily. In the involuntary condition, the participant's finger was attached to the computer key by a little Velcro strap, and the experimenter was able to make the finger press the key by pulling a string that went from the Velcro strap through a hole in the keyboard. From the participants' point of view, it was easy to tell when they were doing the pressing themselves and when they were pressing involuntarily, but the task of estimating the delay to the tone was the same. In other studies, in-voluntary movements have been created by sending a magnetic pulse into the participant's brain (it's supposed to be safe), causing their hand to twitch. No matter how the involuntary movements were produced, participants reported that the delay from the press to the tone was significantly shorter when they pressed themselves compared to when the movement was exter-nally forced. This shows that we have a cognitive bias in favor of binding our actions to their outcomes when a sense of agency—of doing it ourselves—accompanies the action.

The Random and the Perverse

Much of everyday life is a trail of repeated actions. If you watch someone walking down the sidewalk, in most cases, the movements of their legs and the gentle passing of weight from one side to the other is as predictable and regular as the ticking of a metronome. Driving, brushing your teeth, getting dressed, and getting undressed are habitual acts that often verge on the robotic, and to the observer, they do little to dramatize your independence or autonomy. Random actions, in contrast, have more descriptive value. They don't appear to be the result of some ingrained habit or external force and are more often attributed to something in you.

In philosophical debates about free will, some have argued that physicist Werner Heisenberg's quantum uncertainty principle can be applied to the question of free will to show that the world is not entirely deterministic. According to the principle, even under controlled conditions, it is impossible to determine both the location and the momentum of a particle at the same time. Heisenberg believed uncertainty undermined the basic deterministic nature of the universe, but Einstein disagreed, claiming, "God does not play dice with the universe."[32] Scientists still debate this issue,[33] and some philosophers and scientists—including Heisenberg's son, Martin, a biologist—have argued that uncertainty bolsters the possibility of free will.[34] However, the argument over whether uncertainty threatens determinism in the universe is far from settled,[35] and it is not clear how this phenomenon on the level of subatomic particles relates to human choice.

The implications of unpredictable actions are more clear: random behavior—our own or that of other people—appears more free. Wegner and colleague Jeffrey Ebert conducted a pair of studies that showed this effect.[36] In the first study, participants logged into a research website and were prompted to press either the "p" or the "q" keys on their computer keyboard. The computer flashed a letter on the screen and the participant pressed. For one group of participants, the pattern was strict alternation between keys "p-q-p-q-p-q. . . ." A second group of participants was prompted to press in a similar fashion, except that the computer generated a random sequence of p's and q's: "p-q-q-p-q-p-p. . . ." After one hundred trials, both groups were asked how free they felt in pressing keys, with questions such as, "I felt that I was FREELY CHOOSING which keys to press" and "On any trial, I COULD HAVE PRESSED A DIFFERENT KEY THAN I DID." Despite the fact that key presses were completely and equally determined by the computer prompt for both groups, the participants in the random sequence group said that they felt significantly more free.

In a second study, participants watched a "newly discovered" triangular "alien" on a computer screen and were asked to observe its behavior. For one group of participants, the alien followed a rigid sequence of nine moves, which it repeated over and over again. The second group saw the alien move in a random sequence of nine moves, each trial being a different sequence. After observing the alien, both groups were asked about the alien's behavior, with questions such as, "The alien was FREELY CHOOSING how to behave" and "For any action the alien performed, it COULD HAVE ACTED DIFFERENTLY if it wanted to." As expected, the participants whose aliens moved randomly judged it to be significantly more free.

The results of Ebert and Wegner's studies suggest that, although apparent randomness happens often in the natural—and presumably deterministic—world (e.g., if you drop a bag of marbles on the floor or watch a housefly in flight), random behavior appears more free and autonomous. Psychologist Paul Bloom suggested that people engage in related forms of unpredictable behavior for a similar reason.[37] He recounted the story of philosopher Agnes Callard, who, while taking walks at night during her graduate school years, would sometimes lie down on the double-yellow lines on the road, in part because that was not the expected thing to do. Callard called this an example of *unruliness,* a challenge to or rejection of conventional rules of behavior. Bloom called it *perverse action* and described several other cases. For example, in 2016 an online survey was conducted to name a new British research vessel, and the winning name by a large margin was "Boaty McBoatface." Similarly, Bloom pointed out that researchers who interview children are vexed by kids who give silly answers simply because they can. Teenagers are reportedly the worst. According to Bloom, in one study, 19 percent of high school students who said they were adopted were kidding.

Bloom distinguishes perverse actions from rebellion because perverse actions are not goal-directed in the same way. They are not rejecting one set of rules to establish another. Perverse actions are done with full knowledge that they are wrong or bad, and the whole point of the action is to deviate from what is normal and expected. Lying down on the yellow lines appealed to Callard because it was something few other people would do (thankfully!), and it broke from convention. Among the possible explanations for perverse actions, Bloom argues that they provide a sense of autonomy and authenticity. Just as random behavior is interpreted as freer, these perverse acts are more likely to be attributed to individual volition than to the external demands of convention.

Delusions of Inaction

In the upper right-hand box of Figure 9.4 is *automatism,* which is the technical name for unconscious action. Throughout history there have been many popular examples of this separation of the feeling of action from the act.

Three blocks from where I live in Stonington, Connecticut is the former home of James Merrill, the Pulitzer Prize winning poet. The house is on the National Register of Historic Places and has been maintained in much the same condition as Merrill left it upon his death in 1995. On permanent display in his bright coral dining room under a pressed tin dome ceiling are a round milk glass dining table, a Ouija board, and a willowware teacup. Merrill was fascinated with the Ouija board, and over several decades, he and his partner David Jackson spent many evenings at the milk glass table, each with a hand on the overturned teacup, which they used as a simple planchette or pointing device. They received lengthy messages from a variety of characters in the spirit world, including recently departed friends and neighbors, as well as literary luminaries such as Wallace Stevens, W. H. Auden, and W. B. Yeats.[38] Merrill and Jackson transcribed the messages as they came through the board, and much of this testimony found its way into Merrill's poetry. The epic poem, "The Book of Ephraim," recounts conversations with a spirit of the same name who died on the island of Capri in 36 CE, murdered by Emperor Tiberius's guards.[39] Much of the text of the poem is in Ephraim's words, printed in all caps, as transcribed by Merrill and Jackson.

The Ouija board is an example of automatism. The planchette moves, but we don't attribute its movement to our thoughts or actions. Because standard application of the Ouija board involves two people with hands on the planchette (see Figure 9.5), our own movements of the board are easily misattributed to the other person, and when both people are misattributing at the same time, confusion abounds. *I'm not moving it; are you moving it? No, I'm not moving it; you must be moving it!* Whatever our hopes might be for the movement of the planchette, the simple relationship of intention to outcome breaks down due to the actions of our partner. Nonetheless, the players eyes are typically focused on the board, and players find themselves caught up in a process of predicting where the pointer will go next. Despite the fact that they are supposed to be guided by spirits, blindfolded Ouija board players produce gibberish and often stop at blank spots on the board.[40]

Figure 9.5 Norman Rockwell painting, "The Ouija Board," which was used on the cover of the May 1, 1920, issue of *The Saturday Evening Post* magazine.
Source: Wikimedia.

As the Ouija players work together, their predictions about where the planchette will go often come true—even without consciously willing it—via *ideomotor action*. This effect happens when a mere idea (*ideo*) is enough to cause movement (*motor*). An early study of ideomotor action used a super-sensitive planchette made of a plate of glass resting on steel balls.[41] Participants were asked to try to keep their hands still, but they tended to move their hands in a manner appropriate to suggestion. For example, one participant was asked to hide a knife somewhere in the testing room, and once his hand was on the planchette, he was asked to think about the knife. Soon his hand began to move in the direction of the knife. Similarly, another participant was asked to think about a building that was to his left, and his hand began to move left. Just the suggestion was enough to produce subtle movements in the appropriate direction without the participants feeling like they were doing it. Ideomotor action is thought to play an important role in the Ouija board and several other automatisms.

Finally, there is no shortage of lore associated with the Ouija board, which means that anyone who uses the board knows what's supposed to happen. Motivation plays a role in perception. Most players want it to work. The Ouija board would not be much fun if moving the planchette was like playing with a toy car.

The Ouija board was first patented in the United States by Elijah Bond in 1891, and various forms of "talking boards" were a popular long before that.[42] These devices were an outgrowth of nineteenth-century spiritualism, which produced several examples of automatism. The spiritualist movement was driven by an urge to communicate with the dead, and it gained popularity in the years following the Civil War, from which many did not return home. Séances were all the rage, and evidence of contact with the spirit world came in the form of tipping tables, knocking sounds, and ghost-like apparitions. As mentioned in chapter 1, fraud was common among many noted spiritualists, and in addition to William James, the magician Harry Houdini exposed many unscrupulous psychic mediums.[43] But even when the tricksters were eliminated, there remained a few phenomena that may not have been the result of fraud.

Automatic writing was another nineteenth century spiritualist method for receiving messages from beyond. Often the writer would use a planchette outfitted with a pen or pencil at the pointer end or simply hold a pen or pencil in the usual way. As was the case with many mediums, the writer would often go into a trance, and after making some sloppy marks on paper, might begin to write something intelligible. If the medium had any perception of writing at all, they would report feeling their hand move but not being in control of its movements. Only a few people were capable of automatic writing, but those who were claimed to be passive transcriptionists. Often after reading what they wrote, they said they couldn't remember writing the words (see Figure 9.6).

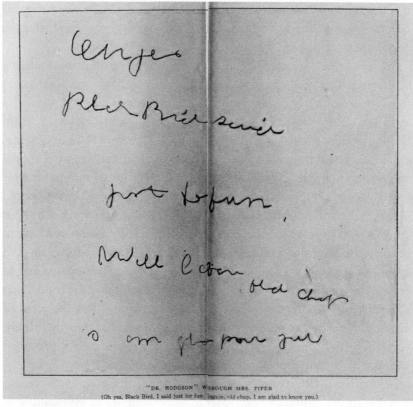

"DR. HODGSON" THROUGH MRS. PIPER
(Oh yes, Black Bird, I said just for fun. ington, old chap. I am glad to know you.)

Figure 9.6 An example of automatic writing produced by the American medium Leonora Piper. It purports to be a message from Dr. Richard Hodgson, a deceased psychical researcher with whom she had worked for many years. *Source*: Wikimedia.

Wegner placed trances in a category of phenomena that involve people projecting action to imaginary agents, something he called *virtual agency*. In ventriloquism, the combination of a funny accent, a doll that moved its mouth, and the lack of human mouth movements gave the impression that Edgar Bergen's dummy, Charlie McCarthy, was speaking. But in the case of ventriloquism, we are all in on the trick. In contrast, *channeling* is advertised as a real effect in which the medium's body is inhabited by the spirit of another person and speaks for that person. Once they snap out of it, *trance channelers* usually claim no knowledge of what went on while they were away. *Conscious channelers* remain aware of their surroundings while their body is being used by the spirit of a dead person. Some channelers are in touch with famous people—Paula Farmer claimed to channel Elvis Presley—but more often the person speaking through the medium is a relative unknown.

Trances, often induced by alcohol or other consciousness-altering substances, have been employed by shamans, magicians, and soothsayers from the beginning of human history, and they gained renewed popularity in the late eighteenth century when German physician Franz Mesmer began treating wealthy Parisian patients with *animal magnetism*.[44] Mesmer some- times used actual magnets applied to the bodies of his patients, but animal magnetism could also shoot out from the fingertips of the mesmerizer and be received through the air by the mesmeree. Many patients tolerated Mesmer's therapy quite well—feeling only mild sensations in their skin—but others would go into a trance, experience violent convulsions, and have to be carted off to special padded rooms to recover. In 1784, King Louis XVI appointed a royal commission that included America's Plenipotentiary to France, Benjamin Franklin, to evaluate Mesmer's methods. After conducting a number of scientific tests, the commission concluded that the patients' imaginations were the source of the effects of Mesmer's magnetic therapy. Franklin agreed with this conclusion but was not convinced it represented sufficient grounds to shut Mesmer down.

Mesmerism led to an interest in hypnosis, another trance-inducing condi- tion that creates virtual agency. Under hypnosis, people can withstand pain, control unwanted thoughts better, forget things that happen while they were hypnotized, and experience a reduced feeling of conscious will. When asked to move body parts they often feel like they are not doing it themselves.

Hypnosis has been extensively researched by physicians and psychologists since the mid-nineteenth century, and a number of theories have been pro- posed to explain hypnotic trances. Fraud—pretending to be hypnotized— was an obvious hypothesis, but for the relatively small percentage of people who are prone to hypnosis, this does not seem to be the answer. Hypnosis is, by definition, a state of suggestibility. It is a well-known phenomenon, and stage hypnotists still perform in Las Vegas and at corporate and college events. In addition, hypnosis is frequently used as a smoking cessation tech- nique and as a clinical tool in the treatment of a number of psychological disorders.[45] As a result, some researchers have proposed that pliable people willingly adopt the role of the hypnotized subject out of a desire for it to work. Another theory suggests that under hypnosis people can achieve a kind of dissociative state in which the thought of a particular action, as presented by the hypnotist, is disconnected from the feeling of doing the action.

None of these theories has emerged as a dominant explanation, but Wegner's view was that normally we have a thought about an act, followed by the action itself, and this sequence gives us a feeling of doing.[46] Under hypnosis, the hypnotist's thoughts influence the subjects thoughts, which in turn influence the action, but the subject has a reduced perception of their own thoughts in the middle of the sequence and, as a result, a diminished sense of agency. Similar to preparing to go to sleep, the process of relaxing hypnotic subjects has the effect of turning off the mental systems associated with planning and executing action. Meanwhile the hypnotist is still speaking and directing and, as a result, it is the hypnotist's thoughts that are salient. All of this leads to a diminished sense of control on the part of the subject.

One of the most dramatic and consequential examples of automaticity is described in Case 2 at the beginning of this chapter. Facilitated communication began in Australia in the late 1980s and was brought to the United States in the early 1990s. It quickly became very popular with parents of children with severe autism, and its early success in the United States was fueled in part by its association with Syracuse University. In 1990, Douglas Biklen, a professor of education at Syracuse, wrote an article entitled "Communication Unbound: Autism and Praxis," in the *Harvard Education Review*, describing his observations of facilitated communication in Australia and proposing the theory that autism was a disorder of expression, not of cognition.[47] Biklen went on to establish a Facilitated Communication Institute at Syracuse, and parents and teachers attended the institute's conferences to learn the technique. Initially it was seen as a wonderful story of children and adults with autism brought out of the shadows to become full participants in a world of human contact and expression. Many uplifting stories appeared on television and in print.

But while this communication revolution was taking off, no one stopped to ask, how had these people learned to read and spell without ever having spoken first? They had never been taught to write before, yet somehow they could suddenly write coherent sentences and paragraphs. Proponents suggested that, merely by observing printed words in the environment, these young people had picked up the language. Eventually doubts emerged, such as those expressed by the psychologists at the O. D. Heck Center, and empirical tests of authorship began to emerge. In 1993, the PBS program

"Frontline" aired a documentary called, "Prisoners of Silence," that outlined the full progression from miracle innovation to discredited method.

For many years, I assigned the "Prisoners of Silence" video in my introductory psychology classes because it was such a clear demonstration of how a simple controlled experiment could reveal a shocking truth. By the end of the film, the students were convinced that facilitated communication didn't work, and the most common question was, "How could the facilitators not know they were doing the typing?" This was the paradox. Despite the obvious possibility of facilitator influence, the people holding the hands of their language-disabled partners appeared to genuinely believe they weren't doing the typing. Furthermore, parents who could afford to pay for facilitators had sent their children off to college, and by now several have graduated with bachelor's degrees.[48] How could the helpers not know they were doing more than helping?

The context of facilitated communication is very similar to the Ouija board, in which the actions of one person are confused with those of another, but this is a case of what Wegner called *action projection*. The actions of the facilitator are projected onto the person with autism. Initial training in facilitated communication sometimes includes considerable help on the part of the facilitator, moving the hand in the area of the correct letters. The training materials proponents give to new facilitators include various methods of getting the process going,[49] and facilitators are often urged to "presume competence."[50] This sets up a fertile mindset for biased perception and unconscious prompting.

The most famous case of unconscious prompting may be Clever Hans, a horse who, after extensive training by Wilhelm von Osten, was capable of doing math, including the addition of fractions. At the command of his trainer, Hans would stamp his hoof the requisite number of times. (In the case of fractions, he would first tap out the numerator, followed by the denominator.) Clever Hans amazed Berlin in the early years of the twentieth century until a psychologist, Oskar Pfungst, came around in 1911 to spoil all the fun. A controversy had developed surrounding the horse, and so an investigation was organized. Simple scientific methods revealed the secret of Hans' brilliance. Pfungst found that Hans could not answer correctly if blindfolded, nor did he respond correctly if the question was spoken into his ear in such a way that von Osten could not hear it. Eventually, Pfungst discovered that Hans was responding to subtle head movements of his trainer as von Osten looked down to observe the hoof stomping and up again once the correct answer was achieved. If von Osten deliberately looked up at the wrong time, the answer was wrong, too. Hans was clever enough to know how to get the praise of his trainer, but he wasn't doing math at all. He was responding to cues provided by von Osten, who was completely unaware.

The same kind of unconscious cueing is likely true in facilitated communication. After many hours, days, and in some cases years of practice, the facilitator and the language-disabled person play out a familiar dance. Similar kinds of tests have been done on facilitation pairs in published peer-reviewed studies, and in every case, when the facilitator did not know the answer, the answers were wrong. At the same time there was no indication that the facilitators were aware they were the authors of the words being typed out on the keyboard. Janyce Boynton, a former facilitator, reported that only when she went through double-blind testing did she begin to doubt the procedure.[51] When the student she was facilitating was asked a simple question that Janyce couldn't answer herself (e.g., "What is the color of your family's car?"), she found herself mentally searching for the correct answer and realized there was something wrong. Like the staff of the O. D. Heck center, Boynton found it very difficult to adjust to the idea that she had been doing the typing all along.

A study done by a group of researchers from the University of Connecticut and Harvard Medical School demonstrates how easy it is for facilitators to fool themselves.[52] Undergraduate students were individually brought into a lab and introduced to facilitated communication. For half of the participants the technique was described in entirely positive terms as a breakthrough in communication, and for the other half it was described as a "controversial method." Next, they were shown part of a training film used to teach people to be facilitators. Finally, the participants were told they would be using the technique with a language-disabled young woman named Jackie, who had been successful with facilitated communication in the past. Prior to Jackie's arrival in the lab, all the participants were given some background information about her, including Jackie's hometown, family, favorite foods, etc. Unknown to the participants, the part of Jackie was played by a typical college senior who was unaware of the background information (which was fictional) given to the participants. Finally, the participants were asked to hold Jackie's hand as shown in the training film and facilitate her typing on a computer in response to basic questions about her family—questions for which the participants now knew the answers. The confederate playing the role of

Jackie was instructed to remain passive and keep her eyes focused on the wall beyond the computer screen.

The results were dramatic. Eighty-four percent of the participants produced meaningful responses on the computer, and 89 percent of the responses corresponded to information given to the participants but unknown to the woman playing the role of Jackie. Furthermore, there was no difference in the level of typing success between the two groups. Presenting facilitated communication as "controversial" did not diminish the number of correct answers produced. After the experiment, the participants were asked to what degree they felt the answers were coming from Jackie versus themselves. Ninety percent said the communication was coming more from Jackie than themselves, and 5 percent said it had come more from themselves than Jackie. The remaining 5 percent said it had come equally from both partners.

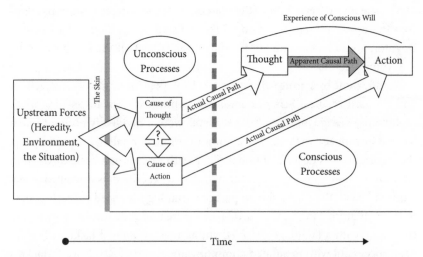

Figure 9.7 The experience of conscious will. This diagram is based and expands on one produced by Wegner (2002, p. 68). Unconscious processes independently give rise to the thought of acting and the action itself, but because the thought emerges sooner, it is experienced as having caused the action. Wegner used a double-headed arrow marked with a question mark to indicate that the unconscious processes may influence each other. I have added the Upstream forces, such as the individual's genetic inheritance, environmental history, and the current situation, which, in turn, give rise to the unconscious processes. The experience of conscious will occurs near the end of a long chain of events.

A Theory of the Doing Delusion

The idea that people have control over many of their actions is embedded in what it means to be human, and yet the forgoing suggests that we often haven't a clue. Sometimes we feel like we are doing something when doing is impossible, and other times we have no feeling of doing when we are. All of this suggests that the feeling of intention is separate from the act of doing. Drawing on the research presented previously—his own studies, Libet's findings, and that of many others—Wegner proposed a theory of the experience of conscious will.[53] I adapted Figure 9.7 from a diagram that Wegner created, but I have added a little detail and extended the causal chain backwards in time to include the upstream influences of the person's genetic inheritance, accumulated environmental experiences, and the current situation.[54] Wegner may or may not have agreed with my modifications of his diagram, but his central theory is the same. In the middle of a longer causal chain, an unconscious process creates the thought of action, and a separate unconscious process causes the action itself. Because they emerge a little earlier in time, it feels like our thoughts cause our actions, but this is a delusion. Wegner left open the possibility that the two unconscious processes might influence each other, which is why he placed a two-headed arrow with a question mark between the two boxes.

The feeling that we choose and cause our actions is not real, but it is not an accident that we have it. Although the sense of volition is a delusion, it is a very valuable delusion—perhaps our most valuable delusion. First, it helps us distinguish the things we've done from those we haven't. Wegner called this the *emotion of authorship*. An important factor in the success of *Homo sapiens* has been our ability to detect cause and effect relationships. We're not always right, but often we are. Part of this detecting involves eliminating certain possibilities. If the steering wheel of your car suddenly turns right, causing the vehicle to veer off the road, it could be quite useful to determine quickly whether or not you caused the wheel to turn. Similarly, dropping down into a chair has a very different meaning if you did so "voluntarily" or involuntarily. The authorship emotion provides us with a very practical way to eliminate a number of causal hypotheses as we stumble through our days trying to figure things out.

In addition, there are tangible benefits to feeling in control. A random world that batters us from pillar to post is not a pleasant place to live. The feeling of conscious will helps us gain a sense of achievement and autonomy.

As we have seen, even an illusion of control contributes to our emotional well-being. Belief in personal agency gives us ownership of our achievements and, as we have seen at several points in this book, the feeling of achievement provides the motivation to keep going.

Finally, it's useful to be able to assign credit and blame. One of the common objections to the idea of this delusion has been that without free will there can be no morality. If we are not responsible, then how can we be praised or punished. As we have seen, beginning in the ancient world, many moral philosophies and religions have depended on the idea that people are free to choose. As a result, some have worried that discarding the notion of freedom might lead to a chaotic postapocalyptic nightmare. If the deterministic view of human behavior is accurate, it may represent a dangerous truth—one that, if abandoned, could be bad for us. Better to be deluded than to adopt some more rational view of human causation. Thankfully, we couldn't stop believing in this delusion, even if we tried. The most ardent determinist would find it difficult to operate without reference to intention in a world so thickly populated with it. Imagine arguing with your spouse and not being able to utter the phrase, "No, honey, I didn't mean it that way. . . . " Just as the enlightened Buddhist knows it is impossible to discard notions of identity in everyday speech, we have no choice (!) but to use the language of intention and will. Furthermore, societies can use the delusion to impose social controls.

For a moment, there seemed to be evidence that believing in determinism encouraged bad behavior. Kathleen Vohs and Jonathan Schooler published the results of two experiments that were designed to allow the possibility of cheating. In both studies, college students were divided into two groups. One group read an essay suggesting that there was no free will and that most scientists now believe in determinism, and the second group read an article about human consciousness that did not raise the issue of free will. Later, when placed in situations where cheating was possible, the groups who read the determinist passage cheated significantly more. For example, in the second experiment, the participants were given a set of problems and told they would be paid $1 for each problem they solved correctly, but after giving the instructions, the experimenter said she had to leave to go to a meeting. The participants would have to score their work themselves and pay themselves out of an envelope containing money, creating a kind of honor system. The participants who read the deterministic material prior to the experiment paid themselves more than those in the neutral condition.[55] Determinism began to look like a dangerous idea, and Vohs and Schooler's study went on to be cited as a cautionary tale by hundreds of philosophers and psychologists, and it was widely described in the media, including *The New York Times* and *The Atlantic*. But, as by now you are well aware, the path of science is iterative: three steps forward and one step back. As of 2020, one attempt by UK researchers failed to reproduce the results of one of Vohs and Schooler's studies, and as a result a group of researchers from the United States, United Kingdom, and Australia attempted a large-scale replication.[56] Across five different studies, all with much larger groups of participants, the researchers were unable to produce deterministic cheaters. Later in 2020 yet another large-scale attempt to replicate Vohs and Schooler's study was published, and again there were no differences in cheating associated with the free-will manipulation, nor did people's expressed belief in free will predict how much they cheated.[57] The authors of both these attempts to replicate concluded that altering people's free-will beliefs may be more difficult than the Vohs and Schooler study suggested.[58] So, we are left with a muddle. The recent studies found it very difficult to induce a belief in the absence of free will, and as a result it is hard to conclude that determinism is a dangerous idea—at least with respect to cheating in the situations used in this research.

The feeling of willing things to happen makes it possible to learn from our experiences in a way that is essential to our success. We feel as though we are consistent people, responsible for what we do, and as we grow up we learn what actions our social group will reward and punish—what things are good and bad. If, after learning these rules, we do something dishonest or unfair, our delusion of having caused it allows us to feel guilt or shame. Alternatively, if we do something admirable, we feel good, whether anyone else has noticed it or not. In a highly interdependent social species such as ours, the feelings accompanying our behavior help us sort out our own actions from those of other people and provide moral signals that help us succeed. As we imagine a course of action, we get a preview of how it might be received and know that, whatever the outcome, it will adhere to us. All of this may be a kind of deterministic dance—a robot play—but we are very lucky to have evolved these extra feelings. They serve us well every day.

10

Odysseus in Rags

I have a longing for life, and I go on living in spite of logic. Though I may not believe in the order of the universe, yet I love the sticky little leaves as they open in spring. I love the blue sky, I love some people, whom one loves you know sometimes without knowing why. I love some great deeds done by men, though I've long ceased perhaps to have faith in them, yet from old habit one's heart prizes them.

—Fyodor Dostoevsky, *The Brothers Karamazov*

The hero of Homer's epic poem, *The Odyssey*, just wants to get home. After fighting the Trojan War, Odysseus finds himself trapped on the island of the beautiful nymph Calypso, who offers him immortality if he will stay with her and be her husband, but he prefers to return to Ithaca where his wife Penelope has been fending off a parade of greedy suitors. On his long journey, he endures a series of perilous adventures and, like many heroic figures, Odysseus shows great leadership and courage. But Odysseus is perhaps best known for his powers of deception and disguise. Homer often describes him as a cunning trickster. He frequently lies about his identity and, when he finally returns to Ithaca, his guardian goddess Athena transforms him into the image of an old beggar. Reunited with his most faithful slave, Eumaeus—but unrecognized by him—Odysseus tells a convoluted false story of who he is and where he has come from.[1]

False identities and disguises have been effective plot devices in literature throughout history, from Odysseus in rags, through Shakespeare's Viola in *Twelfth Night*, to Robin Williams' portrayal of a nanny in *Mrs. Doubtfire*. Disguise is also common in nature. Some butterflies have evolved to be distasteful and poisonous to predators, and they are decorated in bright colors as a warning. In West Africa there is a perfectly tasty form of butterfly that has adapted a protection through mimicry. Females have the ability to produce five different kinds of eggs which grow to look like one of five poisonous varieties of butterfly. Furthermore, the masquerading butterflies match their eggs to the number of poisonous models in the area. If a particular poisonous butterfly is most common, the mimicking species will produce more lookalikes for that variety. Similarly, some birds will feign a broken wing to distract a predator away from the nest. The bird might flop down on the ground with one wing extended and awkwardly walk away from the nest, flying away at the last moment when the predator pounces.[2]

In the previous chapters we have encountered some examples of conscious concealment: lovers who knowingly lied to each other and my own adolescent ploy of putting on the country accent of my summer job coworkers. But when our dissembling is part of a delusion, we are generally not in on the game. There have been examples of a kind of double consciousness, as in the case of Joan Didion, who knew that her husband was not coming home, but still, on some level, believed he would. But most often, when we put on the cloak of these delusions, we wear it fully and without awareness. Overconfident job candidates are convinced they're worth it, and besotted spouses see each other in an unwavering glow. The delusions of continuous personality and conscious will are so convincing that we are incapable of shaking them off. Rather than being a cloak we wear, they are part of our skin.

Often, in the service of deceiving others, it is important that we also deceive ourselves. In chapter 2, we encountered the theory of self-deception proposed by evolutionary biologist Robert Trivers, who suggests that we evolved a propensity for fooling ourselves in order to effectively fool others. Odysseus appears to have been unnaturally talented at deception. When he came home dressed in the rags of a beggar, only his dog Argos recognized him. But most of us are not such good liars. If we are going to get ahead in the world, we will be much more effective if we believe our own lies— if we are deluded. According to Trivers, self-deception has most often been interpreted as a defensive response when we can't accept things as they are. In contrast, he suggests that self-deception can play an offensive role when it helps us overcome our competitors and find success in the marketplace of work, love, and health.[3]

A more charitable view of Odysseus' duplicitousness might be that he has a superb ability to adapt to his surroundings.[4] And, of course, he does survive. Without question, self-deception is not always a good thing. A Pollyannaish view of the world when a freight train—or a pandemic—is headed your way, is not a formula for success. But several of the valuable delusions we have encountered involve a form of self-deception that helps us adapt to our surroundings and achieve things that might not otherwise be possible.

In his book, *Sapiens: A Brief History of Humankind,* Yuval Noah Harari describes how, approximately 70,000 years ago, a cognitive revolution in our species gave us greatly expanding capabilities.[5] Our big brains made imagination possible, and out of imagination came artistic achievements, technological wizardry, and social institutions, including corporations and democracies. The evolving powers of System 2 made it possible to construct cities, travel anywhere on the globe, cure many diseases, invent the internet, paint the *Mona Lisa,* and compose "Sargent Pepper's Lonely Hearts Club Band," among other things. The human brain is arguably nature's greatest achievement and the only one capable of destroying all life on this small blue planet.[6]

This cognitive revolution has been the key to it all. Human knowledge has been accumulating for centuries, making new developments possible, and as individuals we've inherited some of that accumulated knowledge and the ability to remember, calculate, reason, and predict. Given our obvious computing power, it might seem like we should just keep bowing to the god of reason and let science, logic, and technology be our guides, that we should let all our important choices be rational choices. Of course, sometimes we will fall short. We will have failures of self-control. We will choose the strawberry cheesecake when we know we shouldn't or buy things we can't afford. We will burn fossil fuels today and sacrifice a livable planet tomorrow. Although holding to the rational choice model will not always be possible, it seems like a good standard to strive for.

Except in some cases.

Being rational is the best course of action most of the time, but not all the time. As I worked on this book, I often felt somewhat uncomfortable writing about the benefits of delusions and irrationality at a time when there was decreasing agreement about truth and illusion. According to a Reuters/Ipsos poll taken two weeks after the 2020 election, 52 percent of Republicans believed Donald Trump "rightfully won," despite overwhelming evidence to the contrary.[7] A July, 2021 YouGov poll found that 51 percent of those who did not plan to take a COVID-19 vaccine believed that the government was using the vaccines to implant microchips in people.[8] Another poll found that 17 percent of Americans thought the coronavirus pandemic was deliberately launched by the US government, and another 13 percent believed the virus was a complete myth, created by unidentified "powerful forces."[9] Some of those who believed the virus was a myth seem to have assumed the motivation was political. A friend of mine was running in a park a few days after the 2020 election, when a stranger shouted at her: "You can take your mask off now. The election is over!"

Evidence, reason, and science are very important and always will be. Nothing in this book should be construed as challenging that view. But, despite reason's obvious benefits, brain size and intelligence were never the goals. The goal is and always will be survival. In the end, there are no awards for the smartest or most logical creature—just for the creature who gets to live another day. Life is the goal and the reward. In many ways, our powers of reason and computation have helped us survive and live longer and better lives, but reason is a tool among many that we possess. We are a hairless mammal that, at birth, is incapable of feeding itself. Our survival has depended upon the social nature of our species and our ability to bend environments to our needs. Much of what we have achieved is due to our capacity for reason, but some things are both against reason and helpful. Quite often we engage in adaptive forms of self-deception or we simply behave in ways to that don't make sense but are nonetheless helpful to the cause.

This view is consistent with Darwinism and the pragmatist philosophy of William James. American pragmatist philosophy was a direct outgrowth of the success of Darwin's theory of natural selection, and it applied a functionalist approach to ideas as well as to species.[10] The meaning of a thought could only be determined by what action it produced.[11] As we have seen, James suggested some beliefs, though lacking evidence, could be indulged on the basis of their positive effects. This is also consistent with Jonathan Baron's view that, even if our thinking breaks all the laws of logic, it should be considered rational if it leads to a good outcome. The genus *Homo* began 3.5 billion years ago, and the first *Homo sapiens* arrived 200 million years ago.[12] Our ancestors managed to survive a very long time before the cognitive revolution, a mere 70,000 years ago. As brilliant as we have become, much of what got us here long predated our ability to reason in the manner described by the rational choice model. We are born with reflexes, instincts, powers of perception, and tools for adapting to our surroundings that would not fit into philosophy's notions of epistemic and instrumental rationality. Adherence to what we now consider rational thought is a good idea in many cases, but sometimes it's neither desirable nor possible.

At the beginning of this book, I said that some helpful delusions were intrinsic parts of us—built in at the factory—and others seemed more malleable and under voluntary control. Of course, by now we have discarded the notion of voluntary control entirely, so how does this distinction work? Probably the best way to think about this is in terms of *phylogeny*—things that result from our genetic inheritance—and *ontogeny*—things we acquire during the course of our lives. Without DNA evidence, these categories are somewhat speculative, but it seems safe to say that dreaming and consciousness—including but not limited to our sense of conscious will—are largely phylogenic, part of our biology as acquired at birth. Nothing is exclusively nature or nurture, and as a result the contents of our waking and sleeping minds are drawn from our experiences. But pretty much everyone has crazy dreams and the feeling that they themselves cause things to happen.

The sense of continuous identity and character, the self-delusion, also requires a fairly large dose of consciousness, but as social psychology and the Patricia Hearst story suggest, the environment plays a big role. As a result, the sense of self is produced by a more even mix of inherited and acquired characteristics.

All the other delusions we have discussed are greatly dependent upon ontogeny—the luck of our personal experiences. Over the course of our lives we become optimists or pessimists, skeptics or believers, and clear-eyed or doe-eyed lovers. When we first arrive as infants, all of these acquired delusions are undoubtedly possible for most of us, but the accidents of birth—the families we grow up in and other random environmental factors—determine which of these delusions, if any, we acquire. There are undoubtedly temperamental differences that are hard wired, making certain acquired characteristics more or less likely, but many of the delusions we have encountered seem primarily built from experience, and as a result more variable. Some people have gone through the death of a loved one without the kind of magical thinking that Joan Didion and my friend Susan experienced. Others are more pessimistic than optimistic. But for those who possess these delusions, there are clear benefits, and it is the stronger influence of environmental history that makes them feel more malleable.

Can We Still Be Good?

One of the consequences of Odysseus' dissembling is some doubt about whether he is a good person.[13] Given that he so often changes identity and lies about who he is, how should we judge his moral character? Socrates wrestled with this question in a dialogue with the sophist Hippias on the question of who is a better hero, Achilles, the central character of *The Iliad*, or Odysseus. Hippias argued that Achilles was the better man because he was steady and honest, whereas Odysseus was "wily and false."[14] Socrates mounted a defense of Odysseus suggesting that his lies were voluntary and measured and allowed for the defeat of Troy and his eventual homecoming.[15] But it was a difficult sell.

Having come through the last two chapters, we are faced with a similar dilemma. If the continuity of personality and belief in free will are delusions, then are we without moral character? Don't we need that? If our behavior is not really ours but purely a function of nature and nurture, then how can we be responsible for either the good or bad things we do? Doesn't this view excuse the behavior of murders and rapists and diminish the achievements of those who are talented and hardworking?

Not necessarily.

The social nature of our species requires that we live in groups: families, communities, and nations. We are bound together by familial relationships, community structures, cultures, and languages. Within these groups, it will always be important to encourage the kinds of behavior that lead to the success of group members and the group as a whole. Social groups have always established standards of behavior and moral and legal norms, and as long as these systems serve the groups' purposes, they will continue. Parents will reward and punish, as will schools, religious groups, employers, and legal systems.

Exceptions are carved out in certain circumstances. When someone is coerced to do wrong—at gunpoint, for example—many judicial systems recognize that punishing the coerced person will not be a deterrent to future wrongdoing. Similarly, if a bad act is convincingly attributed to mental illness, then it is less likely the usual forms of punishment will be a deterrent. Other measures are needed to discourage this kind of behavior.[16] As a result, the very instances in which we are likely to say, "they had no choice" or "they did not intend to do this," are the ones where social opprobrium is less likely to be effective. Similarly, the concept of *mens rea* or guilty mind, although grounded in the idea of free will, applies in cases that are more amenable to change. Malice aforethought implies a chain of events that might be interrupted if the individual is adequately socialized to feel guilty or have second thoughts. Of course, the evidence points to our not having conscious will in the first place. In addition, we know that observers see deliberate choices in others when they are of a mind to punish them. Thus, the concept of *mens rea* may be objectively misguided—based on a delusion—but it still provides a useful form of social control.

The nondeluded view of personality contradicts the common notion that people have an unwavering essence. Religiously based concepts of good and evil, when applied to people, turn the world into an unrealistic melodrama. When we want to punish people or disregard their needs, we flatten them with labels, such as "murderer," "thief," "criminal," and "liar." In extreme cases, we fashion a suit of clothing from the worst mistake they ever made and insist they wear it for the rest of their lives. Real people are not unidimensional. When we marry or enter into other important relationships we count on a degree of consistency. We need to trust that what we know of the person now will also be true in the future, and their moral makeup is particularly important. But, if circumstances change, all of us are capable of being different people. This is just the chance we take. As time passes, we continue to make our assessments of people, regularly updating a moving average of their strengths and weaknesses, virtues and vices. Those averages are only as predictive of the future as the prevailing winds will allow, but we always take on some level of chance when we enter into any relationship. Groups and individuals can identify what they consider to be permissible and impermissible actions. But we don't live with an action isolated from the person who did it. We live with people who behave in ways we hope we can count on. The illusion of a constant person helps us accommodate the people in our lives.

Emily Wilson's translation of *The Odyssey* into English begins with the line, "Tell me about a complicated man." Odysseus was a complicated man, and one of the goals of this book has been to remind us that we all are complicated people. We are a mixture of reason and magical thinking, intelligence and emotion.

When Camus said, "ridiculous reason is what sets me in opposition to all creation. I cannot cross it out with a stroke of the pen," he was talking about the burdens of consciousness and knowing what we know about life and death.[17] But this book is meant to suggest that we are not in opposition to creation at all. Granted, we are not trees among trees or cats among animals, but we are just as much a part of nature as they are. Furthermore, some of what keeps us going is much older than the ridiculous reason we got in the cognitive revolution. Natural selection is the ultimate pragmatist. It brings to each species whatever characteristics will get it to the next day. For us, much of the work has been done by our remarkable intelligence and computing power, but some of what helps us succeed doesn't strictly make sense. By the usual measures, it isn't rational. But nature doesn't care if it makes sense to us or not. Nature just wants to know if we're in or out. If we hope to remain part of the story of this small planet and have the privilege of greeting the next rosy-fingered dawn, we will need every tool we have.

Acknowledgments

This book is dedicated to two psychologists who greatly influenced my work in general and this book in particular. Although I had a few conversations with Howard Rachlin at conferences and corresponded with him over email, I could not say I knew him well. For several years, I taught a senior seminar called "Irrational Behavior," for which Rachlin's *The Science of Self-Control* was a text. *The Science of Self-Control* was also an important foundation for my book *Going Broke: Why Americans (Still) Can't Hold on to Their Money*. I didn't know Daniel Wegner at all and was unfamiliar with his work until one of his daughters took my introductory psychology course and I discovered that her father was a Harvard psychologist. Subsequently, I designed and taught a seminar on the psychology of free will, for which Wegner's book *The Illusion of Conscious Will* was a primary text. Both men were remarkably creative researchers and, by all reports, very good people. It is unlikely this book could have been written without them.

Another antecedent of this book was a freshman seminar on skepticism that I was lucky enough to co-teach with philosopher Derek Turner, who, as part of his contribution, taught the Clifford-James debate. Several people read and commented on sections of the book, including Ross Morin, Lindsay Crawford, Simon Feldman, and Gary Greenberg. I am grateful to Lindsay Crawford for pointing me to both Alison Gopnik and Berislav Marušić, and I am particularly indebted to Gary Greenberg and Simon Feldman for their comments on the manuscript. I thank my neighbor, Oxford Very Short Introduction brother, and friend Jonathan Post for sonnet consultations.

Much of this book was written in the first American year of the coronavirus plague, a period that made me especially grateful for my many wonderful friends. For companionship and cocktails enjoyed—at a safe distance—in backyards, public parks, and over Zoom and for general companionship and support, I want to thank Lynn Callahan, Jeffrey Callahan, Uta Gossman, Langdon Hammer, Joanna Scott, James Longenbach, Kevin Plummer, Gary Stoner, Ross Morin, Simon Feldman, Kim Stillwell, Lindsay Crawford, Bill Campbell, Danielle Egan, Michael Reder, Frederick Paxton, Sylvia Malizia, Susan Lindberg, Alex Hybel, Jan Hybel, Robert Gay, Sherri Storm, Lee Hisle,

Julie Worthen, Mary Devins, David Jaffee, Rachel Boggia, Perry Susskind, Marc Zimmer, Dianne Zimmer, Gabby Arenge, Kira Goldenberg, and Rachel Dreyer. I also want to thank my family Emily Goda, John Goda, Graham Vyse, Norma Vyse, Keith Vyse, and Kayo Nonaka.

The title of chapter 2 is stolen from a song by the much beloved group, Fountains of Wayne, and the title of chapter 9 is taken from a 2003 article on the illusion of conscious will by Daniel Wegner. I am grateful to Eve Peyser for permission to use one of her tweets, and to Algonquin Books, Springer Nature, and Penguin Random House for permission to use quotes by Tayari Jones, H. G. Wells, and Kurt Vonnegut, Jr., respectively.

Writing is a solitary activity, but the lucky writer is assisted by many others. Fabian Shalini and the staff of Newgen KnowledgeWorks did an excellent job producing the book, and Cheryl Jung contributed essential copyediting. This project started out going in a completely different direction, but a very useful, nondeluded conversation with my wonderful agent Jessica Papin helped it get turned around. The book and I owe much to her good sense. Editors Sarah Harrington and Joan Bossert at Oxford University Press have been loyal supporters of my work for several decades. I am enormously grateful to them.

Notes

Chapter 1

1. Joan Didion, *The Year of Magical Thinking* (New York: Vintage, 2005), 42.
2. Didion, *The Year of Magical Thinking*, 33.
3. Albert Camus, *The Plague: The Fall; Exile and the Kingdom; and Selected Essays* (New York: Knopf, 2004), 534.
4. Michael Lewis, *The Undoing Project: The Friendship That Changed Our Minds* (New York: W. W. Norton, 2016).
5. Veronika Denes-Raj and Seymour Epstein, "Conflict between Intuitive and Rational Processing: When People Behave against Their Better Judgment," *Journal of Personality and Social Psychology* 66, no. 5 (1994): 819.
6. For a variety of similar examples in a more recent study, see Daniel K. Walco and Jane L. Risen, "The Empirical Case for Acquiescing to Intuition," *Psychological Science* 28, no. 12 (2017): 1807–1820.
7. American Psychiatric Association, *Diagnostic and Statistical Manual of Mental Disorders,* 5th ed. (Arlington, VA: American Psychiatric Association, 2013), 87.
8. William Shakespeare, *Henry the VI, Part I*, Open Source Shakespeare, https://www.opensourceshakespeare.org/, line 2747.
9. *Merriam-Webster,* s.v. "delusion," https://www.merriam-webster.com/dictionary/delusion.
10. Katherine Hignett, "Are You a Flat-Earther? More Americans Than Ever Before Are Searching for the 'Truth,'" *Newsweek*, December 1, 2017, http://www.newsweek.com/flat-earth-conspiracy-america-726761.
11. Keith E. Stanovich, *Decision Making and Rationality in the Modern World* (New York: Oxford University Press, 2010).
12. Jon Elster, "Interpretation and Rational Choice," *Rationality and Society* 21, no. 2 (2009): 5–33.
13. Anahad O'Connor, "The Claim: Never Swim After Eating," *New York Times,* June 28, 2005, http://www.nytimes.com/2005/06/28/health/the-claim-never-swim-after-eating.html.
14. See the Flat Earth Society website, https://www.tfes.org/.
15. Adam Smith, *The Theory of Moral Sentiments* (New York: Penguin Books, 2009), 13. Original work published in 1759.
16. William K. Clifford, "The Ethics of Belief, in *The Ethics of Belief and Other Essays*, ed. Timothy J. Madigan (Amherst, NY: Prometheus, 1999), 70–96.
17. Samuel Taylor Coleridge, "Aphorism 25," in *Aids to Reflection*, ed. James Marsh (London: Chauncey Goodrich, 1829).

18. William James, "The Will to Believe," in *The Will to Believe and Other Essays in Popular Philosophy. The Works of William James*, ed. Frederick Burkhardt, Fredson Bowers, and Ignas K. Skrupskelis, vol. 6 (Cambridge, MA: Harvard University Press, 1979). Originally published in 1896.

19. Blaise Pascal, *Pascal's Pensées* (New York: E. P. Dutton, 1958), #277. Original work published in 1670.

20. Linda Simon, *Genuine Reality: A Life of William James* (Chicago: University of Chicago Press, 1999).

21. As quoted in "Books: The Waterspouts of God," an unsigned review of *The Varieties of Religious Experience* by William James, *Time*, July 19, 1963, http://content.time.com/time/magazine/article/0,9171,896918,00.html.

22. Daniel L. Schacter et al., *Psychology*, 3rd ed. (New York: Worth, 2014).

23. Jonathan Baron, *Thinking and Deciding*, 4th ed. (Cambridge: Cambridge University Press, 2008), 61.

24. William James, *Pragmatism* (Toronto: Dover, 1995). Original work published in 1907.

Chapter 2

1. Eve Peyser (@eveypeyser), Twitter, Date, https://twitter.com/evepeyser/status/1204796250366914566?s=20.

2. Calvin Tomkins, "New Paradigms," *New Yorker* 51 (1976): 30–36.

3. Carl R. Rogers, "The Process of the Basic Encounter Group," in *Perspectives in Abnormal Behavior: Pergamon General Psychology Series*, ed. Richard J. Morris (New York: Pergamon, 1974), 369–386.

4. Shelley E. Taylor and Jonathon D Brown, "Illusion and Well-Being: A Social Psychological Perspective on Mental Health," *Journal of Personality and Social Psychology* 103, no. 2 (1988): 193–210.

5. Taylor and Brown used the term illusion rather than delusion, and the line of research that followed their work is placed under the heading *positive illusions*. However, for the reasons explained in chapter 1, I have chosen the term delusion.

6. Ola Svenson, "Are We All Less Risky and More Skillful Than Our Fellow Drivers?" *Acta Psychologica* 47, no. 2 (1981): 143–148.

7. Ezra W. Zuckerman and John T. Jost, "What Makes You Think You're So Popular? Self-Evaluation Maintenance and the Subjective Side of the 'Friendship Paradox,'" *Social Psychology Quarterly* 64, no. 3 (2001): 207–223.

8. Scott L. Feld, "Why Your Friends Have More Friends Than You Do," *American Journal of Sociology* 96, no. 6 (1991): 1464–1477. In nonmathematical terms, the friendship paradox is created by the overrepresentation of popular people on the friends lists of any given group of friends. For example, imagine a network of friends with one individual in the center, Jill, who is quite popular, and three other friends who are less so. Jill has a high number of friends, and as a result she turns up on many people's list of friends. For each person who is friends with Jill, the average number of friends their

friends have will be higher because Jill's score drags up the mean. The effect depends upon the shape of the friend network, and, of course, does not apply to Jill herself. But, on average, your friends will have more friends than you do.

9. Fixx had been a smoker for many years before he began running, and he had a family history of heart disease. Charles Wallace, "Dilemma of Heart Attacks That Strike during Exercise," *Financial Times*, September 8, 2014, https://www.ft.com/content/838810b4-34f6-11e4-aa47-00144feabdc0.

10. Victor A. Benassi, Paul D. Sweeney, and Gregg E. Drevno, "Mind over Matter: Perceived Success at Psychokinesis Victor," *Journal of Personality and Social Psychology* 37, no. 8 (1979): 1377–1386.

11. Neil D. Weinstein, "Unrealistic Optimism about Future Life Events," *Journal of Personality and Social Psychology* 39, no. 5 (1980): 806–820.

12. Kate Sweeny, Patrick J. Carroll, and James A. Shepperd, "Is Optimism Always Best? Future Outlooks and Preparedness," *Current Directions in Psychological Science* 15, no. 6 (2006): 302–306; James A. Shepperd, Angelica Falkenstein, and Kate Sweeny, "Fluctuations in Future Outlooks," in *The Psychology of Thinking about the Future*, ed. Gabriele Oettingen, A. Timur Sevincer, and Peter M. Gollwitzer (New York: Guilford, 2018), 231–249.

13. Roy F. Baumeister and Astrid Schütz, "Positive Illusions and the Happy Mind," in *The Happy Mind: Cognitive Contributions to Well-Being*, ed. Michael D. Robinson and Michael Eid (New York: Springer, 2017), 177–193.

14. Baumeister and Schütz, "Positive Illusions and the Happy Mind," 177–193.

15. Neil D. Weinstein, "Unrealistic Optimism about Future Life Events," *Journal of Personality and Social Psychology* 39, no. 5 (1980): 806–820.

16. Cameron Anderson et al., "Knowing Your Place: Self-Perceptions of Status in Face-to-Face Groups," *Journal of Personality and Social Psychology* 91, no. 6 (2006): 1094–1110.

17. Joseph Heller, *Something Happened* (New York: Alfred A. Knopf, 1974), 13.

18. Dominic D. P. Johnson, *Overconfidence and War: The Havoc and Glory of Positive Illusions* (Cambridge: Harvard University Press, 2004).

19. Roy F. Baumeister, "The Optimal Margin of Illusion," *Journal of Social and Clinical Psychology* 8, no. 2 (1989): 176–189.

20. Joyce Ehrlinger et al., "Why the Unskilled Are Unaware: Further Explorations of (Absent) Self-Insight among the Incompetent," *Organizational Behavior and Human Decision Processes* 105, no. 1 (2008): 98–121.

21. Gary L. Wells and Elizabeth A. Olson, "Eyewitness Testimony," *Annual Review of Psychology* 54, no. 1 (2003): 277–295.

22. Brandon Garrett, *Convicting the Innocent* (Cambridge: Harvard University Press, 2011).

23. David Shariatmadari, "Daniel Kahneman: 'What Would I Eliminate If I Had a Magic Wand? Overconfidence,'" *Guardian*, July 18, 2015, https://www.theguardian.com/books/2015/jul/18/daniel-kahneman-books-interview.

24. Lauren B. Alloy and Lyn Y. Abramson, "Judgment of Contingency in Depressed and Nondepressed Students: Sadder but Wiser?" *Journal of Experimental Psychology: General* 108, no. 4 (1979): 441–485.

25. Chad Otar, "What Percentage of Small Businesses Fail—And How Can You Avoid Being One of Them?" *Forbes*, August 21, 2019, https://www.forbes.com/sites/forbe sfinancecouncil/2018/10/25/what-percentage-of-small-businesses-fail-and-how-can-you-avoid-being-one-of-them/#266c53ef43b5.

26. Barton H. Hamilton, "Does Entrepreneurship Pay? An Empirical Analysis of the Returns to Self-Employment," *Journal of Political Economy* 108, no. 3 (2000): 604–631.

27. Don A. Moore and Tai Gyu Kim, "Myopic Social Prediction and the Solo Comparison Effect," *Journal of Personality and Social Psychology* 85, no. 6 (2003): 1121–1135.

28. Colin Camerer and Dan Lovallo, "Overconfidence and Investment: An Experimental Approach," *American Economic Review* 89, no. 1 (1999): 306–318.

29. Philipp Koellinger, Maria Minniti, and Christian Schade, "'I Think I Can, I Think I Can': Overconfidence and Entrepreneurial Behavior," *Journal of Economic Psychology* 28, no. 4 (2007): 502–527.

30. Daniel Kahneman and Amos Tversky, "Conflict Resolution: A Cognitive Perspective," in *Barriers to Conflict Resolution*, ed. Kenneth J. Arrow et al. (New York: W. W. Norton, 1995), 44–60.

31. This was the September 15, 2016 game. For the ESPN play-by-play record, see https://www.espn.com/mlb/playbyplay?gameId=360915102.

32. E. J. Dionne, "Lendl Winner over McEnroe," *New York Times*, June 11, 1984, https://www.nytimes.com/1984/06/11/sports/lendl-winner-over-mcenroe.html; "John McEnroe: Rankings History: ATP Tour: Tennis," *ATP Tour*, https://www.atptour.com/en/players/john-mcenroe/m047/rankings-history.

33. Dan Barry, *Bottom of the 33rd: Hope, Redemption, and Baseball's Longest Game* (New York: Harper Collins, 2011). In fact, play was suspended at 4:07 a.m. on Sunday, April 19, at the end of the thirty-second inning, and the two teams played the final inning on June 23, 1981.

34. Steve Tignor, "French Open Memories, #4: Ivan Lendl d. John McEnroe, 1984," *Tennis.com*, May 24, 2018, https://www.tennis.com/pro-game/2018/05/french-open-memories-4-ivan-lendl-d-john-mcenroe-1984/73861/.

35. Paul Ekman, Maureen O'Sullivan, and Mark G. Frank, "A Few Can Catch a Liar," *Psychological Science* 10, no. 3 (1999): 263–266.

36. Maria Konnikova, *The Confidence Game: Why We Fall For It . . . Every Time* (New York: Penguin, 2016).

37. Robert Trivers, *The Folly of Fools: The Logic of Deceit and Self-Deception in Human Life* (New York: Basic Books, 2011).

38. Trivers, *The Folly of Fools*; Robert Trivers, "The Elements of a Scientific Theory of Self-Deception," *Annals of the New York Academy of Sciences* 907, no. 1 (2006): 114–131.

39. See also Dominic D. P. Johnson and James H. Fowler, "The Evolution of Overconfidence," *Nature* 477 (2011): 317–320.

40. Lynette L. Craft et al., "The Relationship between the Competitive State Anxiety Inventory-2 and Sport Performance: A Meta-Analysis," *Journal of Sport and Exercise Psychology* 25, no. 1 (2003): 44–65; Edith Filaire et al., "Psychophysiological Stress in Tennis Players during the First Single Match of a Tournament," *Psychoneuroendocrinology* 34, no. 1 (2009): 150–157.

41. Leon Festinger and James M. Carlsmith, "Cognitive Consequences of Forced Compliance," *The Journal of Abnormal and Social Psychology* 58, no. 2 (1959): 203–210.

42. S. Douglas Pugh, Markus Groth, and Thorsten Hennig-Thurau, "Willing and Able to Fake Emotions: A Closer Examination of the Link between Emotional Dissonance and Employee Well-Being," *Journal of Applied Psychology* 96, no. 2 (2011): 377–390.

43. Ellen Heuven and Arnold Bakker, "Emotional Dissonance and Burnout among Cabin Attendants," *European Journal of Work and Organizational Psychology* 12, no. 1 (2003): 81–100.

44. Mathew L. A. Hayward et al., "Beyond Hubris: How Highly Confident Entrepreneurs Rebound to Venture Again," *Journal of Business Venturing* 25, no. 6 (2010): 569–578.

45. Jessica A. Kennedy, Cameron Anderson, and Don A. Moore, "When Overconfidence Is Revealed to Others: Testing the Status-Enhancement Theory of Overconfidence," *Organizational Behavior and Human Decision Processes* 122 (2013): 266–279.

46. Peter Schwardmann and Joël van der Weele, "Deception and Self-Deception," *Nature Human Behaviour* 3, no. 10 (2019): 1055–1061.

47. Michelle Lee, "Fact Check: Has Trump Declared Bankruptcy Four or Six Times?" *Washington Post*, September 26, 2016, https://www.washingtonpost.com/politics/2016/live-updates/general-election/real-time-fact-checking-and-analysis-of-the-first-presidential-debate/fact-check-has-trump-declared-bankruptcy-four-or-six-times/.

48. Si Chen and Hannah Schildberg-Hörisch, "Looking at the Bright Side: The Motivational Value of Confidence," *European Economic Review* 120 (2019): 1–40, https://doi.org/10.1016/j.euroecorev.2019.103302.

49. To simplify this description, I have glossed over a number of technical details of the procedures used in this experiment, but the main features are accurate.

50. Hans K. Hvide, "Pragmatic Beliefs and Overconfidence," *Journal of Economic Behavior and Organization* 48, no. 1 (2002): 15–28.

51. Johnson and Fowler, "The Evolution of Overconfidence."

52. Daniel Kahneman and Amos Tversky, "Conflict Resolution: A Cognitive Perspective," in *Barriers to Conflict Resolution*, ed. Kenneth J. Arrow et al. (New York: W. W. Norton, 1995), 44–60.

53. Robert L. Gandt, *Skygods: The Fall of Pan Am* (New York: Morrow, 1995); Agis Salpukas, "Its Cash Depleted, Pan Am Shuts," *New York Times*, December 5, 1991, https://www.nytimes.com/1991/12/05/business/its-cash-depleted-pan-am-shuts.html.

54. Michael Cohen, "The Best and Worst Foreign Policy Presidents of the Past Century," *Atlantic*, August 1, 2011, https://www.theatlantic.com/international/archive/2011/07/the-best-and-worst-foreign-policy-presidents-of-the-past-century/242781/.

55. Philip Bump, "Analysis | 15 Years after the Iraq War Began, the Death Toll Is Still Murky," *Washington Post*, March 29, 2019, https://www.washingtonpost.com/news/politics/wp/2018/03/20/15-years-after-it-began-the-death-toll-from-the-iraq-war-is-still-murky/.

56. Meta Brown and Sydnee Caldwell, "Young Student Loan Borrowers Retreat from Housing and Auto Markets," *Liberty Street Economics*, April 17, 2013, https://libertystreeteconomics.newyorkfed.org/2013/04/young-student-loan-borrowers-retreat-from-housing-and-auto-markets.html.

Chapter 3

1. Stephen Collinson, "Trump Seeks a 'Miracle' as Virus Fears Mount," *CNN.com*, February 28, 2020, https://www.cnn.com/2020/02/28/politics/donald-trump-coro navirus-miracle-stock-markets/index.html.

2. William Ebbs, "Will Coronavirus Be with Us Forever? American Experts Say It's Possible," *CCN.com*, March 27, 2020, https://www.ccn.com/will-coronavirus-be-with-us-forever-american-scientists-say-its-possible/.

3. Greg Laurie and Tiffany Velasquez, "God Is Bigger Than the Coronavirus," *Harvest*, March 6, 2020, https://harvest.org/resources/gregs-blog/post/god-is-bigger-than-the-coronavirus/.

4. Rob Reich, "The Dangers of Relying on Philanthropists during Pandemics," *Wired*, March 22, 2020, https://www.wired.com/story/opinion-the-dangers-of-relying-on-philanthropists-during-pandemics/.

5. Bill Gates, "The Next Outbreak? We're Not Ready," filmed March 2015, TED video, https://www.ted.com/talks/bill_gates_the_next_outbreak_we_re_not_ready.

6. Quoted in Richard Thaler, "Mental Accounting Matters," in *Choices, Values, and Frames*, ed. Amos Tversky and Daniel Kahneman (New York: Cambridge University Press, 2000), 241–268.

7. For a fuller explanation, see Thaler, "Mental Accounting Matters," 262.

8. Allan Smith, "Fauci: Americans Are 'Going to Have to Hunker down Significantly More' to Fight Coronavirus," *NBCNews.com*, March 15, 2020, https://www.nbcnews.com/politics/meet-the-press/fauci-americans-are-going-have-hunker-down-signif icantly-more-fight-n1159381.

9. Sarah Mervosh, Denise Lu, and Vanessa Swales, "See Which States and Cities Have Told Residents to Stay at Home" *New York Times*, March 24, 2020, https://www.nyti mes.com/interactive/2020/us/coronavirus-stay-at-home-order.html.

10. World Health Organization, *Noncommunicable Diseases Country Profiles 2018* (Geneva: World Health Organization, 2018), https://www.who.int/nmh/publicati ons/ncd-profiles-2018/en/.

11. Melonie Heron, "Deaths: Leading Causes for 2017," *National Vital Statistics Reports* 68, no. 6 (2019); World Health Organization, *Noncommunicable diseases country pro-files 2018*.

12. Heron, "Deaths: Leading Causes for 2017."

13. Marianna Masiero, Claudio Lucchiari, and Gabriella Pravettoni, "Personal Fable: Optimistic Bias in Cigarette Smokers," *International Journal of High Risk Behaviors and Addiction* 4, no. 1 (2015): 1–7; Marianna Masiero et al., "Optimistic Bias in Young Adults for Cancer, Cardiovascular and Respiratory Diseases: A Pilot Study on Smokers and Drinkers," *Journal of Health Psychology* 23, no. 5 (2018): 645–656.

14. Lucy Popova and Bonnie L. Halpern-Felsher, "A Longitudinal Study of Adolescents' Optimistic Bias about Risks and Benefits of Cigarette Smoking," *American Journal of Health Behavior* 40, no. 3 (2016): 341–351; Paul Slovic, "Do Adolescent Smokers Know the Risks?" *Duke Law Journal* 47, no. 6 (1998): 1133–1141.

15. Masiero et al., "Optimistic Bias in Young Adults for Cancer, Cardiovascular and Respiratory Diseases."

16. Bonnie L. Halpern-Felsher et al., "Perceived Risks and Benefits of Smoking: Differences among Adolescents with Different Smoking Experiences and Intentions," *Preventive Medicine* 39, no. 3 (2004): 559–567.

17. Gary S. Becker and Kevin M. Murphy, "A Theory of Rational Addiction," *Journal of Political Economy* 96, no. 4 (1988): 675–700. See also Jared C. Carbone, Snorre Kverndokk, and Ole Jørgen Røgeberg, "Smoking, Health, Risk, and Perception," *Journal of Health Economics* 24, no. 4 (2005): 631–653; Athanasios Orphanides and David Zervos, "Rational Addiction with Learning and Regret," *Journal of Political Economy* 103, no. 4 (1995): 739–758.

18. Milton Friedman, *Theory of the Consumption Function* (Princeton: Princeton University Press, 1957); Franco Modigliani, "The Life Cycle Hypothesis of Saving, the Demand for Wealth and the Supply of Capital," *Social Research* 33, no. 2 (1966): 160–217.

19. Jon Elster, "More Than Enough," *University of Chicago Law Review* 64 (1997): 749–764; Howard Rachlin, *The Science of Self-control* (Cambridge: Harvard University Press, 2000).

20. Geoffrey T. Fong et al., "The Near-Universal Experience of Regret among Smokers in Four Countries: Findings from the International Tobacco Control Policy Evaluation Survey," *Nicotine and Tobacco Research* 6, Suppl. 3 (2004): 341–351.

21. Paul Slovic, "Cigarette Smokers: Rational Actors or Rational Fools?" in *Smoking: Risk, Perception, and Policy*, ed. Paul Slovic (Thousand Oaks, CA: Sage, 2001), 97–126.

22. Rachlin, *The Science of Self-Control.*

23. Taylor and Brown, "Illusion and Well-Being."

24. Shelley E. Taylor and David K Sherman, "Self-Enhancement and Self-Affirmation: The Consequences of Positive Self-Thoughts for Motivation and Health," in *Handbook of Motivation Science*, ed. James Y. Shah and Wendi L. Gardner (New York: Guilford, 2008), 57–70.

25. Lise Soleberg Nes and Suzanne C. Segerstrom, "Dispositional Optimism and Coping: A Meta-Analytic Review," *Personality and Social Psychology Review* 10, no. 3 (2006): 235–251; Suzanne C. Segerstrom, Charles S. Carver, and Michael F. Scheier, "Optimism," in *The Happy Mind: Cognitive Contributions to Well-Being*, ed. Michael D. Robinson and Michael Eid (New York: Springer 2017), 195–213.

26. Nes and Segerstrom, "Dispositional Optimism and Coping: A Meta-Analytic Review"; Heather N. Rasmussen, Michael F. Scheier, and Joel B. Greenhouse, "Optimism and Physical Health: A Meta-Analytic Review," *Annals of Behavioral Medicine* 37, no. 3 (2009): 239–256; Michael F. Scheier and Charles S. Carver, "Dispositional Optimism and Physical Health: A Long Look Back, a Quick Look Forward," *American Psychologist* 73, no. 9 (2018): 1082–1094.

27. Variations on this quotation have been attributed to George Bernard Shaw, Oscar Wilde, and others, but the original author is unknown.

28. Barbara S. Held, "Why Clinical Psychology Should Not Go 'Positive'—and/or 'Negative,'" in *The Wiley Handbook of Positive Clinical Psychology*, ed. Alex M. Wood and Judith Johnson (Malden, MA: Wiley, 2016), 31–45.

29. Weining C. Chang and Ruben Wen Sivam, "Constant Vigilance: Heritage Values and Defensive Pessimism in Coping with Severe Acute Respiratory Syndrome in Singapore," *Asian Journal of Social Psychology* 7, no. 1 (2004): 35–53.

30. Julie K. Norem and Edward C. Chang, "The Positive Psychology of Negative Thinking," *Journal of Clinical Psychology* 58, no. 9 (2002): 993–1001.

31. Chang and Sivam, "Constant Vigilance."

32. Ingrid Gilles et al., "Trust in Medical Organizations Predicts Pandemic (H1N1) 2009 Vaccination Behavior and Perceived Efficacy of Protection Measures in the Swiss Public," *European Journal of Epidemiology* 26, no. 3 (2011): 203–210.

33. Chang and Sivam, "Constant Vigilance."

34. Edward E. Jones and Steven Berglas, "Control of Attributions about the Self through Self-Handicapping Strategies: The Appeal of Alcohol and the Role of Underachievement," *Personality and Social Psychology Bulletin* 4, no. 2 (1978): 200–206.

35. Rachel A. Millstein et al., "The Effects of Optimism and Gratitude on Adherence, Functioning and Mental Health Following an Acute Coronary Syndrome," *General Hospital Psychiatry* 43 (2016): 17–22; Rasmussen, Scheirer, and Greenhouse, "Optimism and Physical Health"; Cecilia C. Schiavon et al., "Optimism and Hope in Chronic Disease: A Systematic Review," *Frontiers in Psychology* 7 (2017): 1–10, https://doi.org/10.3389/fpsyg.2016.02022.

Chapter 4

1. Barack Obama, *A Promised Land* (New York: Crown, 2020), 200.

2. Chris Chase, "Barack Obama Played Election Day Basketball Game with Scottie Pippen," *USA Today*, November 06, 2012, https://www.usatoday.com/story/gameon/2012/11/06/barack-obama-scottie-pippen-election-day-pickup/1686751/.

3. "Tabasco Shots, Baths and Gross Gloves: The Best Rituals and Superstitions on All 32 NFL Teams," ESPN, October 02, 2019, https://www.espn.com/nfl/story/_/id/27699107/tabasco-shots-baths-gross-gloves-best-rituals-superstitions-all-32-nfl-teams.

4. Jane L. Risen and Thomas Gilovich, "Why People Are Reluctant to Tempt Fate," *Journal of Personality and Social Psychology* 95, no. 2 (2008): 293–307. There has been some controversy about this tempting-fate effect. There have been two peer-reviewed attempts to replicate it, one successful and one unsuccessful, but in my opinion the evidence is still in favor of this being a genuine phenomenon.

5. Risen and Gilovich, "Understanding People's Fear of Tempting Fate."

6. Holly Rhue, "11 Celebrities on Their Weird Superstitions," *Elle*, July 13, 2018, https://www.elle.com/culture/celebrities/g22071946/celebrity-superstitions/.

7. Lysann Damisch, Barbara Stoberock, and Thomas Mussweiler, "Keep Your Fingers Crossed! How Superstition Improves Performance," *Psychological Science* 21, no. 7 (2010): 1014–1020.

8. Robert J. Calin-Jageman and Tracy L. Caldwel, "Replication of the Superstition and Performance Study by Damisch, Stoberock, and Mussweiler (2010)," *Social Psychology* 45 (2014): 239–245.

9. Niko Tinbergen, "'Derived' Activities; Their Causation, Biological Significance, Origin, and Emancipation during Evolution," *Quarterly Review of Biology* 27, no. 1 (1952): 1–32.

10. David J. Foster, Daniel A. Weigand, and Dean Baines, "The Effect of Removing Superstitious Behavior and Introducing a Pre-Performance Routine on Basketball Free-Throw Performance," *Journal of Applied Sport Psychology* 18, no. 2 (2006): 167–171.

11. Michael I. Norton and Francesca Gino, "Rituals Alleviate Grieving for Loved Ones, Lovers, and Lotteries," *Journal of Experimental Psychology: General* 143, no. 1 (2014): 266–272.

12. Study 1 of Alison Wood Brooks et al., "Don't Stop Believing: Rituals Improve Performance by Decreasing Anxiety," *Organizational Behavior and Human Decision Processes* 137 (2016): 71–85.

13. Brooks et al., "Don't Stop Believing," study 2.

14. Allen Ding Tian et al., "Enacting Rituals to Improve Self-Control," *Journal of Personality and Social Psychology* 114, no. 6 (2018): 851–876.

15. Brooks et al., "Don't Stop Believing," 6.

16. Tian et al., "Enacting Rituals to Improve Self-Control," study 4.

17. Nicholas M. Hobson et al., "The Psychology of Rituals: An Integrative Review and Process-Based Framework," *Personality and Social Psychology Review* 22, no. 3 (2018): 260–284.

18. Chris Chase, "The Definitive Guide to Rafael Nadal's 19 Bizarre Tennis Rituals," *USA Today*, June 5, 2014, https://ftw.usatoday.com/2014/06/rafael-nadal-ritual-tic-pick-water-bottles.

19. Brooks et al., "Don't Stop Believing," pilot study.

20. André Bouquet, "The Walmart Cheer," *The Talkative Man*, January 03, 2016, https://www.talkativeman.com/the-walmart-cheer/. I lightly edited the cheer as reported by Bouquet. Interested readers can find videos of the cheer being performed by Walmart employees on YouTube.com.

21. William K. Clifford, "The Ethics of Belief, in *The Ethics of Belief and other Essays*, ed. Timothy J. Madigan (Amherst, NY: Prometheus, 1999): 70–96.

22. David G. Myers and Ed Diener, "The Scientific Pursuit of Happiness," *Perspectives on Psychological Science* 13, no. 2 (2018): 218–225.

23. All these examples were drawn from Myers and Diener, "The Scientific Pursuit of Happiness."

24. Myers and Diener, "The Scientific Pursuit of Happiness."

25. Much of this section on religion and morality is drawn from Paul Bloom, "Religion, Morality, Evolution," *Annual Review of Psychology* 63 (2012): 179–199.

26. Justin McCarthy, "Less Than Half in U.S. Would Vote for a Socialist for President," Gallup.com, November 23, 2020, https://news.gallup.com/poll/254120/less-half-vote-socialist-president.aspx.

27. Cited in Bloom, "Religion, Morality, Evolution," 192.

28. Jeremy Ginges, Ian Hansen, and Ara Norenzayan, "Religion and Support for Suicide Attacks," *Psychological Science* 20, no. 2 (2009): 224–230.

29. Ginges et al., "Religion and Support for Suicide Attacks," 228.

30. This is a simplified definition of a "dictator game."

31. These examples come from Bloom, "Religion, Morality, Evolution," 190.

Chapter 5

1. Centers for Disease Control, "Provisional Number of Marriages and Marriage Rate: United States, 2000-2016," National Center for Health Statistics, https://www.cdc.gov/nchs/data/dvs/national_marriage_divorce_rates_00-16.pdf

2. Krista K. Payne, *Median Duration of First Marriage and the Great Recession, FP-14-20* (Bowling Green, OH: National Center for Family & Marriage Research, Bowling Green State University, 2014), https://www.bgsu.edu/content/dam/BGSU/college-of-arts-and-sciences/NCFMR/documents/FP/FP-14-20-median-duration-first-marriage.pdf.

3. The actress Jennifer O'Neill, who starred in the 1971 hit "Summer of '42" has been married nine times, including remarrying and re-divorcing her sixth husband.

4. Ruqaiyyah Waris Maqsood, "Religions—Islam: Weddings," BBC, September 08, 2009, https://www.bbc.co.uk/religion/religions/islam/ritesrituals/weddings_1.shtml; "The Ketubah, or Jewish Marriage Contract;" My Jewish Learning (website), https://www.myjewishlearning.com/article/the-ketubah-or-marriage-contract/; Nathan B. Oman, "How to Judge Shari'a Contracts: A Guide to Islamic Marriage Agreements in American Courts," *Utah Law Review* (2011): 287–334.

5. Paul Rampell, "A High Divorce Rate Means It's Time to Try 'Wedleases,'" *Washington Post*, August 04, 2013, https://www.washingtonpost.com/opinions/a-high-divorce-rate-means-its-time-to-try-wedleases/2013/08/04/f2221c1c-f89e-11e2-b018-5b8251f0c56e_story.html.

6. Berislav Marušić, "Promising against the Evidence," *Ethics* 123, no. 2 (2013): 292–317; Berislav Marušić, *Evidence and Agency: Norms of Belief for Promising and Resolving* (New York: Oxford University Press, 2015).

7. William Berry, "Why Does the Heart Want What It Wants?" *Psychology Today*, December 22, 2015, https://www.psychologytoday.com/us/blog/the-second-noble-truth/201512/why-does-the-heart-want-what-it-wants.

8. Dick P. H. Barelds and Pieternel Barelds-Dijkstra, "Love at First Sight or Friends First? Ties among Partner Personality Trait Similarity, Relationship Onset, Relationship Quality, and Love," *Journal of Social and Personal Relationships* 24, no. 4 (2007): 479–496.

9. Julian Barnes, *The Only Story* (New York: Vintage, 2018), 3.

10. "Tell Me a Lie," written by Barbara Wyrick and Charles M. Buckins.

11. Clancy Martin, "Good Lovers Lie," *New York Times,* February 07, 2015, https://www.nytimes.com/2015/02/08/opinion/sunday/good-lovers-lie.html.

12. Alison Clarke-Stewart and Cornelia Brentano, *Divorce: Causes and Consequences* (New Haven: Yale University Press, 2006).

13. Norman P. Li et al., "Confidence Is Sexy and It Can Be Trained: Examining Male Social Confidence in Initial, Opposite-Sex Interactions," *Journal of Personality* 88, no. 6 (2020): 1235–1251.

14. Delroy L. Paulhus et al., "The Over-Claiming Technique: Measuring Self-Enhancement Independent of Ability," *Journal of Personality and Social Psychology* 84, no. 4 (2003): 890–904.

15. Paulhus et al., "The Over-Claiming Technique."

16. Sean C. Murphy et al., "The Role of Overconfidence in Romantic Desirability and Competition," *Personality and Social Psychology Bulletin* 41, no. 8 (2015): 1036–1052, studies 1 and 2.

17. Murphy et al., "The Role of Overconfidence in Romantic Desirability and Competition," studies 3–5.

18. Sean C. Murphy, Fiona Kate Barlow, and William von Hippel, "A Longitudinal Test of Three Theories of Overconfidence," *Social Psychological and Personality Science* 9, no. 3 (2018): 353–363.

19. Kevin Koban and Peter Ohler, "Ladies, Know Yourselves! Gentlemen, Fool Yourselves! Evolved Self-Promotion Traits as Predictors for Promiscuous Sexual Behavior in Both Sexes," *Personality and Individual Differences* 92 (2016): 11–15; Christopher Dana Lynn, R. Nathan Pipitone, and Julian Paul Keenan, "To Thine Own Self Be False: Self-Deceptive Enhancement and Sexual Awareness Influences on Mating Success," *Evolutionary Behavioral Sciences* 8, no. 2 (2014): 109–122.

20. Damian R. Murray et al., "A Preregistered Study of Competing Predictions Suggests That Men Do Overestimate Women's Sexual Intent," *Psychological Science* 28, no. 2 (2017): 253–255.

21. Richard Fry, "More Americans Are Living without Partners, Especially Young Adults," *Pew Research Center*, May 30, 2020, https://www.pewresearch.org/fact-tank/2017/10/11/the-share-of-americans-living-without-a-partner-has-increased-especially-among-young-adults/.

22. Stuart Vyse, "Looking Back on Life" (unpublished study), Connecticut College, New London, CT, doi:10.17605/osf.io/nvwgk.

23. Interestingly, when I asked the participants to imagine what "other people like you" would choose, "being well-off financially," which had been at number five on the list, shot up to number one. "Successful family" dropped to number two, and "fulfilling marriage or love relationship" dropped to number four. The truth may be somewhere between these self and other ratings.

24. Sarah Flèche et al., *The Origins of Happiness: The Science of Well-Being over the Life Course* (Princeton: Princeton University Press, 2019).

25. McNulty, James K., Carolyn A. Wenner, and Terri D. Fisher, "Longitudinal Associations Among Relationship Satisfaction, Sexual Satisfaction, and Frequency of Sex in Early Marriage," *Archives of Sexual Behavior* 45, no. 1 (2016): 85–97; Ed Diener and Robert Biswas-Diener, *Happiness: Unlocking the Mysteries of Psychological Wealth* (New York: John Wiley & Sons, 2011).

26. Claire M. Kamp Dush, Miles G. Taylor, and Rhiannon A. Kroeger, "Marital Happiness and Psychological Well-Being across the Life Course," *Family Relations* 57, no. 2 (2008): 211–226.
27. Gary S. Becker, *A Treatise on the Family* (Cambridge: Harvard University Press, 1991).
28. Bernard I. Murstein, Mary Cerreto, and Marcia G. Mac Donald, "A Theory and Investigation of the Effect of Exchange-Orientation on Marriage and Friendship," *Journal of Marriage and the Family* (1977): 543–548; Bernard I. Murstein and Marcia G. MacDonald, "The Relationship of 'Exchange-Orientation' and 'Commitment' Scales to Marriage Adjustment," *International Journal of Psychology* 18, no. 1–4 (1983): 297–311.
29. Robert H. Frank, *Passions within Reason: The Strategic Role of the Emotions* (New York: W. W. Norton, 1988).
30. "Forget Good Times, David Sedaris Is Far More Interested in Bad Behavior," *NPR. com*, May 29, 2018, https://www.npr.org/transcripts/615132917.
31. Pamela C. Regan et al., "Partner Preferences," *Journal of Psychology & Human Sexuality* 12, no. 3 (2000): 1–21.
32. Sandra L. Murray et al., "Tempting Fate or Inviting Happiness? Unrealistic Idealization Prevents the Decline of Marital Satisfaction," *Psychological Science* 22, no. 5 (2014): 619–626.
33. Paul J. E. Miller, Sylvia Niehuis, and Ted L. Huston, "Positive Illusions in Marital Relationships: A 13-Year Longitudinal Study," *Personality and Social Psychology Bulletin* 32, no. 12 (2006): 1579–1594.
34. Sandra L. Murray et al., "Kindred Spirits? The Benefits of Egocentrism in Close Relationships," *Journal of Personality and Social Psychology* 82, no. 4 (2002): 563–581.
35. Sandra L. Murray, John G Holmes, and Dale Wesley Griffin, "The Self-Fulfilling Nature of Positive Illusions in Romantic Relationships: Love Is Not Blind, but Prescient," *Journal of Personality and Social Psychology* 71, no. 6 (1996): 1155–1180.
36. Claire M. Kamp Dush, Miles G. Taylor, and Rhiannon A. Kroeger, "Marital Happiness and Psychological Well-Being across the Life Course," *Family Relations* 57, no. 2 (2008): 211–226.
37. Miller, Niehuis, and Huston, "Positive Illusions in Marital Relationships."

Chapter 6

1. Didion, The Year of Magical Thinking, 225–226.
2. Didion, The Year of Magical Thinking, 226.
3. Ronald W. Pies, "The Bereavement Exclusion and DSM-5: An Update and Commentary," *Innovations in Clinical Neuroscience* 11, no. 7–8 (2014): 19–22.
4. American Psychiatric Association, *Diagnostic and Statistical Manual of Mental Disorders*, 5th ed. (Arlington, VA: American Psychiatric Association, 2013).
5. In fairness, I am reporting the nature of Susan's grief as best I recall it, but memories are not photographs.

6. Elisabeth Kubler-Ross, *On Death and Dying* (New York: Scribner, 2011). Original work published in 1969.

7. Sigmund Freud, "Mourning and Melancholia," in *The Standard Edition of the Complete Psychological Works of Sigmund Freud* 14 (London: Hogarth Press, 1917): 152–170.

8. John Bowlby, "Processes of Mourning," *International Journal of Psycho-Analysis* 42 (1961): 317–340; Paul K. Maciejewski et al., "An Empirical Examination of the Stage Theory of Grief," *Journal of the American Medical Association* 297, no. 7 (2007): 716–723.

9. George A. Bonanno, *The Other Side of Sadness: What the New Science of Bereavement Tells Us about Life After Loss*, rev. ed. (New York: Basic Books, 2019).

10. Bonanno, *The Other Side of Sadness*; Christopher Hall, "Bereavement Theory: Recent Developments in Our Understanding of Grief and Bereavement," *Bereavement Care* 33, no. 1 (2014): 7–12.

11. Joan Didion, *Blue Nights* (New York: Alfred Knopf, 2011).

12. Karina Stengaard Kamp et al., "Bereavement Hallucinations after the Loss of a Spouse: Associations with Psychopathological Measures, Personality and Coping Style," *Death Studies* 43, no. 4 (2019): 260–269.

13. Bonanno, The Other Side of Sadness.

14. Susan Nolen-Hoeksema and Judith Larson, *Coping with Loss* (Mahwah, NJ: Routledge, 1999), 168.

15. Kamp et al., "Bereavement Hallucinations after the Loss of a Spouse."

16. Jacqueline Hayes and Ivan Leudar, "Experiences of Continued Presence: On the Practical Consequences of 'Hallucinations' in Bereavement," *Psychology and Psychotherapy: Theory, Research and Practice* 89, no. 2 (2016): 194–210.

17. Christopher Hall, "Bereavement Theory: Recent Developments in Our Understanding of Grief and Bereavement," *Bereavement Care* 33, no. 1 (2014): 7–12.

18. Barnes, Levels of Life, 111.

19. Barnes, Levels of Life, 111.

20. Barnes, Levels of Life, 112.

Chapter 7

1. This section on George Smith is drawn from David Damrosch, *The Buried Book: The Loss and Rediscovery of the Great Epic of Gilgamesh* (Macmillan, 2007); Andrew George, *The Epic of Gilgamesh: The Babylonian Epic Poem and Other Texts in Akkadian and Sumerian* (New York: Penguin, 1999).

2. F. N. H. Al-Rawi and A. R. George, "Back to the Cedar Forest: The Beginning and End of Tablet V of the Standard Babylonian Epic of Gilgameš," *Journal of Cuneiform Studies* 66 (2014): 69–90.

3. George, *The Epic of Gilgamesh*, 10–11.

4. George, *The Epic of Gilgamesh*, 30.

5. A. Leo Oppenheim, "The Interpretation of Dreams in the Ancient Near East with a Translation of an Assyrian Dream-Book," *Transactions of the American Philosophical Society, New Series* 46, no. 3 (1956): 179–373.

6. Homer, *The Iliad*, trans. Robert Fagles (New York: Penguin, 1990), 99–100.

7. Homer, *The Odyssey*, trans. Robert Fagles (New York: Penguin, 1996), 149–150.

8. J. Donald Hughes, "Dream Interpretation in Ancient Civilizations," *Dreaming* 10, no. 1 (2000): 7–18.

9. Daniel E. Harris-McCoy, *Artemidorus' Oneirocritica* (Oxford: Oxford University Press, 2012).

10. J. Donald Hughes, "Dream Interpretation in Ancient Civilizations," *Dreaming* 10, no. 1 (2000): 7–18.

11. Sigmund Freud, *The Interpretation of Dreams*, 3rd ed., trans. Abraham Arden Brill (New York: Macmillan, 1913).

12. Carl Gustav Jung, *Dream Analysis 1: Notes of the Seminar Given in 1928–30* (London: Routledge, 2013).

13. Sudhansu Chokroverty, "Overview of Normal Sleep," in *Sleep Disorders Medicine: Basic Science, Technical Considerations and Clinical Aspects*, 4th ed., ed. Sudhansu Chokroverty (New York: Springer, 2017), 5–27.

14. Jussara M. R. Maragno-Correa et al., "Sleep Deprivation Increases Mortality in Female Mice Bearing Ehrlich Ascitic Tumor," *Neuroimmunomodulation* 20, no. 3 (2013): 134–140; Allan Rechtschaffen et al., "Physiological Correlates of Prolonged Sleep Deprivation in Rats," *Science* 221, no. 4606 (1983): 182–184.

15. Mike Birbiglia, "Fear of Sleep," *This American Life*, June 18, 2019, https://www.thisamericanlife.org/361/fear-of-sleep.

16. Avi Karni et al., "Dependence on REM Sleep of Overnight Improvement of a Perceptual Skill," *Science* 265, no. 5172 (1994): 679–682. See also Robert Stickgold et al., "Visual Discrimination Task Improvement: A Multi-Step Process Occurring during Sleep," *Journal of Cognitive Neuroscience* 12, no. 2 (2000): 246–254.

17. Robert Stickgold, "Sleep-Dependent Memory Consolidation," *Nature* 437, no. 7063 (2005): 1272–1278; Lea Winerman, "Let's Sleep on It: A Good Night's Sleep May Be the Key to Effective Learning, Says Recent Research," *Monitor on Psychology* 36, no. 1 (2006): 58, http://www.apa.org/monitor/jan06/onit.aspx.

18. Ross Levin and Tore Nielsen, "Nightmares, Bad Dreams, and Emotion Dysregulation: A Review and New Neurocognitive Model of Dreaming," *Current Directions in Psychological Science* 18, no. 2 (2009): 84–88.

19. James M. Wood et al., "Effects of the 1989 San Francisco Earthquake on Frequency and Content of Nightmares," *Journal of Abnormal Psychology*, 101, no. 2 (1992): 219–224.

20. Levin and Nielsen, "Nightmares, Bad Dreams, and Emotion Dysregulation";Tore Nielsen and Ross Levin, "Nightmares: A New Neurocognitive Model," *Sleep Medicine Reviews* 11, no. 4 (2007): 295–310.

21. Rosalind Cartwright et al., "Role of REM Sleep and Dream Variables in the Prediction of Remission from Depression," *Psychiatry Research* 80, no. 3 (1998): 249–255; Antti Revonsuo, "The Reinterpretation of Dreams: An Evolutionary Hypothesis of the Function of Dreaming," *Behavioral and Brain Sciences* 23, no. 6 (2000): 877–901.

22. J. A. Hobson and R. W. McCarley, "The Brain as a Dream State Generator: An Activation-Synthesis Hypothesis of the Dream Process," *American Journal of Psychiatry* 134, no. 12 (1977): 1335–1348.
23. Hobson and McCarley, "The Brain as a Dream State Generator."
24. Damrosch, *The Buried Book.*

Chapter 8

1. H. G. Wells, "The Illusion of Personality," *Nature* 153, no. 3883 (1944): 395–397.
2. The details of the Patricia Hearst story are largely drawn from Jeffrey Toobin, *American Heiress: The Wild Saga of the Kidnapping, Crimes and Trial of Patty Hearst* (New York: Doubleday, 2016).
3. Toobin, *American Heiress*, 126.
4. David Curran, "Patty Hearst a Double Winner at the Westminster Dog Show," *SFGate*, February 14, 2017, https://www.sfgate.com/sports/article/Patty-Hearst-a-double-winner-at-the-Westminster-10931892.php#photo-12366200.
5. Dahlia Lithwick, "The Return of the 'Brainwashed' Defense," *Slate*, January 28, 2002, https://slate.com/news-and-politics/2002/01/the-return-of-the-brainwashed-defense.html.
6. Michael Adorjan, Tony Christensen, and Benjamin Kelly, "Stockholm Syndrome as Vernacular Resource," *Sociological Quarterly* 53 (2012): 454–474.
7. Brian Holoyda and William Newman, "Between Belief and Delusion: Cult Members and the Insanity Plea," *Journal of the American Academy of Psychiatry and the Law* 44 (January 2016): 53–66.
8. Joshua Knobe, "Intentional Action and Side Effects in Ordinary Language," *Analysis* 63, no. 3 (2003): 190–194.
9. Toobin, *American Heiress*, 296.
10. Nina Strohminger, "Moral Character Is the Foundation of a Sense of Personal Identity," *Aeon*, November 17, 2014, https://aeon.co/essays/moral-character-is-the-foundation-of-a-sense-of-personal-identity.
11. Lyndsay A. Farrall, "The History of Eugenics: A Bibliographical Review," *Annals of Science* 36, no. 2 (1979): 111–123.
12. Stanley A. Mulaik, *Foundations of Factor Analysis*, 2nd ed. (Boca Raton, FL: CRC Press, 2009).
13. John Ceraso, Howard Gruber, and Irvin Rock, "On Solomon Asch," in *The Legacy of Solomon Asch: Essays in Cognition and Social Psychology*, ed. Irvin Rock (New York: Psychology Press 2014), 3–19. Originally published in 1990.
14. Solomon E. Asch, "Opinions and Social Pressure," *Scientific American* 193, no. 5 (1955): 31–35; Solomon E. Asch, "Studies of Independence and Conformity: I. A Minority of One Against a Unanimous Majority," *Psychological Monographs: General and Applied* 70, no. 9 (1956): 1–70.
15. Kirsten Fermaglich, *American Dreams and Nazi Nightmares: Early Holocaust Consciousness and Liberal America 1957–1965* (Lebanon, NH: University Press of New England, 2006).

16. Hannah Arendt, *Eichmann in Jerusalem: A Report on the Banality of Evil* (New York: Penguin, 2006), 276. Original work published in 1963.

17. Thomas Blass, *The Man Who Shocked the World: The Life and Legacy of Stanley Milgram* (New York: Basic Books, 2004), 62–63.

18. Stanley Milgram, "Behavioral Study of Obedience," *Journal of Abnormal and Social Psychology* 67, no. 4 (1963): 371–378.

19. Arendt, *Eichmann in Jerusalem*, 276.

20. Stanley Milgram, *Obedience to Authority: An Experimental View* (New York: Harper, 2009), 7.

21. Jerry M. Burger, "Replicating Milgram: Would People Still Obey Today?" *American Psychologist* 64, no. 1 (2009): 1–11.

22. Rachel Manning, Mark Levine, and Alan Collins, "The Kitty Genovese Murder and the Social Psychology of Helping: The Parable of the 38 Witnesses," *American Psychologist* 62, no. 6 (2007): 555–562.

23. Bibb Latané and John M. Darley, *The Unresponsive Bystander: Why Doesn't He Help?* (Englewood Cliffs, NJ: Appleton-Century-Crofts, 1970); Bibb Latané and Steve Nida. "Ten Years of Research on Group Size and Helping," *Psychological Bulletin* 89, no. 2 (1981): 308–324.

24. Zimbardo Philip, *The Lucifer Effect: Understanding How Good People Turn Evil* (New York: Random House, 2007).

25. Peter Fischer et al., "The Bystander-Effect: A Meta-Analytic Review on Bystander Intervention in Dangerous and Non-Dangerous Emergencies," *Psychological Bulletin* 137, no. 4 (2011): 517–537; Richard Philpot, "Would I Be Helped? Cross-National CCTV Footage Shows That Intervention Is the Norm in Public Conflicts," *American Psychologist* 75 (2019): 66–75.

26. Walter Mischel, *Personality and Assessment* (New York: John Wiley & Sons, 1968); Walter Mischel, "Toward an Integrative Science of the Person," *Annual Review of Psychology* 55 (2004): 1–22; Lee Ross and Richard E. Nisbett, *The Person and the Situation: Perspectives of Social Psychology* (Pinter & Martin Publishers, 2011).

27. Theodore Mead Newcomb, *The Consistency of Certain Extrovert-Introvert Behavior Patterns in 51 Problem Boys* (New York: Teachers College, Columbia University, 1929). See also H. Hartshorne and M. A. May, *Studies in Deceit. Book I. General Methods and Results. Book II. Statistical Methods and Results* (Oxford, England: Macmillan, 1928).

28. Ross and Nisbett, *The Person and the Situation*.

29. Strohminger, "Moral Character Is the Foundation of a Sense of Personal Identity." Much of the following paragraphs is indebted to this article by Strohminger.

30. Gordon W. Allport, "What Is a Trait of Personality?" *Journal of Abnormal and Social Psychology* 25, no. 4 (1931): 368–372.

31. Strohminger, "Moral Character Is the Foundation of a Sense of Personal Identity."

32. Kristján Kristjánsson, "Selfhood, Morality, and the Five-Factor Model of Personality," *Theory & Psychology* 22, no. 5 (2012): 591–606.

33. M. W. Hughes, "Personal Identity: A Defence of Locke," *Philosophy* 50, no. 192 (2016): 169–187.

34. I should make clear that the decision in *Madison v. Alabama* made no mention of Locke's memory-based theory of identity. The comparison offered here is my own.

35. Aurora Barnes, "Madison v. Alabama," *SCOTUSblog*, https://www.scotusblog.com/case-files/cases/madison-v-alabama/.

36. "Vernon Madison, Whose Case Challenged Execution of Prisoners with Dementia, Dies on Alabama's Death Row," *Death Penalty Information Center*, https://deathpenaltyinfo.org/news/vernon-madison-whose-case-challenged-execution-of-prisoners-with-dementia-dies-on-alabamas-death-row.

37. John Locke, *An Essay Concerning Human Understanding* (Indianapolis, IN: Hackett, 1996), 142–143. Originally published in 1689.

38. Derek Parfit, "Personal Identity," *Philosophical Review* 80, no. 1 (1971): 3–27.

39. Harry Frankfurt, *On Truth* (New York: Knopf, 2006), 72.

40. René Descartes, *Discourse on the Method of Rightly Conducting One's Reason and of Seeking Truth in the Sciences* (London: Penguin Classics, 2000).

41. David Hume, *A Treatise of Human Nature* (Mineola, MN: Dover, 2003), 180. Originally published in 1740.

42. Endel Tulving, "Precis of Elements of Episodic Memory," *Behavioral and Brain Sciences* 7, no. 2 (1984): 223–238.

43. Larry R. Squire, "The Legacy of Patient H. M. for Neuroscience," *Neuron* 61, no. 1 (2009): 6–9.

44. Céline Souchay et al., "Subjective Experience of Episodic Memory and Metacognition: A Neurodevelopmental Approach," *Frontiers in Behavioral Neuroscience* 7 (December 2013): 1–16.

45. Alison Gopnik, *The Philosophical Baby: What Children's Minds Tell Us about Truth, Love, and the Meaning of Life* (New York: Farrar, Straus and Giroux, 2009), 145–146.

46. James Giles, "The No-Self Theory: Hume, Buddhism, and Personal Identity," *Philosophy East and West* 43, no. 2 (2012): 175–200.

47. Alison Gopnik, "Could David Hume Have Known about Buddhism? Charles François Dolu, the Royal College of La Flèche, and the Global Jesuit Intellectual Network," *Hume Studies* 35, no. 1–2 (2009): 5–28; Alison Gopnik, "How David Hume Helped Me Solve My Midlife Crisis," *Atlantic,* September 14, 2015, https://www.theatlantic.com/magazine/archive/2015/10/how-david-hume-helped-me-solve-my-midlife-crisis/403195/.

Chapter 9

1. This episode is taken from something that actually happened to Daniel Wegner, as reported in Daniel M. Wegner, *The Illusion of Conscious Will* (Cambridge, MA: MIT Press, 2002), 9–10.

2. Bronwyn Hemsley et al., "Systematic Review of Facilitated Communication 2014–2018 Finds No New Evidence That Messages Delivered Using Facilitated Communication Are Authored by the Person with Disability," *Autism & Developmental Language Impairments* 3, (2018): 1–8.

3. Jon Palfreman, *Frontline*, "Prisoners of Silence," videotape (Boston: WGBH Public Television, 1993); Douglas L. Wheeler et al., "An Experimental Assessment of Facilitated Communication," *Mental Retardation* 31, no. 1 (1993): 49–60.

4. *Gateways to the Mind*, made by Owen Crump for the Bell Laboratory Science Series, (1958), accessed January 10, 2018, https://lucian.uchicago.edu/blogs/sciencefilm/human-sciences-on-film/consciousness/506-2/.

5. Jessica Riskin, "Machines in the Garden," *Republics of Letters: A Journal for the Study of Knowledge, Politics, and the Arts* 1, no. 2 (2010): 16–43.

6. Gert-Jan Lokhorst, "Descartes and the Pineal Gland," *Stanford Encyclopedia of Philosophy* (Fall 2020 ed.), ed. Edward N. Zalta, https://plato.stanford.edu/archives/fall2020/entries/pineal-gland/.

7. Sarah Broadie and Christopher Rowe, *Aristotle, Nicomachean Ethics: Translation, Introduction and Commentary* (Oxford: Oxford University Press, 2002).

8. John H. Wright, "Divine Knowledge and Human Freedom: The God Who Dialogues," *Theological Studies* 38, no. 3 (1977): 450–477.

9. Ilham Dilman, *Free Will: An Historical and Philosophical Introduction* (London: Routledge, 1999).

10. David Hume, *A Treatise of Human Nature* (Mineola, MN: Dover, 2003), 295. Originally published in 1740.

11. Hume, *A Treatise of Human Nature*, 292.

12. "The PhilPaper Surveys," https://philpapers.org/surveys/results.pl.

13. Hagop Sarkissian et al., "Is Belief in Free Will a Cultural Universal?" *Mind & Language* 25, no. 3 (2010): 346–358.

14. Felipe de Brigard, Eric Mandelbaum, and David Ripley, "Responsibility and the Brain Sciences," *Ethical Theory and Moral Practice* 12, no. 5 (2009): 511–524; Eddy D. Nahmias, Justin Coates, and Trevor Kvaran, "Free Will, Moral Responsibility, and Mechanism: Experiments on Folk Intuitions," *Midwest Studies in Philosophy* 31, no. 1 (2007): 214–242.

15. Bertram Malle and Joshua Knobe, "The Folk Concept of Intentionality," *Journal of Experimental Social Psychology* 33, no. 2 (1997): 101–121.

16. Cited in Cory J. Clark et al., "Free to Punish: A Motivated Account of Free Will Belief," *Journal of Personality and Social Psychology* 106, no. 4 (2014): 501–513.

17. Fiery Cushman, Joshua Knobe, and Walter Sinnott-Armstrong, "Moral Appraisals Affect Doing/Allowing Judgments," *Cognition* 108, no. 1 (2008): 281–289, experiment 2.

18. Clark, "Free to Punish."

19. The author acknowledges a certain irony in this statement.

20. Thomas H. Maugh, "Benjamin Libet, 91; Physiologist Probed Consciousness," *Los Angeles Times*. August 27, 2007, https://www.latimes.com/archives/la-xpm-2007-aug-27-me-libet27-story.html.

21. Benjamin Libet, "Unconscious Cerebral Initiative and the Role of Conscious Will in the Initiation of Action," *Behavioral and Brain Sciences* 8 (1985): 529–566, Benjamin Libet, C. A. Gleason, E. W. Wright, and D. K. Pearl, "Time of Conscious Intention to Act in Relation to Onset of Cerebral Activity (Readiness-Potential). The Unconscious Initiation of a Freely Voluntary Act," *Brain* 106 (1983): 623–642.

22. "Remembering Daniel M. Wegner," Association for Psychological Science, December 31, 2013, https://www.psychologicalscience.org/observer/remembering-daniel-m-wegner.

23. Bryan Marquard, "Daniel M. Wegner, 65; Harvard Social Psychologist Unraveled Mysteries of Thought and Memory," *Boston.com*, July 11, 2013, https://www.boston.com/news/local-news/2013/07/11/daniel-m-wegner-65-harvard-social-psychologist-unraveled-mysteries-of-thought-and-memory.

24. Daniel M. Wegner, *White Bears and Other Unwanted Thoughts: Suppression, Obsession, and the Psychology of Mental Control* (New York: Guilford Press, 1994), 9.

25. Wegner, *White Bears and Other Unwanted Thoughts.*

26. Daniel M. Wegner, *The Illusion of Conscious Will* (Cambridge, MA: MIT Press, 2002), 8.

27. Wegner, *The Illusion of Conscious Will*, 9–10.

28. Christopher Mele, "Pushing That Crosswalk Button May Make You Feel Better, But . . . ," *New York Times.* October 27, 2016, https://www.nytimes.com/2016/10/28/us/placebo-buttons-elevators-crosswalks.html.

29. Stuart Vyse, *Believing in Magic: The Psychology of Superstition—Updated Edition* (New York: Oxford University Press, 2014).

30. Vyse, *Believing in Magic.*

31. J. Bryan Lowder, "When Did Humans Realize That Sex Leads to Pregnancy?" *Slate*, January 10, 2013, https://slate.com/technology/2013/01/when-did-humans-realize-sex-makes-babies-evolution-of-reproductive-consciousness-of-the-cause-of-pregnancy.html.

32. James W. Moore, Daniel M. Wegner, and Patrick Haggard, "Modulating the Sense of Agency with External Cues," *Consciousness and Cognition* 18, no. 4 (2009): 1056–1064.

33. Mindy Weisberger, "'God Plays Dice with the Universe,' Einstein Writes in Letter About His Qualms with Quantum Theory," *LiveScience*, June 12, 2019, https://www.livescience.com/65697-einstein-letters-quantum-physics.html.

34. Paul S. Wesson, "Space-Time Uncertainty from Higher-Dimensional Determinism (or: How Heisenberg Was Right in 4D Because Einstein Was Right in 5D)," *General Relativity and Gravitation* 36, no. 1 (2003): 451–457.

35. Martin Heisenberg, "Is Free Will an Illusion?" *Nature* 459 (2009): 164–165; Robert Kane, *A Contemporary Introduction to Free Will* (Oxford: Oxford University Press, 2005).

36. Wesson, "Space-Time Uncertainty from Higher-Dimensional Determinism."

37. Jeffrey P. Ebert and Daniel M. Wegner, "Mistaking Randomness for Free Will," *Consciousness and Cognition* 20, no. 3 (2011): 965–971.

38. Paul Bloom, "The Strange Appeal of Perverse Actions," *New Yorker*, July 19, 2019, https://www.newyorker.com/culture/annals-of-inquiry/perverse-incentives; Robert Wright, "Agnes Callard on Acting against Your Interests," *Nonzero*, https://nonzero.org/post/agnes-callard-akrasia.

39. James Merrill, *The Changing Light at Sandover* (New York: Knopf, 2011).

40. Langdon Hammer, *James Merrill: Life and Art* (New York: Knopf, 2015), 194.

41. A demonstration of blindfolded Ouija board playing can be seen in "Do You Believe?" Brain Games video series, National Geographic, February 5, 2015, https://www.yout ube.com/watch?v=PRo8TytvIDw.

42. Joseph Jastrow and Helen West, "A Study of Involuntary Movements," *American Journal of Psychology* 4, no. 3 (1892): 398–407.

43. Stoker Hunt, *Ouija: The Most Dangerous Game* (New York: Harper, 1985).

44. Theodore Flournoy, *Spiritualism and Psychology* (New York: Harper & Row, 1911).

45. Douglas J. Lanska and Joseph T. Lanska, "Franz Anton Mesmer and the Rise and Fall of Animal Magnetism: Dramatic Cures, Controversy, and Ultimately a Triumph for the Scientific Method," in *Brain, Mind and Medicine: Essays in Eighteenth-Century Neuroscience*, ed. Harry Whitaker, Christopher Upham Murray Smith, and Stanley Finger (New York: Springer, 2007), 301–320.

46. Steven Jay Lynn and Irving Kirsch, *Essentials of Clinical Hypnosis: An Evidence-Based Approach* (Washington, DC: American Psychological Association, 2006).

47. Wegner, *The Illusion of Conscious Will*, chapter 8.

48. Douglas Biklen, "Communication Unbound: Autism and Praxis," *Harvard Educational Review* 60, no. 3 (1990): 291–314.

49. See, for example, Sue Rubin's website, https://sites.google.com/site/suerubin696/.

50. Rosemary Crossley and Jane Remington-Gurney, "Getting the Words Out: Facilitated Communication Training," *Topics in Language Disorders* 12, no. 4 (1992): 29–45; Diane Twachtman-Cullen, *A Passion to Believe: Autism and the Facilitated Communication Phenomenon* (Boulder, CO: West View Press, 1997).

51. Jamie Burke and Douglas Biklen, "Presuming Competence," *Equity and Excellence in Education* 39, no. 2 (2006): 166–175.

52. Janyce Boynton, "Facilitated Communication—What Harm It Can Do: Confessions of a Former Facilitator," *Evidence-Based Communication Assessment and Intervention* 6, no. 1 (2012): 3–13.

53. Cheryl A. Burgess et al., "Facilitated Communication as an Ideomotor Response," *Psychological Science* 9, no. 1 (1998): 71–74.

54. Wegner, *The Illusion of Conscious Will*, chapter 9; Daniel M. Wegner and Thalia Wheatley, "Apparent Mental Causation: Sources of the Experience of Will," *American Psychologist* 54, no. 7 (1999): 480–492.

55. For comparison, Wegner's diagram can be found in Wegner, *The Illusion of Conscious Will*, 68.

56. Kathleen D. Vohs and Jonathan W. Schooler, "The Value of Believing in Free Will: Encouraging a Belief in Determinism Increases Cheating," *Psychological Science* 19, no. 1 (2008): 49–54. I have simplified the description of experiment 2.

57. Thomas Nadelhoffer et al., "Does Encouraging a Belief in Determinism Increase Cheating? Reconsidering the Value of Believing in Free Will," *Cognition* 203 (2020): 1–13.

58. Nicholas R. Buttrick et al., "Many Labs 5: Registered Replication of Vohs and Schooler (2008), Experiment 1," *Advances in Methods and Practices in Psychological Science* 3, no. 3 (2020): 429–438.

Chapter 10

1. Homer, *The Odyssey,* trans. Emily Wilson (New York: Norton, 2018).
2. These examples come from Robert Trivers, *The Folly of Fool: The Logic of Deceit and Self-Deception in Human Life* (New York: Basic, 2011).
3. William Von Hippel and Robert Trivers, "The Evolution and Psychology of Self-Deception," *Behavioral and Brain Sciences* 34, no. 1 (2011): 1–16.
4. This idea of Odysseus adapting to his surrounding was inspired by this interview with Emily Wilson, a translator of *The Odyssey*: Stephen Metcalf, Dana Stevens, and Julia Turner, "Murder on the Orient Express Is Richly Upholstered Nonsense," *Slate Magazine*, November 15, 2017, https://slate.com/culture/2017/11/murder-on-the-orient-express-louis-c-k-and-emily-wilsons-odyssey-translation.html.
5. Yuval Noah Harari, *Sapiens: A Brief History of Humankind* (New York: Harper Collins, 2015).
6. Admittedly, this is probably a bit if hyperbole. I am not sure whether we are actually capable of destroying all life on the planet or not, given all the microscopic species, etc. Consider the tardigrade. But you get the point.
7. Chris Kahn, "Half of Republicans Say Biden Won Because of a 'Rigged' Election: Reuters/Ipsos Poll," *Reuters*, November 18, 2020, https://www.reuters.com/article/us-usa-election-poll/half-of-republicans-say-biden-won-because-of-a-rigged-election-reuters-ipsos-poll-idUSKBN27Y1AJ.
8. Kathy Frankovic, "Why Won't Americans Get Vaccinated?" YouGov, July 15, 2021, https://today.yougov.com/topics/politics/articles-reports/2021/07/15/why-wont-americans-get-vaccinated-poll-data.
9. Jon Henley and Niamh McIntyre, "Survey Uncovers Widespread Belief in 'Dangerous' Covid Conspiracy Theories," *Guardian*, October 26, 2020, https://www.theguardian.com/world/2020/oct/26/survey-uncovers-widespread-belief-dangerous-covid-conspiracy-theories.
10. Frithjof Nungesser, "The Evolution of Pragmatism: On the Scientific Background of the Pragmatist Conception of History, Action, and Sociality," *European Journal of Sociology* 58, no. 2 (2017): 327–367, https://doi.org/10.1017/S0003975617000121.
11. William James, *Pragmatism* (Toronto: Dover), 1995. Original work published in 1907.
12. Harari, *Sapiens: A Brief History of Humankind.*
13. For a discussion of whether Odysseus is a good person, see Madeline Miller and Emily Wilson, "Reimagining the Classics," recorded conversation, November 20, 2020, https://www.crowdcast.io/e/_reimaginingclassics?utm_campaign=discover&utm_source=crowdcast&utm_medium=discover_web.
14. Plato, *Lesser Hippias*, trans. Benjamin Jowett. Project Gutenberg, 2008.
15. Laurence Lampert, "Socrates Defense of Polytropic Odysseus: Lying and Wrong-Doing in Plato's Lesser Hippias," *Review of Politics* 64, no. 2 (2002): 231–259.
16. Steven Pinker, "The Fear of Determinism," in *Are We Free? Psychology and Free Will*, ed. John Baer, James C. Kaufman, and Roy F. Baumeister (New York: Oxford University Press, 2008), 311–324.
17. Albert Camus, *The Plague: The Fall; Exile and the Kingdom; and Selected Essays* (New York: Knopf, 2004), 534.

Index

For the benefit of digital users, indexed terms that span two pages (e.g., 52–53) may, on occasion, appear on only one of those pages.

Tables and figures are indicated by *t* and *f* following the page number